TEACHING PEOPLE TO SPEAK WELL

Training and Remediation of Communication Reticence

SCA Applied Communication Publication Program

Gary L. Kreps, Editor
Northern Illinois University

The SCA Program in Applied Communication supports the Speech Communication Association mission of promoting the study, criticism, research, teaching, and application of artistic, humanistic, and scientific principles of communication. Specifically, the goal of this publication program is to develop an innovative, theoretically informed, and socially relevant body of scholarly works that examine a wide range of applied communication topics. Each publication clearly demonstrates the value of human communication in addressing serious social issues and challenges.

TEACHING PEOPLE TO SPEAK WELL
Training and Remediation of Communication Reticence

Lynne Kelly
University of Hartford

Gerald M. Phillips
Pennsylvania State University

James A. Keaten
University of Northern Colorado

HAMPTON PRESS, INC.
CRESSKILL, NEW JERSEY

SPEECH COMMUNICATION ASSOCIATION
ANNANDALE, VIRGINIA

Printed in the United States of America

Library of Congress Cataloging-in-Publication Data

Kelly, Lynne.
    Teaching people to speak well : training and remediation of communication reticence / Lynne Kelly, Gerald M. Phillips, James A. Keaten
       p.   cm. -- (Speech Communication Association/Hampton Press applied communication program)
    Includes bibliographical references (p. 303) and index.
    ISBN 1-881303-50-0. -- ISBN 1-881303-51-9 (pbk.)
    1. Public speaking. 2. Communication--Study and teaching.
I. Phillips, Gerald M. II. Keaten, James A. III. Title. IV. Series.
PN4121.K3395   1995
808.5'1--dc20
                           95-23134
                                 CIP

Hampton Press, Inc.
23 Broadway
Cresskill, NJ 07626

In loving memory of Gerald M. Phillips

—L.K.
—J.A.K.

CONTENTS

PART IV: EVALUATION OF THE TRAINING APPROACH

PREFACE

When it comes to social conversation I am not very good. I don't know how to begin or what to say. I think too long about things I want to say, and usually never end up saying them. This happens a lot at parties or other similar situations. I am uncomfortable when I am with a group of mostly strangers. I will stand around and not really say much. I would like to be able to speak more freely with others and to participate openly in social conversations—Student in Penn State Reticence Program

A student wrote this description of himself as a communicator upon entering a training program for reticent communicators offered through the Speech Communication Department at The Pennsylvania State University. The program, known as the "Reticence Program," started in 1965 to help college students like this one improve their ability to speak.

Although all of us can use some improvement, the students who enroll in the Reticence Program suffer because of their communication incompetencies. They find it difficult to make friends, traumatic to speak in class, and impossible to give a public speech. They often call themselves *shy*; we refer to them as *reticent* or *incompetent communicators*.

The world abounds with such people. We all know them. Many of us were, at one time, just like them. Fortunately, there are ways to help them. This book describes one of those ways.

Written as a companion to *Communication Incompetencies: A Theory of Training Oral Performance Behavior* by Gerald M. Phillips, founder of the Reticence Program, this book provides an in-depth look at the model of instruction underlying the Reticence Program and the specific techniques used by instructors to help people become better communicators. This book is intended for teachers and trainers who want to: (a) institute a program of remediation for individuals with communication skills deficiencies; (b) incorporate techniques from a successful program like that at Penn State into an existing program; or (c) offer training workshops for reticent speakers.

In the introduction we provide the background of and rationale for the skills training approach used as the treatment model. We also introduce the reader to the Penn State Reticence Program—how it got started, how it evolved, and what it is like.

In the first part of the book, we take the reader through the content and methods used in the training program. We begin with a discussion of how to assess inept communication behaviors (Chapter 2), assuming that accurate diagnosis must precede treatment. In Chapter 3 we describe two of the essential skills the program develops—goal setting and audience and situation analysis—and the particular methods and activities employed to teach those skills. Similarly, in Chapter 4, we discuss the instructional techniques designed to help people acquire skills for social conversation, class or meeting participation, small group discussion, job interviewing, and public speaking. Chapter 5 presents our ideas on how to teach invention (idea generation) and organization of ideas. Chapter 6 concludes Part I with a description of ways instructors teach oral delivery skills.

In Part II, "Theoretical and Philosophical Underpinnings of the Training Approach," we explain the instructional model in its entirety. Chapter 7 clarifies the nature of the communication problems we call *reticence* or *communication incompetencies*. We present the basic premises of the system of pedagogy in Chapter 8, and in Chapter 9 we describe the role of criticism in the improvement of speech performance.

It is not always possible, due to logistical and resource considerations, to institute a program like the one we describe. As an alternative, we have written Part III to help teachers structure speaking assignments and the general classroom environment (chapter 10) to minimize the impact of reticence on students' academic achievement. The model workshop described in Chapter 11 can be offered in schools or community and business organizations to train people in communication skills.

We summarize the supporting research and other treatment models in the final section of the book. Finally, we compare the models and offer a critique of the evaluation literature.

We wish to acknowledge the many people who played a part in the production of this book. Over the years, many talented instructors have taught in the PSU Reticence Program, who have been instrumental in giving the program its current shape and who have made it successful. Especially noteworthy are Nancy Metzger and Kent Sokoloff, who worked with Gerald Phillips in the 1970s to incorporate goal analysis as the heart of the pedagogy. To the thousands of students who have enrolled in the Reticence Program, we are grateful for their participation, trust, and helpful feedback about the course. We also appreciate their willingness to serve as participants in the many research projects undertaken to study the Reticence Program and reticent people.

We appreciate the respect, encouragement, and patience shown by Barbara Bernstein, the publisher at Hampton Press. To the other staff members at Hampton Press, who assisted with the production of the book, we are very grateful. Our thanks to Gary Kreps, editor of the Speech Communication Association Series on Applied Communication, of which this book is a part, and to SCA for giving us the opportunity to be included in this excellent series. We also thank Tim Hopf of Washington State University, for his important review of an earlier draft of the manuscript.

On a more personal note, each of us appreciates the love and support we have received from family, friends, and colleagues throughout this process. I, Lynne, especially want to thank my dean, Gary Waller, for his constant encouragement; my chair, Harvey Jassem, for his support and longstanding friendship; and my daughter, Megan Rose, for reminding me of what life is all about. I, James, would like to thank my parents for their love and support; my brother, for his assistance in solving the world's problems; my Colorado parents, Lee and Sandy, for their wit and affection; and Heather, for a whole new world.

Finally, during the last phases of producing this book, Gerald Phillips, creator of the Penn State Reticence Program, passed away. It is fitting that this, his final academic book, tells the story of his Reticence Program. Information about how the program was developed and implemented will no longer be stored only in the memories of those of us who had the privilege of working side by side with Jerry. We want to thank him for the tremendous influence he has had on our lives and careers. If it was not for his recognition of the problem of reticence and his

hard work in instituting this remarkable program, this book
would never have been written. The words of Lao-tzu capture the
vision and foresight of Gerald M. Phillips: "To see things in the
seed, that is genius."

Lynne Kelly
James A. Keaten

1

INTRODUCTION

Many people cannot speak very well. For a variety of reasons, they either cannot, or find it difficult to perform necessary social tasks. They are ineffective in some aspects of social life, competent in other aspects.

Most of us do not think much about our speaking. Because we do not test ourselves, we are rarely sure of our capabilities. Professionals at speaking, like actors or politicians, have learned their capabilities through experience and training and take chances accordingly. Most of the rest of us just blunder forward. If something goes wrong when we communicate with others, we often blame the other person. We generally do not plan for social situations or rehearse our communications, but we might worry about such interactions until we are paralyzed with fear.

There is no universal reason for communication incompetence. We are all qualified and disqualified in our own ways. Incompetent speaking, sometimes called shyness or reticence, is not a disease and consequently there is no cure for it. There is only remediation. Various experts have made claims about the

1

nature of the problem. Some say it results from anxiety about speaking; others blame it on defective training in the home; still others pin it on being socially marginal.

There are many labels used for communication incompetence. We have communication apprehension (McCroskey, 1970, 1984a), reticence (Phillips, 1968, 1984a), interaction and audience anxiety (Leary, 1983), unwillingness to communicate (Burgoon, 1976a), and a host of definitions of shyness (Buss, 1984; Cheek & Buss, 1981; Jones & Russell, 1982; Pilkonis, 1977a; Zimbardo, 1977). These labels are sometimes useful and sometimes misleading. Some ineffective speakers are apprehensive about speaking; some are not. Some inept speakers know their deficiencies and care about them. Some have no idea how poorly they communicate. Some know and do not care.

We regard communication apprehension as a separate problem, sometimes, but not necessarily, associated with incompetent speaking. We do not believe that modifying social fears necessarily changes the way a person speaks. In the final analysis, we must see a person write a page or give a speech in order to be convinced of his or her competency. Observing people perform in one context offers some prognosis about how they might perform in a similar context.

Anxiety may be a part of the problem. There are fine performers who are terrified all the time but perform well, and others whose anxiety gets in their way. Some people cannot communicate effectively but are not at all concerned. There are people who are laconic and taciturn and still quite effective at accomplishing what they set out to do. In Chapter 7, we explore the nature of the problem in greater detail. In general, however, this book is not about theory or causes. We start with the assumption that there are people who have problems speaking and most of them can improve with effective instruction.

THE CENTRAL ROLE OF COMMUNICATION IN SOCIAL LIFE

The importance of developing speaking competence cannot be overstated. Human talk is an advertisement of who we are. Our personalities unfold through our discourse. The distinguished psychiatrist, Harry Stack Sullivan (1953), defined *personality* as the regularly occurring patterns of behavior people come to expect from an individual. Most of that behavior is talk, and we use it to judge other people.

Speech has a purpose. An individual may want to have a good time with a friend or may want to sell $1 million yacht. Regardless of its goal, speech requires a certain level of competence. Consider the possibilities:

- We speak to show others we like them. We exchange pleasantries. We inquire about their health. We say "I like you," or "I love you." We might also use speech to push others away.
- We ask others for favors. "Please pass the salt." "Loan me $500." "Vote for me!" "Make love to me." "Take $100 off the price and I'll buy it."
- We solicit support and friendship from others. We arrange a dinner date or call someone just to chat because we are lonely.
- We use talk to support exchanges of goods and services. We conduct our business. We work together. We buy and sell. We go to the dentist or consult with a garage mechanic.
- We attempt to persuade others to support our point of view. We become active in organizations. We work for political causes or even run for office.
- We argue about what is right and wrong. We tell our children to stop smoking. We are pro life or pro choice. We take a stand on living wills.
- We discuss our course of action to combat a common problem. We belong to committees or lobby the legislature. We become citizen advisors or simply plan a family picnic. We decide whether to put grandma in a nursing home.
- We give and receive information about social and vocational matters. All manner of counselors are ready to give us advice about our personal, social, and work lives. Our bosses often have a lot to say about our work.
- We inspire others with lofty thoughts. We recite poetry. We indulge in philosophical speculation. We pray.
- We entertain each other with narratives, jokes, and remarks. We amuse our guests at a dinner party. We tell one neighbor what another neighbor said. We make witty remarks about the issues of the day.
- We express approval and disapproval. Sometimes a nod will do. Sometimes we have to vote.
- We instruct others in doing and/or understanding in school or through informal learning.

- Occasionally, we speak just to hear ourselves talk, to confirm that we are alive, alert, and opinionated.

We believe in the importance of communication skills because we operate under the assumption that truth will prevail if all sides have an equal opportunity to be heard. Competent communication is essential to equity in competition between individuals and to sustain a democratic society. Citizens must be competent in speech to make their voices heard and to debate ideas in the public forum. A competent speaker is one who is master both of language and situation. Ineptitude can be identified by inability to size up situations and select and perform speech appropriate to it.

Oral communication is also central to human socialization. Incompetent speakers may have trouble managing their own personal relationships. We establish and maintain relationships with others primarily through speech.

Success on the job, in school, in life itself often depends on skill at speaking. Those who are not competent at communicating may lose their opportunity to participate fully in life.

WHAT THIS BOOK IS ABOUT

This book is designed for teachers and trainers who need a method for helping reticent communicators improve their skills. Ultimately, the people we hope will benefit from this book are those who cannot perform the ordinary social tasks on the job or in their personal life. The new skills they learn can help them improve dialogue with fellow employees, solve problems with spouses and children, and play some role in shaping the political, social, and economic community in which they live.

In this book we raise a basic question: What can be done to help people become competent at communication? We are not addressing how people feel about communicating, although we assume they will feel better about themselves as they improve. In fact, our experience with our trainees supports this assumption. Those who succeed feel good about it; they are ready to take on additional tasks. It is important, therefore, to provide people with adequate skills so they experience successful communication. This book deals with the vast majority of people who lack skills because they have simply never learned.

Our main premise is that most people who have problems

with oral communication can be trained to be more effective in the context of their lives. We examine the kinds of problems they have, and describe some training techniques and programs that have been demonstrably effective in remedying those problems. Specifically, we present, in its entirety, the Pennsylvania State University (PSU) Reticence Program, including the philosophy of the program and details of its implementation.

BACKGROUND OF THE PSU RETICENCE PROGRAM

The Beginnings

The Pennsylvania State University opened its Reticence Program in the early 1970s. The program was designed to deal with students who were kept from graduation because they were unable to successfully complete the required speech course. The existence of incompetent speakers was empirically demonstrated in 1964 when a psychologist confronted the speech faculty at PSU with a group of students who were prepared to drop out of school rather than attempt the basic, required speech course. None qualified for treatment by speech pathologists and none were considered psychologically or physiologically impaired. The question was, could some form of instruction be devised that would enable these inept speakers to qualify with at least a "C" in the required course. A special, experimental section was inaugurated to attempt accomplishing that goal.

The original teaching staff depended largely on the Hawthorne effect for its success, for they simply did not know what kind of instruction might work. Initially, they relied on a lot of individualized faculty attention plus peer support. The students, however, clearly illustrated the pervasive problems shared by many inept speakers:

- They did not seem to be aware of how speech was used to carry on social business.
- Virtually all had inept delivery styles.
- All could report occasions where their inability to speak well got them into trouble.
- Most could remember friends or family commenting on their speech incompetency.

All qualified as incompetent. Their speech drew the attention of others, caused them difficulty, and caused both themselves and their listeners to be upset (Van Riper & Emerick, 1984). They had no speech defects, but they seemed to share the qualities just mentioned. Many sprinkled their speech with "and uh" and other vocalized pauses, displaying poor organization of ideas. All of them were afraid to and had difficulty presenting public speeches. Most could not carry on ordinary social conversation; they were essentially quiet.

The stake, their graduation, was high enough to motivate a response to instruction. All passed and went out into the world. Most of them felt that they were more effective speakers as a result of what went on.

These students were only the tip of the iceberg. The school had a required public speaking course, but when the administration mandated screening all students in advance of placement, a test was devised for deficiencies. About 10% were proficient enough to exempt the course. About 25% could not perform in a simple interview situation. The question of how to identify these students for special help was particularly taxing. Most preferred to hide or simply take a "C" rather than try a course that might improve their performance. In interviews, they all made it clear that their anticipated losses from speaking outweighed any possible gain. In short, they knew that they could not handle the normal speaking tasks life demanded of them.

They approached speaking, in most situations, with trepidation, knowing they would not succeed. They saw the most likely outcome of every social engagement as failure and possibly insult or humiliation. Measures of anxiety did not catch these feelings. They were too personal.

Early Speculations About the Problem

Interviews with students and adults who sought special help were most revealing. Virtually all indicated there were some social situations that seemed to be consistently difficult for them. These included:

- Meeting and initiating conversation with strangers.
- Making dates and appointments with strangers and authority figures.
- Having interviews with authority figures in general and especially employment interviews.

- Asking and answering questions in class and on the job.
- Participating in task groups and public meetings.
- Speaking formally in public, especially on assignment (e.g., giving reports, lectures, or presentations).
- Making and sustaining friendships.

The situations had one element in common; something obvious was at stake. In each case, personal rejection was an issue; grades, money, and status were involved. The incompetent speakers were not consciously aware of the stake and could not explain it, but they had a general sense they could lose something. Explaining how their speaking ability related to their general satisfaction was not easy.

In general, however, inept speakers do not appear to have any more psychological disturbances or physical impairments than the population at large. Although a number of authorities argue that the tendency to shyness is genetic, we had insufficient data to confirm or contradict this proposition. In fact, the reason speakers are inept became irrelevant. The question was how their performance could be improved.

For most of them, the problem was not global personality deficit, but rather situational ineptitude. Most were perfectly comfortable and capable in some social encounters. They might be able to deal with friends, but not strangers, for example. They were successful on the job, but not in social situations like dating. Various scholars have debated whether communication disabilities are "state" or "trait" in nature. Our findings indicate the label does not matter.

The diversity of incapabilities mandated individualized instruction. Students of all ages came with different combinations of difficulty. For teaching purposes, it seemed sensible to develop methodologies directed at modifying particular ineptitudes. Concern for causes proved irrelevant. Only in a very few cases that were clearly psychological or physiological in origin was discovering the cause important so appropriate referral could be made.

Enter Robert Mager

The industrial training systems designed by Robert Mager (1972) provided the direction for the program. The instructional techniques focus on modification of oral behavior to achieve relevant social goals. Specifically, his notion of goal analysis, explained in detail in Chapter 3, became a cornerstone of instruction. The

analogy between industrial training (Mager's specialty was vocational education) and modification of speech performance was
based on the insight that spoken rhetoric is made up of small
skills, each of which must be mastered, then combined and
applied to appropriate situations. Speakers must understand
what skills they need to accomplish a social goal and then get
training in the component skills. Conservation of effort is especially important, that is, avoiding situations where success is not
possible. By teaching speakers how to analyze situations for specific performance requirements, we were able to offer training in
individual skills.

    We assumed trainees did not know how to cope with a
social situation rather than presuming ability was innate. We
helped trainees build repertories of social behavior to apply to
everyday social situations. This approach meant starting with
simple tasks and proceeding to more difficult ones, learning to
store successful behaviors and then modify and adapt them to
new social situations. Trainees were taught that they could not
control the behavior of others. They had to determine a connection between their behavior and that of others, and then plan and
schedule their own performance.

    Speakers need methods that will help them evaluate situ-
ations and make decisions about what is needed and expected in
a given case. They must assess the probabilities in Aristotelian
fashion. "Rhetoric is the art of finding in any given case, all the
available means of persuasion," said Aristotle.

    How does one identify a given case? What is a means of
persuasion? How does one know which means of persuasion are
available when? The work of Beck (1976) in cognitive restructuring provided the basis for our analysis. We had to find ways to
reorganize how people think about social situations and their
personal responsibility in them. The speakers would have to
learn what was possible as opposed to dreaming about the ideal
outcome. The rule of thumb became distinguish between the
doable and the desirable.

    For example, it is desirable that all participants take
equal responsibility for maintaining the talk in a social situation.
Although this goal is desirable, it is also unrealistic. Often, the
person doing the talking has to demand and hold the attention of
the listener. The listener either wants to talk or leave. Rarely do
two people come together with equal motivation and willingness
to take turns. Because the goal became repair of the rhetoric, the
process of training became known as *rhetoritherapy*. This was not
a facetious label.

Rhetoritherapy is a training process that combines cognitive restructuring and behavior modification. It is based on a set of simple questions divided into the main headings of the rhetorical canons:

- Invention: This is the process of sizing up a social situation to discover the relevant participants and what they have at stake. What do they seek to gain and at whose expense? What can I gain and from whom? What can I talk about? What are the available "sayables" from which I can select?
- Disposition: This is the sequence of ideas I have to present in this situation. To whom are the ideas directed? What is the sequence I should use?
- Style: What are the words I use to make this presentation? What exactly do I say?
- Delivery: What is the process of presentation? Once the script is written and the scene set, what constitutes skillful presentation?
- Memory: What resources do I have? What has been successful in similar situations that I can apply to this situation? Also included in this category is mastery of the process of sizing up the new situation created by our talk. How did they react to me and what must I do now?

Components of the Program Today

The Reticence Program has been standardized since about 1973, with relatively minor modifications (see sample syllabus in Appendix 1.1). The approach discussed in the previous section on the work of Mager still holds in the 1990s. Since the program began, more than 5,000 students and adult trainees have taken instruction. In addition, several hundred programs have been conducted in industrial facilities and community programs. Instructional programs have been designed for training teachers in formal programs for the elementary and secondary schools.

The program can be divided into three major components: teaching students to rethink communication, learning key skills applicable to all situations, and instruction and practice in techniques for specific types of situations. In this section we provide an overview of these components. Each is discussed more fully in other chapters.

Rethinking Communication. Students come into the program with misconceptions or destructive ways of thinking about communication. These have been alluded to and will be further developed in later chapters. The first instructional task is to help trainees look at communication in a new way. This is part of the cognitive restructuring component of the Reticence Program.

First, students are given an understanding of the role communication plays in human relationships. Although it is not necessary to understand a process in order to perform a task (e.g., driving a car), failure to understand how communication influences other humans can account for lack of commitment to learning specific skills. In short, it is necessary to know when and how to communicate in order to select the appropriate script.

The concept of *script* is a useful metaphor we train students to use. The script defines *roles* we play in various human scenes. Others' expectations of us are fulfilled through communication. Failure to meet these expectations affects the evaluation others make of us. The script we use with family, for example, may be very different from the script required on the job. Confusion of one scene with another may account for defective selection of communication behaviors that in turn accounts for social failure. Confusion as a cause of communication ineptitude can be addressed by training.

The training refutes the popular belief that persuading others is a process of pushing buttons. We plant the idea that the only control a speaker has over his or her personal behavior and, therefore, over effective performance is based on sensible planning and skillful execution of behavior. Trainees learn their responsibility to support others by listening carefully and being sensitive to others' needs. This skill is both a matter of courtesy and a strategic move. Only by listening and watching carefully is it possible to learn what others seek in the social situation and adapt to the listeners and situation. Trainees are also taught they have to give in order to get because social relationships are a matter of exchanging goods, services, and expressions of sentiments (exactly as theorized by Homans, 1974).

Teachers also emphasize the notion that personalities develop out of a repertoire of behaviors. As noted earlier, Sullivan (1953) defined *personality* as the behaviors others come to expect of us. Some of these behaviors, more than we like to think, are defined by social roles. Parents, employees, bosses, children, and friends exhibit behaviors associated with their roles. Instructors try to convince students that improving their communication skills is vital because how they speak influences how others see them, how they see themselves, and what they are and become.

Trainers make the point that communication skills can be learned, that to be competent one does not need some special talent for speaking. Inept communicators often believe that only other people are lucky enough to possess the talent to speak well. Instructors explain that the communication process involves a set of skills that need to be developed. Learning may come easier to some people, but there are always specific skills that must be honed to become truly good at the activity.

Students are also taught to view communication as a primary means by which to exert influence over their lives and the world. Being an effective communicator, of course, does not guarantee achievement of individual goals, but remaining silent makes successful goal achievement virtually impossible.

Finally, teachers explain that nervousness and discomfort are natural experiences during the communication process, and that all people feel tense about speaking in some situations. Students are told that they will not be able to eliminate all feelings of anxiety or discomfort. Instead, as in performing any other set of skills like dancing or driving a car, nervousness tends to decline with increased ability. Trainers emphasize that as speakers learn specific skills and techniques and acquire the ability to use them effectively, they will probably feel much more relaxed.

Key Skills. Five skills central to successful speaking in all types of situations are then taught: goal analysis (Chapter 3), audience and situation analysis (Chapter 3), organizing ideas (Chapter 5), delivery (Chapter 6), and self-evaluation (Chapter 3). Teachers explain that these abilities are important for any kind of interaction, and that before any techniques for particular situations can be taught, students need to begin mastering these five.

Goal analysis involves learning to set realistic, "doable" communication goals like "I will say hello to three people in my neighborhood this week," rather than vague, unrealistic goals such as, "I want to be popular." Through the goal analysis method, students learn to identify specific behavioral criteria that indicate success. Finally, students are taught to follow a particular format to prepare for situations. They can then routinely think through their behavioral options before interacting.

A second key skill is audience and situation analysis. Inept communicators are disabled because they may not be able to identify what is expected of them or what is appropriate in a given situation; and even if they select correctly, they may not be able to perform the behaviors. Training incompetent communicators becomes a combination of teaching them to analyze situations to discover appropriate roles and then learning the simple skills required to play those roles adequately.

Each social situation is a new scene even if it contains old actors. The major principle of general semantics is "No one ever steps into the same river twice." Trainees learn that new scripting is essential in every situation; that one could proceed only by analogy, not by rule of thumb.

This subtle proposition is central to success. Most speakers have a repertoire of stock phrases and clichés that help to maintain their position in the group, but do little to advance their particular cause. To succeed rhetorically in a social situation requires adaptation of the clichés in the repertoire to make them situation-specific, that is, designed to appeal to the people present, to take in their motives.

The third key skill is the organization of ideas or disposition, as the rhetorical canon is called. Teachers explain the particular method of structuring, described in detail in Chapter 5. Structuring is a method for organizing ideas for any type of speaking situation. The method emphasizes the ability of the structures to help generate new ideas. Although idea organization is considered one of the central skills, it usually is taught along with social conversation and is reinforced in the public speaking unit.

Another of the essential skills is the ability to deliver speech in an intelligible and interesting way. Speech can be organized and adapted to the audience and the situation, but it will not be effective or perceived as competent if poorly delivered. Most people recognize the importance of good delivery only when they observe an incompetent public speaker. They may not consider the role of delivery in everyday conversation. Some people are seen as interesting conversationalists and others as great joke tellers. These perceptions are in large measure a result of competent delivery. Thus, an essential skill of the effective speaker, regardless of the situation, is the ability to present ideas in a way that maintains listener interest and attention. We discuss specific techniques for teaching delivery skills in Chapter 6.

The last of the key skills emphasized in the program is self-evaluation. Improving communication skills is a lifelong process; the primary way trainees can continue to develop as speakers is to learn a method for evaluating their own performance. A teacher will not always be there to provide criticism. If students depend solely on an instructor for feedback, they are not likely to develop further after the course is over. Students are taught to assess their own behavior, which is an essential component of the goal analysis process (described in Chapter 3), so they can continue to improve. Through realistic appraisal of their performance, students can identify specific behaviors that need to be changed or strategies that failed to accomplish a desired end.

These five skills—goal analysis, audience and situation analysis, organization, delivery, and self-evaluation—are the core abilities that trainees must develop to become more competent communicators. These skills are required regardless of the speaking context, and when they are well developed, the individual has the foundation on which to build specific techniques for handling a variety of interactions.

Techniques for Specific Situations. Students are provided with training in a wide range of situations, including social conversation, speaking to authority figures, class participation, small group communication, job interviewing, oral interpretation of literature, and public speaking (discussed in Chapters 4 and 6). Teachers discuss the unique aspects of each situation and lead students in activities designed to develop their abilities to speak effectively in each one. Later chapters provide more detail about the mechanisms of instruction in these skill areas.

In the chapters to follow, we discuss in detail implementation of the training program. Our intent is to provide the reader with the information needed to develop a program based on the PSU Reticence Program.

IMPLEMENTING THE
TRAINING APPROACH

2

ASSESSING INEPT COMMUNICATION BEHAVIOR

People who experience difficulty communicating, like individuals with most kinds of problems, usually do not know precisely what their problem is. They may feel uneasy about talking to others or have the general sense that they are not very good communicators. A remediation plan that targets an individual's specific communication problems depends on a teacher or trainer to identify the nature of those difficulties.

Practitioners have a number of methods available for diagnosing communication behavior problems. In this chapter, we present three methods of assessment: standardized scales, observation, and screening interviews. We discuss the details of implementing them, and consider their limitations. We close the chapter with a summary of the specific methods used in the PSU Reticence Program to assess the skill level of the trainees who participate in the program.

A few general comments at the outset are in order. There are two primary ways that the trainer or teacher comes in contact with people who need remediation of their communication skills: self-identification or referral from others. Perhaps the ideal situation is when an individual is aware of a problem and seeks help. Assessment in that case is a matter of identifying specific deficient behaviors. The teacher or trainer is not confronted with the ethical problem of whether or not to tell the individual about his or her communication deficiencies. The person is already aware of the need to improve.

Throughout this chapter we generally advise against telling people they have problems unless they have sought help. We have two concerns. The obvious one is that instructors may create problems for individuals who are happy with themselves by making them feel self-conscious or inferior and creating stress. An additional concern is that individuals who are told that they need remediation, unlike those who seek help, simply may not have the motivation to change.

In other instances, people may be referred to the teacher because someone else perceives that an individual's communication skills are deficient. Although we prefer the situation when a person seeks help, there are times when it is necessary and appropriate to advise people they need improvement. Employees, for example, are often evaluated, both informally and in performance appraisals, on their communication skills. Students are frequently graded in part on their ability to participate in class discussions or present material in formal presentations.

In both cases, we believe it is appropriate for someone to talk with these individuals about their communication skills, but only if two conditions can be met. First, the problem being identified must be a communication problem and not the result of a personality clash between the individuals involved. Second, the organization must offer a program to assist the person in the development of his or her communication skills or must be able to refer the individual to someone who can help. People should not be told they have problems with their communication behavior without giving them a program or other assistance to help them improve.

A second issue is that assessment implies judgment. All of the methods we describe are only as good as the expertise of the trainer or teacher using them. Only experienced professionals should be involved in the assessment process. At times individuals will be referred by unqualified persons to the teacher or trainer who is responsible for the remediation program. This type of referral can be easily handled if the individual conducting the actual assessment of communication skills is a qualified professional.

Finally, no assessment procedure is flawless. All methods have their limitations, and, when possible, it makes sense to use a combination approach. All instructors work within time and financial constraints. Trainers must make do with the resources they have, so it may not be possible to use extensive behavioral observation or in-depth interviews. Well-qualified instructors can do more with fewer resources.

STANDARDIZED SCALES

Researchers have developed and tested a number of paper-and-pencil measures to assess communication problems. These assessment instruments are generally self-report measures that the instructor administers and scores. In this section we identify many of the available measures, considering a few of them in more detail.

Available Measures

Measures of communication difficulties cover a broad range of types of problems. For example, some measure anxiety about communicating, whereas others assess shyness. We have grouped the measures by types in our descriptions here.

Tendency to Communicate. There are three scales designed to assess a person's general tendency to communicate or to avoid interaction. First is the Willingness-to-Communicate scale (McCroskey & Richmond, 1987). This is a 20-item scale that measures an individual's willingness to talk in a variety of contexts. The assumption is that, although situational factors influence the degree to which one is willing to talk, people have a predisposition to be more or less willing to communicate (McCroskey & Richmond, 1991).

A similar assumption is made by the authors of the Predispositions Toward Verbal Communication scale (Mortensen, Arnston, & Lustig, 1977). This 25-item scale (see Appendix B) also measures the degree to which a person tends to be quiet or talkative in communication situations. The third measure of a general tendency to approach or avoid communication is the

Unwillingness-to-Communicate scale (Burgoon, 1976a). This is a 20-item test that measures two dimensions, perceived communication rewards and apprehension about communication. The rewards dimension is the one relevant here because it assesses the tendency to approach or avoid communication.

Apprehension about Communicating. There are many measures of fear or apprehension about communication, especially for the public speaking context. We will consider only those that assess a person's general or traitlike tendency to be apprehensive about talking. This discussion does not include measures of situational apprehension or fear in specific contexts such as public speaking or interpersonal settings.

Two measures of a person's tendency to be apprehensive or anxious are the Personal Report of Communication Apprehension (PRCA-24; McCroskey, 1982) and the Interaction Anxiousness scale (Leary, 1983). The PRCA-24 is a 24-item scale (see Appendix C) that measures one's level of fear or anxiety in four situations: dyadic interaction, groups, meetings or classrooms, and public speaking. In addition, the instructor can calculate an overall communication apprehension score.

The McCroskey scale is undoubtedly the one most commonly used by teachers and researchers in the field of speech communication. Scores range from 24 to 120, with an average score of about 65 (McCroskey, 1981). Scores below 59 and above 85 indicate very low and very high levels of communication apprehension respectively (Richmond & McCroskey, 1992).

The Interaction Anxiousness scale has 15 items and assesses the level of anxiety people generally feel in social situations such as parties, groups, job interviews, and on the telephone. The scale was specifically designed to measure only self-reported feelings of anxiety and not anxious behaviors (Leary, 1983).

Shyness. Quite a few instruments have been developed to measure shyness. The developers of the measures make differing assumptions about what shyness is, and as a result, the scales differ. For example, McCroskey developed a 14-item Shy scale (McCroskey, Andersen, Richmond, & Wheeless, 1981) that taps shy behavior because he views shyness as a problem of being quiet and withdrawn in communication situations. Most of the items assess the extent to which one is generally talkative or quiet.

A second measure of shyness is the Social Reticence scale (Jones & Russell, 1982). This scale includes 22 items (see

Appendix D) that tap four dimensions of the problem of shyness: (a) difficulties in meeting people, making friends, and poor self-projection; (b) problems in communicating; (c) self-consciousness and negative affect; and (d) feelings of isolation. Trainers can calculate overall scores (Jones & Russell, 1982) and scores for the four dimensions (Kelly & Keaten, 1992).

Cheek and Buss (1981) created a 9-item test of shyness. This scale measures awkwardness, tension, and discomfort in social situations. A similar instrument was developed by Morris (1982). This measure consists of 14 items that assess the amount of discomfort people experience when around others.

A final measure is the Stanford Shyness Survey (Zimbardo, 1977). This is not a scale in that the items are not summed to determine a person's level of shyness. Instead, it consists of 44 questions that address a range of issues related to shyness, such as others' perceptions, reactions to shyness, and consequences. Whether or not a person is considered shy is determined by the response to question one: "Do you consider yourself to be a shy person?" Other questions measure the degree of shyness and the situations that elicit it.

Uses and Limitations of Self-Report Scales

Because self-report measures are easy to administer, they are frequently used to assess communication problems. There are other reasons, however, to use self-report instruments. Certainly the best source of information about communication difficulties is the person who experiences them. People can report on their internal states when communicating—how they feel, what they are thinking, and how they perceive situations. These states, of course, are aspects of human experience that cannot be directly observed. Self-report measures are most useful when we are interested in assessing how people feel and what they think. They are not as useful for assessing performance behavior.

Self-report scales are also able to measure a variety of aspects of communication problems (e.g., cognitive, affective, behavioral). They can examine experience in a range of communication situations (public speaking to cocktail parties), and they can assess situational reactions or more general tendencies.

These features of self-report measures suggest some guidelines for their use in the assessment of communication problems. First, the trainer or teacher must select the measure(s) carefully, which means reading the literature about any scale under consideration. This research provides information about what a particular measure is designed to assess, how it is scored, its reliability and validity, and what constitutes a high, moderate, or low score.

Second, more than one scale may be needed to assess a variety of problems. For instance, a measure of communication apprehension (e.g., the PRCA-24) combined with a measure of shy behavior (e.g., the McCroskey et al., 1981, Shy scale) would provide the trainer with information about the extent to which an individual generally experiences fear of communication and how quiet or talkative that person describes him- or herself to be.

People can see themselves as quiet but not anxious, both nervous and talkative, or both anxious and quiet. Although both the PRCA-24 and the Shy scale rely on self-assessments, a teacher could use them to make an educated guess about a student's behavior, based on his or her self-perceptions.

A third guideline is actually a warning about the use of self-report scales. Trainers need to exercise caution and to use their judgment in the interpretation of scores. Published norms for scales give a trainer a sense of what constitutes a high score, but a high score does not mean that a person is having a problem. If people seek help because they feel they have communication problems, the scale scores can help determine the nature of those difficulties. Blanket administration of the measures followed by instructor identification of those with problems on the basis of scores is dangerous at worst and inefficient at best. It is quite likely that such a procedure would identify perfectly contented people and convince them that they have communication apprehension or shyness or some other problem. Thus, using the scale alone could generate unnecessary problems. Also, keep in mind that authors of self-report scales have not always demonstrated their correlation with performance behaviors.

We have used self-report scales with individuals who have sought help from us. When we have administered such measures to students in the PSU Reticence Program, on the average they receive high scores on apprehension, shyness, and unwillingness to communicate measures (Kelly, Duran, & Stewart, 1990; Kelly & Keaten, 1992; McKinney, 1980). Some individuals, however, do not receive particularly high scores but still feel they have a problem and want help. Some receive high scores on measures of apprehension but do not score high on a shyness measure. Thus, the scores can help us diagnose specific aspects of an individual's difficulties with communication, but we only administer scales to people who have sought help on their own. Our objective is to see the student in action and evaluate performance.

OBSERVATION

Another method for diagnosing communication problems is observation. Although self-report scales are most useful for assessing internal experiences such as feelings, thoughts, and perceptions, observation is the appropriate method to focus on actual communication behavior. In this section we discuss two types of observation and then identify limitations of using observation as a mode of assessment.

Types of Observation

To observe is to watch, to see what people do. The process sounds simple and it can be, but watching to identify specific communication problems may not be so simple. We can loosely categorize observation procedures as either formal and systematic or informal and random. By formal, systematic observation we mean any set of carefully designed, specified procedures for collecting observational data about a person's communication behavior. Observation can include a wide range of procedures, but the trainer attempts to be planned and consistent during the observation process. In contrast, informal and random observation is essentially unplanned and includes no specified procedures.

Formal, Systematic Observation. In conducting formal and systematic observations, trainers have choices to make. First they must decide whether to observe ongoing behavior and make judgments on the spot or to record the behavior (e.g., on videotape) for later assessment. The decision can be affected by the availability of time and equipment and the skill of the observer in rendering judgments quickly. Video or audiotaping can also be very intrusive, and some people may refuse to allow it or may be quite uncomfortable in the presence of the recording device.

A second choice concerns choosing the observer. Conducting all of the observations can be time consuming for a trainer or teacher. If a skilled observer trained in the observation criteria makes the assessment, the likelihood of agreement with the teacher is very high (Sours, 1979). Having trained observers available can save time and allow for more observations. Having untrained or unskilled observers can result in serious disagreements, so adequate training in observation is mandatory.

Trainers also need to make decisions about when, where, and how long observations will be. These choices represent some of the greatest difficulties of using observation as a method for assessing communication problems. The more time and varied the observed situations, the greater the validity of the assessment. Generally, observations are done in the "laboratory," by researchers who watch while the individual interacts with another person. This method is popular because the alternative is to observe people as they go about their lives. *In vivo* observations often are not accurate because the observer is always an intrusive factor. It is also unethical to "spy" on a shy person as well as potentially disturbing for that individual. The situation is somewhat analogous to a patient's rise in blood pressure when taken in the doctor's office.

In a work setting, the screener can use reports from supervisors. In a school, teacher observations are often useful. More typically, however, students are screened through some kind of interview process. In the PSU program, students enrolled in the required public speaking course are told about the opportunity for special training and invited to an interview if they feel they need help. This process guarantees that those who come for screening are informed volunteers. It also provides a legitimate pretext for conducting a planned interview on which to base decisions.

A final problem is whether to make global or specific observations. To make a global observation, the screener carries on a conversation with the potential student to get a Gestalt of performance. A general decision is made about whether or not the student would benefit from training. The details of the training are worked out later. A second option is to have a protocol of questions about students' behavior in real-life situations and ask them directly if they have particular kinds of problems. The screener has the benefit of the potential student's self-diagnosis as well as impressions about fluency, ability to answer questions, behaviors associated with speaking, and other relevant criteria.

Specific observations target particular behaviors or finer skills. Such observations are more difficult to make and often require the aid of videotape or a type of behavioral measure or checklist. For example, the Behavioral Assessment of Speech Anxiety (BASA; Mulac & Sherman, 1974) is an 18-item instrument developed to assess the degree to which people display speech anxiety (see Appendix E). Other behavioral measures are available that enable observers to make judgments about specific skills and behaviors.

Informal Observation. Because informal observation is unplanned and unsystematic, it should only be undertaken by an experienced teacher or trainer. Over time, as teachers and trainers work with people to remedy their communication problems, they develop the ability to "know it when they see it." Experienced instructors may choose, as one element of an assessment procedure, to informally observe people who seek remediation. Such informal observation has the advantages of taking little time, requiring no special planning or facilities, and being comparatively unobtrusive. The trainer simply takes advantage of an opportunity to observe the communication behavior of people seeking help.

This type of observation provides only a holistic impression, and the teacher is usually unable to identify specific communication skill deficiencies. If the method is used in conjunction with other modes of assessment, it may be very effective and efficient as an initial screening device. In the PSU Reticence Program, informal observation is coupled with a screening interview, which we describe later, to assess the communication difficulties of those enrolling in the program.

Limitations of Observation

The key limitation of behavioral observation as an assessment method is that a standard of competence is required. In order to observe someone's behavior and make a determination of its quality or effectiveness, the teacher or trainer must have judgment criteria. These criteria become clearer and easier to apply with experience. Communication professionals have been attempting to identify competence and how to assess it (Aitken & Neer, 1992; Goulden, 1992; Hay, 1992; Rubin, 1982), but the task is far from complete. Less experienced instructors might benefit from using behavioral observation instruments like the BASA because these instruments contain the assessment criteria to be used.

Another limitation of observation is more obvious but no less important—its inability to capture the individual's own view of his or her behavior. This limitation is relevant to the issue discussed earlier, not telling people they have problems just because they receive high scores on standardized scales. Such a practice may create problems where none exist.

The same caveat applies to observation. People whose communication skills do not meet our criteria for competence simply may not perceive they have a problem or may be content with their abilities. When those skill deficiencies influence classroom or workplace performance, however, it may be appropriate and even necessary to point them out in office conferences or performance appraisals. Until we talk to these individuals, we have no way of knowing what they think or feel about their communication abilities.

We have already alluded to the practical but important issues of using behavioral observation. If people are observed in a single situation, the trainer cannot know how those people perform in other situations. As McCroskey (1984b) noted, "Behavioral observation is probably most useful for assessing states and least useful for assessing traits" (p. 85).

Finally, one must contend with the problem of the obtrusiveness of observation and its subsequent effect on the behavior being observed. All methods of assessment are obtrusive to some extent, but intrusion poses a special problem because observers need to view the behavior as it usually occurs. If the presence of an observer enhances the performance or generates high levels of anxiety that interfere with performance, the assessment will not be valid.

SCREENING INTERVIEWS

A third way to identify and assess communication problems is to use an interview process for screening. This approach assumes that people can discuss their problems and the trainer can use that information to more specifically identify skill deficiencies. This method can be used whether individuals seek help for themselves or are referred by someone else. In this section we describe the PSU Reticence Program interview and screening procedures as a model for using this method. Then we consider the use of screening interviews more generally.

Screening Interviews in the PSU Reticence Program

The PSU Speech Communication Department offers four options of Speech Communication 100 to meet the general speech requirement. One is the special skills training program for reticent communicators. Students (freshmen through seniors) enroll in one of three options of the basic speech course. The special option, the Reticence Program (called Option D), is not listed in the course schedule, so unless students have heard about it through word of mouth, they are not aware there is a fourth option. The only way into the program is to register for one of the three options of Speech Communication 100.

On the first day of class in all sections of the three options, students are given a handout (see Appendix F) that lists seven communication problems, such as nervousness about talking to authority figures, extreme fear of public speaking, difficulties carrying on social conversation, avoidance of class participation, trouble communicating in small groups, and feelings of shyness. The handout informs students that if they feel they have any or all of the concerns listed, they should consider Option D of Speech Communication 100. The handout specifies that if they are considering Option D or would like to find out more about it, they should report to a particular room during designated hours to talk to a special section instructor. Those students who show up to find out more about Option D are interviewed by one of the special section teachers.

Not everyone is an appropriate candidate for the special program, so the screening objective is to enroll only those students who need the program. Generally, there are two types of students who are accepted. First is the student who reports having trouble communicating across most situations. This type of person typically describes him- or herself as shy, quiet, or introverted. Most of the students who enroll in the program are in this category. They find a variety of types of communication situations uncomfortable and try to avoid them. Second is the person abnormally afraid of speaking in front of a group and reports class participation and public speaking as two dreaded situations. Although this person may survive a regular speech class, the experience is likely to be extremely unpleasant.

Students who experience occasional situational difficulties and who express a normal fear of public speaking are encouraged to return to regular speech classes for three main reasons. First, there are only so many seats available in the special program, and accepting marginal students would mean excluding those who have more severe problems communicating. Second, because only the last quarter of the semester is devoted to public speaking in the special program, these students are likely to be bored and frustrated with the course. Third, students with relatively mild stage fright would appear to be far better off in a regular speech course in which material on public speaking is covered earlier and in more depth. Instructors in the regular course are trained to deal with "normal" speech apprehension.

Those conducting the screening interviews have been trained to teach in the program. Interviews generally range between 5 and 15 minutes per student. Interviewers follow a set procedure.

1. *The interviewer greets the student and asks him or her to sit down.*

2. *The interviewer introduces him- or herself and waits to see if the student does the same.* Most students will introduce themselves, but sometimes the most highly reticent do not. If the student does not, the interviewer asks for the student's name.

3. *The interviewer then asks the student why he or she has come for the interview.* Generally, the student will mention being in a speech class and receiving a handout about a special option. Other students will say they heard about the special program from a friend or teacher and that they came to find out more about it. At schools where there is not a required speech class, students usually say they read about the special course in the schedule of classes. After the student states his or her reason, the interviewer produces a copy of the handout (see Appendix F) that briefly describes the program and lists seven communication concerns.

4. *The interviewer goes through the handout with the student, asking him or her to identify which of the concerns he or she feels.* The interviewer asks probing questions to get a sense of the breadth and depth of a student's communication problems. For example, if the student reports difficulty carrying on social conversation, the interviewer will ask with whom this is a problem and in what types of situations. The interviewer is trying to determine if the problem is fairly generalized or situation specific. Probing further, the interviewer will ask what kinds of difficulties the student experiences during social conversation. Does the student have trouble initiating talk, maintaining conversation, or ending it? The interviewer probes to get more information about the nature and extent of a problem in each of the areas the student identifies as troublesome.

The interviewer does not ask questions about the student's home life, personal relationships, or seek any information other than what is related to specific communication concerns (except perhaps major and year in college). All instructors in this type of program are just that—instructors, not psychologists or counselors. On a rare occasion, the student may offer a bit of personal information, but the interviewer is trained to move back to the topic of communication problems.

5. *Once the interviewer and the student have completed the discussion of the seven communication concerns listed on the handout, the interviewer describes the program to the student.* The description begins by emphasizing that the course is designed for people who feel any or all of the concerns listed, and that it is a

course that will allow the student the opportunity to learn skills for tackling these problems. The interviewer stresses that the course is not an escape from public speaking or other feared situations; rather, the student will be required to confront communication problems by setting and carrying out communication goals. The student is told that he or she will be asked to complete communication goals both in and out of class. For example, a student who reports being unable to participate in class discussions will be expected to set goals such as, "I will participate at least twice in my Spanish class." The interviewer informs the student that during class sessions there will be lecture material, discussion, and activities designed to prepare the student to meet these goals, and that he or she can approach the goals by starting with the least feared situation. The student is also informed that he or she will have to present public speeches in class.

6. *Following the interviewer's description of the program, the student asks questions.*

7. *After the student's questions have been answered, the interviewer asks if the student feels the special program is better suited to meet his or her needs than the regular section.* (The interviewer only asks this question if the student has reported experiencing communication problems. If the student has not expressed communication concerns, the interviewer uses the procedure described later.) If the student says yes, the interviewer will generally say that the decision is a good one, and will explain which sections are open, when they meet, and so on, and will sign the student up for the section of his or her choice.

Some students who show up at the interviews are not appropriate for the program because they do not experience difficulties communicating. These individuals show up for a variety of reasons. They are curious; they do not like the instructor of their regular section; they are looking for a class that better fits into their schedules; they have a close friend who is enrolled in the course, and so forth. It is easy for an interviewer to recognize these people because of the way they approach the interview situation. They usually come into the interview office, announce that they are there to find out about the special program, and introduce themselves. (Those who truly need the program tend to hang around outside the door and wait to be addressed by the interviewer.)

When these students appear for an interview, the interviewer asks them to sit down, and begins going through the handout to determine if any situations on the list present difficul-

ty to them. They generally report no troubles except some nervousness about public speaking. At that point the interviewer
explains what the program is about and why the student is not
an appropriate candidate for it. The interviewer tells the student
that fear of public speaking is a natural response and that his or
her regular section instructor can work with him or her on overcoming anxiety. In nearly every case, the student says that he or
she will stick with the regular section and leaves.

These seven steps are followed by all interviewers. There
are times, however, when the interviewer has to do some additional probing or take an alternative tack. For instance, occasionally, students will show up for interviews who do not appear to
have problems (they appear comfortable, can maintain eye contact, speak loudly and clearly, etc.), but who claim to have problems. These individuals tend to fall into two groups: those looking
for an easy course and those who are very frightened at the
prospect of having to give public speeches in their regular classes
and are trying to avoid speaking.

The interviewer can usually spot students looking for an
easy course because they ask a lot of questions about workload
and grading. Some even say that they heard this is easier or ask,
"Wouldn't this be easy for someone who isn't afraid of speaking?"
When the instructor is getting a lot of these types of questions, he
or she is trained to describe the program and the work that is
involved. The interviewer explains that the student will take two
exams, present several speeches, participate in a group project,
write two self-as-communicator papers, and complete at least five
goals requiring two papers each. Because the course involves
much more writing than the regular sections, the student generally perceives it as having a heavier workload. This description is
enough to discourage the student looking for an easy course.

The interviewer can easily identify students who are afraid
of public speaking but who do not have other communication concerns. (Some of those students are appropriate candidates for the
course, as is explained shortly.) These students will also appear to
be comfortable in the interview situation and will point to public
speaking as their only concern. The interviewer pursues the topic
of public speaking by asking if the student has ever given a public
speech. If the student says no, the student is probably experiencing normal apprehension about public speaking. If the student
has given a speech before, the interviewer asks him or her to
describe the experience. Students generally answer by either saying that it went "ok" or by describing a bad experience such as
blanking out, nausea, or other symptoms of severe nervousness. If

the student has never given a public speech or did not have a bad experience with it, the interviewer recommends that the student go back to his or her regular section or enroll in a regular section. This student is probably experiencing very normal fear of public speaking and does not need the special program. (The reasons for this recommendation were discussed earlier.)

If the student has had a bad experience with public speaking, the interviewer asks the student his or her year in school. If the student is a second semester senior, the interviewer will recommend that he or she enroll in the special program. The fact that the student has put off taking the course until the last semester is considered evidence of more-than-average fear of public speaking. In addition, if the student attempts to complete the regular speech course and cannot, his or her graduation will be delayed.

In summary, the screening interview is a standardized procedure designed to identify individuals who have problems communicating across situations and individuals who have a severe fear of public speaking and speaking out in groups. However, the vast majority of students who enroll in the program have generalized communication difficulties.

A study by Sours (1979) provides support for the validity of the screening interview procedure. Sours had trained interviewers make evaluations of the degree of reticence exhibited and described by students who were interviewed. In addition, the classroom instructors of those students who enrolled in the special course made similar evaluations based on their more extensive contact with the students. Sours found that interviewers and instructors generally agreed as to whether or not a student was reticent, and they were in agreement regarding the severity of the problem. When interviewers and instructors disagreed, the interviewers tended to see problems as more severe. This discrepancy may be due to an unwillingness by interviewers to exclude anyone from the course who might actually need it.

Conducting Screening Interviews

In general, there are several considerations to establish a screening procedure. The persons conducting the screening interviews must be well qualified to assess the communication skills of others because judgments must be made fairly rapidly. An interview protocol should be prepared so that interviews become standardized. Clearly, deviations from the protocol may be necessary at times, but it is much easier to make judgments regarding the nature and severity of people's communication problems if the interviews are fairly standardized. Preparing a protocol has the added benefits of streamlining both the interviewing process and the training of interviewers.

The teacher or trainer also needs to decide whether the screening interview will be the only assessment or if it will be followed by more extensive evaluation. At PSU the interviews are brief because they are intended as a means to identify those who should enroll in the program. Once enrollment is determined, additional assessment, as described later, is conducted by the section instructors. We recommend this procedure rather than using one lengthy interview to both screen individuals for remediation and target their specific areas in need of improvement.

Separating the two processes has several advantages. First, the screening interviews can be brief, including the interviews with people who turn out to be inappropriate for the program. Second, it is possible to use interviewers who are qualified to conduct the screening but who may not have the credentials to do a more thorough assessment. Finally, the extensive assessment should be made by the person who conducts the training because that individual will have to understand the specific needs of the participants. If the two processes are incorporated in a single interview, the interviewer must be the teacher or trainer.

Uses and Limitations of Screening Interviews

Interviews may be the best method of assessing communication skill deficiencies for several reasons. They are moderately standardized so results can be compared and others can be trained to conduct them, but they are not as rigid as standardized scales. Moreover, screening interviews allow individuals to talk in their own terms about their communication abilities and provide the interviewer with an opportunity to observe communication behavior. Interviewers can probe where necessary and ask for specific examples of behaviors and situations. Interviews are also quite feasible, requiring limited time and money.

Like all methods, screening interviews have limitations. They are probably more time and labor intensive than standardized scales. Furthermore, they are still essentially self-reports; observation of the person's behavior is limited to that exhibited during the interview. Not everyone is able to provide detailed descriptions of his or her skills deficits, and if the individual is extremely apprehensive about communicating, it may be very difficult for the interviewer to elicit much information.

CHOOSING ASSESSMENT METHODS

The person responsible for assessment must select from the available methods. Our intent is to provide enough information about the three major methods of standardized scales, observation, and screening interviews to enable one to make an informed decision. Methods can be used alone or in combination. The two primary bases for making the decision should be what is feasible and what is effective.

Feasibility hinges on the availability of resources such as time, space, personnel, and budget. Using standardized scales is the least resource intensive of the three methods and behavioral observation is undoubtedly the most.

The other issue concerns the method or set of methods the teacher is able to employ effectively. The instructor must be competent at using a particular assessment method and feel comfortable with it. The other aspect of effectiveness is the success of the method in identifying communication skill deficits. We have the least faith in standardized scales because they are inherently rigid and limit assessment to the content of the items. On the other hand, if they are chosen carefully to be broad in scope, this limitation can be overcome. Behavioral observation must include enough instances of observation to allow the instructor to make informed judgments about communication abilities and problems. Screening interviews must be planned carefully and be conducted by qualified interviewers to be effective tools for assessing skills.

Remediation is a process and can be modified as necessary, thus assessments can be revised. The successful assessment procedure identifies those who need skills remediation and targets a starting point for training. As the trainer or teacher works with an individual, the trainer gathers more information about that person's communication strengths and weaknesses. Thus, the training program can be modified to fit the instructor's expanding assessment and the changing needs of the individuals.

ASSESSMENT PROCEDURES IN THE RETICENCE PROGRAM

At this point, the reader has some sense of how the communication competence of individuals in the PSU program is evaluated through the screening interview. In this section we complete the picture by discussing the additional assessment procedures.

Observations During the First Class Session

Because there are a number of interviewers, instructors may meet students in their sections for the first time at the opening class session. Teachers are trained to use that session to make some initial assessments of the kinds and severity of communication problems students exhibit. There are three procedures that teachers use to try to elicit and assess student responses. First, the trainer calls roll and may ask a question or make a comment to each student. Some students display signs of discomfort or simply do not speak, only indicating their presence through nonverbal means.

Next, teachers have students fill out cards that provide information about their major, year in school, career goals, interests, home town, and so forth. Once those have been collected, the instructor goes through the cards and asks each student questions. "How did you get interested in veterinary science," or "How did you like growing up in Chicago?" are typical kinds of questions. The instructor uses the opportunity to appear friendly, supportive, and perhaps humorous. He or she also is evaluating the communication skills of the students. Although almost all display some level of discomfort at being "put on the spot," some demonstrate much greater difficulty responding to questions. Individuals may provide minimal response or may not answer at all.

Finally, teachers give students a chance to meet others in the class and chat with them. This exercise provides trainers with a chance to observe who initiates conversations, who hangs back and refuses to meet anyone, and so forth. It also enables students to begin feeling more comfortable in the classroom and with each other.

The Self-as-Communicator Papers

At the first class session, students are instructed to write a paper (about two pages) in which they describe themselves as communicators. They are asked to focus on their strengths and weaknesses as communicators, to provide specific details and examples of their behavior, and to specify the ways they would like to change their behavior. This procedure is used to encourage students to think about their skills and how they would like to improve, but it also is a major component of the assessment process used by trainers. At the end of the program, students write a second self-as-communicator paper in which they evaluate the progress, if any, that they have made and set goals for their continued improvement.

The Conference

Each trainee is scheduled to participate in a 15- to 20-minute conference with the instructor. This schedule is established at the opening class session, and the teacher tries to have a conference with each student prior to the second meeting. The student brings the self-as-communicator paper to the conference, and it becomes the basis for the discussion.

The instructor reads the paper, and then goes through it with the student, asking for clarification, examples, and greater detail. Students have a tendency to focus on their feelings about speaking in these papers, so a primary goal of the instructor is to get them to talk about their behavior. Where possible, the teacher asks the student to describe what happens when he or she tries to give a speech, ask a question in class, or initiate a conversation with a stranger.

Throughout the conference, the teacher takes notes on the general areas (e.g., public speaking, group discussion, social conversation) that the student identifies as difficult and in need of improvement. Teachers also note the more specific types of problems students describe (e.g., "I can initiate a conversation, but then I'm at a loss as to what to talk about").

Once the teacher has read the paper, asked questions, and prepared a list of areas in which the student wants to improve, he or she reviews that list with the student, asking if there is anything else that needs to be added. After the list has been completed, the instructor explains that the student will be self-selecting communication goals throughout the semester, and that he or she will be choosing goals in each of the areas on the list. The instructor explains goal assignments to the student, and then assists him or her in selecting an area for a first goal. The teacher suggests that the student begin with the least difficult. If, for example, social conversation presents fewer problems for the student than the other items on the list, the first goal assignment should be in that area.

If the student does not mention a particular area, such as speaking to authority figures, the instructor asks about that situation and whether or not it presents any difficulties. Sometimes students simply overlook a particular context, and when it is mentioned, consider it an area in need of improvement. An instructor also may point out an observation he or she has made of the student ("I noticed that you tend to speak very softly," or "In class you seemed to be uncomfortable answering my questions"). In these instances, the student may say the reaction was situational or that he or she does not usually have this difficulty. The student may actually agree with the instructor's assessment.

In essence, the assessment approach used in the PSU program for reticent communicators is a multimethod procedure. It begins with the screening interview to determine entrance into the course. The instructor makes observations of a student's communication behavior and solicits self-reports of difficulties. Once the student is in the program, he or she provides a more detailed discussion of communication strengths and weaknesses through the self-as-communicator paper and the individual conference. The instructor observes the trainees' behavior in class, especially during the first session, and in the conference.

3

GOAL SETTING AND AUDIENCE AND SITUATION ANALYSIS

One of the central components of the training program is a procedure called goal analysis, based on Mager's (1972) work, as discussed in Chapter 1. Largely because of the goal-setting method, the teaching program can be tailored to meet the individual needs of trainees.

Through the assessment process described in Chapter 2, students identify the skill areas they wish to improve. They target those areas by concentrating their efforts on them, although they are exposed to a wide array of skill areas by virtue of being enrolled in the program. In this chapter we describe the training contract established with each individual, and how that contract is carried out through the goal analysis method. An essential element of the goal analysis procedure is the process of listener and situation analysis, which we discuss at length.

THE TRAINING CONTRACT

Agreement About What the Training Includes

To reiterate several ideas introduced earlier, there are three occasions at which the teacher and the student discuss what the PSU program is about. The first is the screening interview. At the interview, trainers explain that the program is essentially skills-based. The skill areas addressed are social conversation, class participation, interviewing, speaking to authority figures, group meetings, reading aloud, and public speaking. Prospective trainees are informed that, with the help of their instructor, they will develop an improvement plan, targeting those skill areas they most need to improve. Skill areas are targeted by setting specific goals that the students will plan and complete. For example, if they want to improve conversational skills, they might set two or three goals to engage in conversation in particular situations. Interviewers inform them that they will be required to complete a minimum number of goals in their selected areas, and that one of those goals must be a public speech. The interviewer is clear about what the program entails because students should be giving informed consent when they agree to register for the training.

The second time information about the program is presented is at the first session of class. Instructors provide students with a detailed syllabus (see Appendix A) that describes the fundamental skills-based approach utilized in the program and the specific requirements the student is expected to fulfill. The syllabus also includes information on how the students will be evaluated because this is a three-credit course and students receive a letter grade. The grading method is in large part contractual. The teacher tells the students that they must complete a minimum number of goals to receive a "C" in the course and how many they must complete to receive grades of "B" or "A."

Grading is not entirely contractual, however, in that students take two tests, complete a group project, and are evaluated on the quality of the papers they submit with each goal. For the most part, however, students can choose the grade they wish to receive in the course and usually receive that grade because the goals they complete are the most important component of the course.

Between the first class session and the second, students have a 15- to 20-minute conference with their instructors. To this meeting they bring their self-as-communicator paper (described in Chapter 2). At this time, the teacher again explains how the training works, what is expected of the student, and how he or she will be evaluated. It is also at this time that the individualized contract is outlined. The teacher reads the self-as-communicator paper and discusses it with the student. Students are asked to talk about the specific communication problems they experience and how they want to change their behavior. By the end of the conference, the teacher has a list of the skill areas the student wishes to target and the types of behaviors he or she will attempt to change. In addition, the student roughly prioritizes the areas and identifies which one he or she will work on first. This, then, is the basis of the contract between the student and the teacher. It is a "loose" contract in that it does not specify exactly how many goals the student will attempt to accomplish and can be modified as the student progresses through training. Often students discover other skills they want to work on or get motivated by their progress to work on additional areas. Students and instructors remain in contact throughout the program to discuss these changes in the contract.

The Role of the Trainer and Trainee

The training is carried out both individually and in the larger group, which usually consists of 20 students. The teacher's role includes several elements, beginning with running the course and all that it involves (preparing lectures, making plans for class sessions, administering tests, grading, and so forth). Beyond that, instructors are there to meet individually with students to help them identify which goals to work on, to offer advice about how to approach those goals, and to assist the students as they evaluate their attempts.

Instructors do not force students to work on particular goals with the one exception that all students must complete one public speech. The teacher does not tell students what situations they should choose for their goals in order to allow the students to practice their communication skills in situations meaningful for them. One student may find it difficult to talk to strangers of the opposite sex at dormitory parties and may want to complete several goals in such a situation. For another student that situation may be irrelevant; he or she may want to learn to carry on conversation with acquaintances at work. So teachers do not dictate goals, but guide students in goal selection. They attempt to make sure students are ready to tackle a particular goal so that successful accomplishment is the most likely outcome.

The students' role is to identify goals, complete the preparation for each goal, carry out the goals, and evaluate their behavior. In essence, they must motivate themselves to improve because beyond the minimum number of goals required to pass the course, they can complete as many or as few goals as they choose. It is also the students' responsibility to be honest about the goals they have actually completed and in their assessment of their behavior. Trainees often ask how the instructor will know if they actually carried out the goals they set. The standard response is that the students are there to improve. If they are dishonest about the goals they have completed, they are hurting themselves. They may never have another opportunity like this to improve their communication skills.

TRAINING PRELIMINARIES

Before the goal analysis method can be taught, some preliminary training must be delivered. Students are told that classroom instruction is designed to teach performance skills encompassing seven rhetorical subprocesses (Phillips, 1977):

- how to identify a situation in which some goal can be achieved through talk,
- how to select the person(s) to be modified by talk,
- how to set communication goals,
- how to analyze audience and situation and adapt talk to meet the requirements of propriety for that audience and situation,
- how to select and arrange words appropriate for audience and situation,
- how to speak the words and adapt to changing conditions, and
- how to observe and evaluate responses to assess message effectiveness.

Beyond that, a kind of informal "cognitive restructuring" takes places. Students need to be convinced of several points as outlined in Chapter 1. First, instructors stress the notion that communication skills can be learned. Often, these students feel that they were born "shy" or don't have a "talent" for speaking and so cannot really change. Teachers compare speaking to other learned sets of skills that can be developed with training and practice. They emphasize that we generally are not taught to communicate; instead, we learn by modeling and muddling along.

Next, the issue of anxiety about speaking is addressed, and three main points are covered. Teachers argue that some tension about speaking is natural and to be expected, particularly when the person's skills are weak. Who wouldn't feel anxious performing in front of others when one's skills are deficient? They also make it clear that the program does not deal with anxiety directly. Rather, it takes the approach that if people can be trained to be better communicators, they will become less anxious about speaking. The final point is that some level of tension is desirable because it can infuse life into the speaker's delivery. That optimal tension level can usually be achieved by improving one's skills and having successful communication experiences.

Instructors also attempt to persuade students about the value of speaking, because many of them have chosen silence to avoid the anxiety associated with talking. Teachers explain that our sense of self is developed through interaction with others. When we speak, other people respond to us, and those responses in part shape how we see ourselves. If people often yawn and look away when we talk, we can come to see ourselves as boring or as poor conversationalists. Our own responses to ourselves as we talk also affect our self-concept. "Gee, I was very witty just now," or "I did not give those instructions clearly" are thoughts that might lead us, if repeated on many occasions, to define ourselves as humorous or disorganized. The value of speaking for developing and maintaining relationships with others and having an impact on one's world is also stressed. Students are told that a primary way we can make things happen is through communication. We cannot get a job if we will not go to the interview. The teacher will not change a course grade if we do not talk to him or her. And it is difficult, if not impossible, to become close to people if we say little to them.

Generally, teachers introduce this material by putting students into small groups to participate in a forced choice exercise. Students are given a sheet (see Appendix G) listing several statements about the communication process. As a group they decide the extent of their agreement or disagreement with each statement. The purpose of this activity is to stimulate discussion of the principles of communication.

GOAL ANALYSIS

Once the preliminary material is covered, students are ready to learn about goal analysis. Goal analysis is a procedure derived from Mager (1972). It takes students through the steps of setting specific communication goals, preparing for those goals, carrying them out, and evaluating their behavior. This procedure is designed to help students acquire three skills: (a) the ability to clearly define their goals, (b) the ability to list criteria that would indicate successful goal accomplishment, and (c) the ability to plan and prepare to execute a specific goal. Until students learn this procedure, they cannot complete the assignments for the course. In this section we explain the three skills that goal analysis involves, how each is used in the training program, and how each is taught.

Three Skills of Goal Analysis

Setting Specific Goals. Students in the Reticence Program often set unrealistic goals for themselves or do not know what their goals should be for a situation. A student may set an unrealistic goal such as, "I will carry on a conversation with a stranger and we will become friends." Because it is highly unlikely that two people will become friends after a brief initial interaction, the student is setting him- or herself up to fail. Any vague or unrealistic goal increases the likelihood that the individual will be unsuccessful.

Furthermore, the person may be immobilized because the goals are too large and overwhelming. Mager (1972) called vague, unclear ideas "fuzzies." Statements like, "I want to be impressive," or "I want to be popular" are fuzzies to avoid. Fuzzy goals do not give the individual any sense of what to do or how to make "it" happen. Instead, students are taught to set specific, realistic goals, like, "I will carry on a 5-minute conversation with a stranger at the reception," or "I will ask two questions in my accounting class."

Instructors emphasize stating goals in terms of the students' behavior. We cannot control another person's behavior; we can only attempt to control our own. If we state goals in terms of what we want the other person to do (e.g., "She will offer me the job," or "The teacher will give me an 'A' on my speech"), we set ourselves up for failure. A clear goal statement provides direction to our behavior. When we identify goals, they should be stated in terms of what we want to do or how we want to behave. "I want to be a valuable member of my group," and "I want the audience to applaud at the end of my speech" are two inappropriate goal statements. "I will bring a list of possible project topics to my group meeting and share them with the group" is a clear goal that gives direction to the goal setter's behavior.

Setting Criteria for Success. The next skill the goal analysis method develops is the ability to list criteria indicating successful goal achievement. The method develops this skill by forcing students to be specific about what success would look like. Teachers in the program continually ask students, "What would success look like? How will you know when you have achieved your goal?" This concept is difficult for trainees to deal with at first, because people in general do a poor job of evaluating their own behavior. Similar to students in the program, most people have a tendency to evaluate themselves in terms of how they felt about their communication, not how they actually behaved.

If, for example, a student gave a speech judged by the instructor and the audience to be very good, but the student felt nervous, he or she would assume the speech had been a total failure. Students are taught instead to make a list of behaviors indicating they had successfully completed a goal. For example, for the goal, "I will carry on a 5-minute conversation with a stranger at the reception," the student might generate the following criteria for success:

"I will introduce myself during the conversation."
"I will maintain eye contact about 50% of the time while talking and 75% of the time while listening."
"I will contribute about half of the conversation."
"I will close the conversation by saying, 'Nice talking to you' or some other permanent closing."

Instructors emphasize that the items on the list must be phrased in terms of behaviors, not feelings. Students' lists must focus on their behavior, not the other person's behavior. Criteria lists give students a concrete tool for assessing their behavior in a specific situation. Furthermore, the lists allow them to see themselves as partially successful rather than as a total failure. When individuals evaluate themselves on the basis of some overall impression, they tend to declare themselves successes or failures. If they have a list of standards, they may discover they did some things well and need to improve in other areas. The value of developing this skill of self-evaluation is that trainees can continue to improve after the training is over. To improve, one needs to know what to change. If people cannot assess their own performance, they will not know what specific behaviors to change because there is almost never anyone there to tell them what they did well or not so well.

Formulating a Specific Plan for Goal Accomplishment. The final goal analysis skill is the ability to prepare for a communication goal. Perhaps because students in the Reticence Program often think good speakers are born with a special talent, they do not recognize the importance of preparation. Effective class participation, for example, requires being prepared for class, paying close attention, and mentally formulating questions and answers. Students are taught to make written plans of how they will prepare for, initiate, carry out, and complete their communication goals. Instructors stress that even seemingly unplanned situations, like social conversation, require a plan of action. Otherwise, students are likely to behave as they usually do, falling back on the habits, especially the habit of being quiet, they have developed over the years. Teachers explain that they cannot write out a script, but they can and should plan for the situation. Trainees should, for instance, anticipate possible topics of conversation that might be appropriate to initiate or which are likely to come up. They should think about how they will decide with whom to initiate a conversation and how they might open the conversation. When they enter the situation, they have some possibilities for their own behavior. Even if they deviate radically from the plan (which they rarely do, and usually only when circumstances dictate such a change), they enter the situation feeling more confident and having some direction.

How Goal Analysis is Used in the Training

Students use the goal analysis procedure throughout the training program. As soon as the instructor has taught goal analysis, trainees begin using it. For each goal a student selects, there is a specific procedure to follow that continually develops the three goal analysis skills. Students are given a handout (see Appendix H) to complete every time they are preparing to carry out a communication goal. This goal analysis preparation sheet helps students learn goal analysis by requesting that they state a specific goal, list criteria for success, and list the steps they will take to prepare for and implement the goal.

The goal preparation sheet also requires that students

consider various alternative outcomes and how they will handle each. Communication is not totally predictable because we cannot control the other person's behavior or the unforeseen circumstances that might occur. Teachers train students to consider the possible alternatives. First, they must consider the best, worst, and most likely outcomes that could occur when they attempt their goals. They also need to specify what they will do if and when each happens.

There are two reasons why it is valuable to consider these possible outcomes. Instructors explain that by anticipating different scenarios, students can be better prepared with a course of action. Students usually have a difficult time identifying a worst case scenario that is sufficiently bad. They often end up writing something intended to be humorous like "The building collapses," or "The other person punches me in the face and walks away." Through this exercise, they discover the worst thing that could happen is usually not so bad. If the worst does occur, they are prepared with a response.

Second, students are asked to consider the possibility of something going wrong when they try to carry out their goals. They must answer the questions, "If something goes wrong, when would it be my fault? The other person's fault? The fault of circumstances?" This is an important set of questions because trainees often are too willing to accept the blame for failure. If a goal does not go well, they tend to blame themselves automatically. These questions encourage them to consider that failure might not be their fault. For people who too readily find fault with themselves, this is an important lesson.

Upon completion of a goal, the students write a goal report (see Appendix I). This form asks students to state their end goal, describe their behavior during the goal attempt, and evaluate success on the basis of the criteria listed during goal preparation. Students are also asked, if something went wrong, to determine if it was their fault, the fault of the other person, or the fault of circumstances. They also respond to the question, "If you could do the goal again, what would you do differently?"

For each goal that a student carries out either in or outside of the classroom, he or she completes a goal analysis paper, gets instructor approval for the goal and the paper, executes the goal, and writes a goal report evaluating his or her performance. Students who complete six goals for the course (which is not unusual), write 12 papers. It should be clear to the reader that the goal analysis method is a critical part of the training program. Without it, the program would be something entirely different.

How Goal Analysis Is Taught

The amount of class time devoted to instruction in goal analysis is not great, but the concepts need to be reinforced at various points and on individual papers. Trainers begin with a brief lecture on goal analysis and the three skills it is designed to teach. They spend time providing the rationale for the procedure too. Students participate in activities such as generating criteria of success for various sample goals or identifying fuzzy goal statements, and they receive a sample goal analysis (Appendix J) to guide them.

Students are tested on the material at the next session to encourage their rapid learning of goal analysis. Students are asked to write their first goal analysis paper within the first 2 weeks of class, preferably by the third class meeting. Most students have to rewrite the first goal analysis preparation paper because the papers are full of fuzzies or lack detail. Students need to get used to this rather unusual way of thinking about and planning for communication.

Throughout the program, instructors write comments on students' papers to reinforce their understanding of and ability to use the goal analysis method. On occasion, if a number of students have been making the same mistake, the teacher will review that point. For example, if students are consistently writing criteria focusing on the other person's behavior, it may be necessary to reinforce their skills by having a brief lecture on how to write criteria for success accompanied by some in-class exercises. In addition, after students complete their first and second goals, they sit in a circle and discuss their goals, what they did, and their evaluation of their goal attempts. Trainers use this time to go over points about goal analysis as needed.

The goal analysis method is a central part of the program. Students learn it early and use it consistently throughout the course. Its primary purpose is to force trainees to think about their behavior, not their feelings, and to plan for communication situations. Some students resist goal analysis at first because they find it so difficult to think only in terms of their behavior or to identify "what success would look like." Once mastered, the process becomes a relatively easy one for them and helps them see when they have been successful.

AUDIENCE AND SITUATION ANALYSIS

To complete the goal analysis process, students must develop the ability to analyze a communication situation and the other people involved in it. Teachers explain that all communication occurs in a context, a specific time and place in which a person feels he or she can accomplish something by speaking (Kelly & Watson, 1986). The audience is any person or group of people involved in the act of communication. Students are trained to use a set of heuristics to conduct an audience and situation analysis. Instructors explain that *situation analysis* means observing the context to determine what is appropriate behavior. What do people talk about in that situation? What do they do? How do they greet each other?

Audience analysis refers to assessing the other people involved in the communication in terms of their needs, interests, goals, and so forth. Thus, students are taught to examine potential communication situations in terms of time of day, time available, the physical setting, social rules and norms for behavior, relationship(s) to the other(s) involved, possible goals of the other(s), and appropriateness of the goal for the particular audience. We provide more detail about these heuristics in this chapter.

Instructors also try to persuade students to see the value of listener and situation analysis. These analyses are important because they enable the speaker to select behaviors appropriate for the audience and the situation. Although we often communicate almost automatically, and we are influenced by the behavior of others, we do make choices when we interact. We choose what to talk about or not talk about, our language, and the verbal responses we convey to others. Teachers stress that effective speakers are people who can adapt to varying situations and listeners.

A second reason for developing the skill of analysis is to increase our confidence. When people spend time observing and analyzing situations and thinking about the other people involved, they remove some of the ambiguity and gain a sense of being prepared.

In this section we discuss the skills of audience and situation analysis by describing the guidelines students are taught and the methods of instruction used in this segment of the program. Like the goal analysis method, this material is taught early in the training program and is reinforced throughout the semester. These two sets of skills are fundamental to the rest of the training program, which, for the most part, focuses on various contexts (social conversation, interviewing, small groups, etc.). Although the methods of situation analysis and audience analysis are essentially the same, we separate them here for purposes of discussion. They are rejoined in our discussion of how instructors teach these skills.

Situation Analysis

Situation analysis involves observing the features of situations that provide clues about appropriate communication behaviors. Most people assess situations to some degree, although they may not be systematic about it. The procedure taught in the Reticence Program includes thinking about and observing each of several situational features described in the next section.

Features of Communication Situations. Special section instructors discuss time, place, and norms for behavior as three features of situations. Students are taught that there are two ways to look at time in sizing up situations. First, speakers must consider the time of day and day of the week in making choices about when to initiate an interaction or make sense of one that is occurring. Certain times of the day are more conducive to successful conversation. Many people, for instance, are not interested in serious talk early in the morning or very late at night. Teachers generally are eager for lunch at 11:45 a.m. and for the weekend at 3:45 on Friday afternoon. Students are told to consider the influence that time of day and day of the week may have on communication, especially on the response they receive from others.

The other aspect of time is how much time is available for the interaction. Students are encouraged to determine how much time they either want or need for a specific interaction. For example, in trying to straighten out a relationship problem with a friend or family member, one needs to pick a suitable time allowing the conversation to reach resolution. Both people feel frustrated when there is not enough time to finish a discussion. There are also time limits, especially for a public speech or an interview. Students need to consider what they can realistically hope to accomplish in the time allotted. People who speak beyond the limit set tend to annoy their listeners and lose their interest.

The second situational feature is the place where interaction is taking or will take place. People gather in all kinds of places, and the place itself influences the communication process. For instance, when people try to talk at parties where the music is loud, they tend to speak very little and about highly superficial topics. It is hard to discuss an important issue when you have to shout and then strain to hear the response. In these situations people tend to rely heavily on brief remarks and a great deal of nonverbal communication.

Consider a second example. Students often work in small groups on class projects. Sometimes groups choose to meet at one member's apartment or dorm room, which may not be large enough or have enough seating for all members to sit comfortably in a circle. Instead, members are scattered awkwardly, some seated on the floor, some on a couch, and others in chairs. This arrangement of group members makes it difficult or impossible for all to address each other, and encourages the occurrence of coalitions or side conversations.

Both of these examples illustrate how the place in which communication occurs influences, often inhibits, interaction. Students in the special program learn to consider the effects of place and choose locations that enhance communication. Specifically, they are trained to examine the following four aspects of a physical setting having the potential to affect communication:

Size of the room. How large or small a room is can have an effect on communication. If a small number of people, who are strangers to each other, attend a party held in a large space, they may be uncomfortable and gravitate toward the edges of the room. Students often have more difficulty participating in classes in large lecture halls simply because of the number of people present. They also find they must project their voices to be heard.

Distractions. In any location there can be unexpected distractions such as noise out in the hallway, coughing audience members, or a crying baby. When distractions occur, speakers need to adapt by changing location, speaking louder, or waiting for the distraction to cease. Trainees learn to consider likely and/or certain distractions and to choose places more conducive to communication or devise plans for coping. Distractions cause people's attention to wander, even for those who are highly motivated to listen or participate.

Organization of the setting. Arrangement of space and furnishings can either impede or encourage interaction between people. Party guests often end up in the kitchen because kitchens usually have no furniture in the middle, giving people space to stand and counters or appliances to lean against. In a living room area there may not be enough seating for everyone, and it is awkward for people to converse when some are standing and others have settled into sofas and chairs. Trainers teach students to look at how spatial arrangements may affect communication and, when possible, arrange space to be appropriate for communication goals.

Presence of others. In some ways, other people's presence in a setting can be considered a type of distraction. However, here we are concerned with others in the setting who are not directly involved in the interaction. Kelly and Watson (1986) referred to these bystanders as a *nonimmediate audience.* These people are not directly involved in the interaction, but have the potential to listen to the conversation and shape the behavior of the communicators. Teenagers who do not have a telephone in their rooms, for instance, may censor their conversations with friends because a parent is within earshot. People can refrain from saying what they want to say or choose words carefully in case they may be overheard. On other occasions a person may be more interested in impressing members of the nonimmediate audience than in actually communicating with the person ostensibly involved in the conversation. Again, it is the presence of other people that affects the nature and quality of the interaction.

Students learn to consider all aspects of place that can affect the communication process. When possible they should choose places conducive to interaction and their specific goals. In other instances, they can try to make the best of a poor location or at least understand how the interaction is being shaped by the place.

The third major situational feature instructors discuss is the norms for communication and other behavior. Students are trained to examine situations to determine what expectations for behavior (norms) exist so they can communicate in ways that do not violate those norms. When they do violate norms, it should be a conscious choice rather than a faux pas. One way to determine the norms is to consider the nature or purpose of the situation. People gather for many purposes, and the purpose for a particular interaction sets some of the behavioral norms. For example, when the purpose is to conduct an employment interview, there are expectations about appropriate topics, language choices, and how much each communicator should speak. Purpose interacts with place and time, of course, and so considering time and place in addition to the nature of the situation helps one identify norms.

Our ability to identify norms depends in part on how much experience we have in various situations or how much vicarious exposure we have had through reading, watching films or television, or listening to others talk about their experiences. If one has never taken an oral comprehensive exam, it is difficult to assess the norms for that situation. To build the requisite experience, teachers encourage students to expose themselves to varied situations and take the time to observe carefully what people do, what they talk about, and how they talk.

Audience Analysis

Besides examining the situation in which communication occurs, students learn to assess their audience, the other person or persons with whom they intend to speak. Similar to situation analysis, the purpose of audience analysis is to make appropriate and effective communicative choices. To maximize the possibility of goal achievement, we must communicate in ways appropriate to the particular audience. Trainers emphasize that we are unlikely to accomplish our own goals if we fail to address the needs, interests, and goals of the audience. Specifically, they teach students to examine three aspects of their audience: the nature of the relationship between speaker and audience; the goals of the listener; and audience needs, values, and interests.

Relationship Between Speaker and Audience. Instructors discuss the idea that the nature of the relationship we have with another person has a strong influence on the communication process. How intimate we are with the other, the social roles we enact, and the status of each person in relation to the other all bear on the topics discussed, the language used, and how meanings are interpreted. For example, the range of conversational topics is generally restricted in nonintimate relationships when communicators are of unequal status. On the other hand, we can discuss many subjects with intimate others in a relationship of relative equality. Students are taught to consider the type of relationship they have with the audience and the history of that relationship to help them make informed and appropriate communicative choices. Teachers give them the general advisory that we must rely more on situational norms when communicating with nonintimate others. It is very important that students learn what is appropriate in various situations. Violations of propriety are a major source of trouble in interpersonal communication. Students are advised to be careful of divulging personal information to relative strangers.

Goals of the Audience. Most of us cannot get away with a

"Do-it-because-I-said-so" approach to speaking; we must take the goals of our audience into account and design our communication so all people involved can achieve their goals. Goals often are compatible, but when they are not, it is much more difficult for everyone to be satisfied. In many situations, however, we do not know exactly what the other's goals are, but we can infer what those goals might be. For a speaker at a publicized lecture, for example, the goals of the audience members must be considered. Why are they attending the lecture? They must have either some interest in the topic, the speaker, or the sponsoring organization. The speaker faced with this task has a relatively easy job of making effective behavioral choices because speaker and audience goals do not appear to be incompatible. If, however, one roommate wants to study and the other wants to listen to loud music, their interaction goals are conflicting. The studious roommate must keep the other's goal in mind when devising strategies for talking about the conflict.

Sometimes people know what the audience's goals are; at other times, they must infer those goals from knowledge of the audience, from what happens during the interaction, and from the nature and history of their relationship with one another. However this inference is made, the objective is to create a win-win situation so that all parties at least partially achieve their goals. Students are told that creating a win-win situation does not mean they must defer to others or relinquish their own goals. Rather, they should try to achieve their goals and satisfy those of the other simultaneously, or they may want to consider modifying their goals at times in the interest of longer range objectives or the relationship itself.

It is important not to stereotype others when assessing an audience. It has long been customary to advise students that women, elderly people, African Americans, and teenagers have certain goals and motivations in common. This is a dangerous way of thinking. There are some general human needs; for example, we all seek self-esteem. We all welcome a good listener, and we like to talk about ourselves. Beyond that, students are trained to look for conversational cues to what the other person seeks and what his or her interests are.

Audience Needs, Interest, and Values. Finally, trainees are encouraged to assess both general needs, interests, and values of the audience and those relevant to the specific communication context. It is important to use effective delivery to maintain listener attention as we discuss later; another way to maintain attention is to speak to people about their interests or to incorporate their interests into the interaction. People pay attention when their needs are addressed by a speaker or when the speaker relates ideas to their needs and interests.

Furthermore, if we do not consider the audience's values, we may be surprised to discover we have offended them or provoked a hostile reaction. We do not need to change our values to suit others; we do need to recognize value differences and communicate in ways that maximize our chance of being heard and listened to. Instructors advise students to make inferences about needs, values, and interests on the basis of information provided by the context, the audience, and the history of their relationships with those listeners.

Because we generally can only make assumptions about our listeners, students are taught to be ready to adapt their goals and strategies as they learn more about their audience. Trainees must listen and observe throughout the interaction, and their plans must be flexible. The goal analysis procedure allows them to retain this level of flexibility and requires them to construct alternative scenarios for how a situation might unfold.

Methods for Teaching Audience and Situation Analysis

Trainers lecture on audience and situation analysis, and there is material on the topic in the course text. Following the lecture, students may be asked to complete an exercise taking them through the process of analyzing a situation and an audience and selecting communication strategies appropriate for both. Appendix K provides a sample exercise for an interpersonal situation. Later students analyze the situation and audience for the public speaking context.

The goal analysis procedure is the primary way the skills of audience and situation analysis are taught and reinforced. As described earlier in this chapter, the goal analysis preparation sheet requires students to consider situational issues of time, place, and norms, as well as audience issues such as goals and reactions of that audience. The goal report format used in the program asks students to assess what happened, how the audience responded, how they adjusted to the response, and what they would do differently. By completing the goal analysis preparation and report papers, students acquire experience analyzing audiences and situations and how they might better their communication in future encounters.

CONCLUSION

This chapter focused on two central components of the training program: goal setting and audience and situation analysis. Both are considered to be essential skills in developing communication competence. They are general skills required for communicating in all contexts, from social conversation to public speaking. These skills are taught early in the program of instruction to serve as the basis for other more context-specific skills and to give students many opportunities for developing them. Throughout the program, these skills are referred to and reinforced as specific situations such as class participation, group communication, and public speaking are examined. The next chapter addresses the critical social situations included in the PSU Reticence Program and the methods of instruction designed to help students improve their communication in those situations.

4

MODIFYING CRITICAL SOCIAL SITUATIONS

In the previous chapter we dealt with the skills essential for competent communication performance across situations: goal setting, audience analysis, and situation analysis. We gave examples of the kinds of goals students in the Reticence Program pursue, such as initiating a conversation with a stranger at a party or asking a question in class.

As Phillips and Sokoloff (1979) noted, the goal-setting process is "a form of systematic, individualized instruction directed at improving speech performance in mundane, task, and social situations" (p. 389). Although trainees occasionally set goals for highly involved or novel situations, most goal assignments center on mundane sorts of communication exchanges. These situations occur frequently, and those who enroll in the Reticence Program find routine interactions difficult. The commonality of situation types enables us to generalize instruction to some extent. Although students may be seeking different goals, they are, at least, seeking the same type of goals.

In this chapter, we describe the types of communication situations students choose for major focus. These include social conversation (including speaking to authority figures), class participation, small group discussion, job interviewing, and public speaking. We discuss these contexts in the order in which they are presented to students in the PSU program. In each case, we describe the methods instructors use to help students learn this material and requisite skills.

SOCIAL CONVERSATION

Many trainees are eager to learn "the art of small talk" because they realize they are not very good at it. They observe others handling conversation effectively, whereas they see themselves as uncomfortable, awkward in response, and often at a loss for words when they try to engage a stranger in a conversation. In the unit on social conversation, instructors discuss four topics: the importance of small talk, how to initiate conversation, techniques for maintaining conversation, and how to terminate social conversations.

The Value of Small Talk

Many trainees enter the Reticence Program with the belief that small talk is superficial, hence, meaningless and to be avoided. They rationalize to themselves that they are not good at small talk because it is pointless. Instructors must persuade students that this belief about small talk is misguided. Small talk or *phatic communion* (Malinowski, 1923) is a fundamental type of communication that serves several important purposes. Trainers use a lecture and discussion format to discuss the nature and function of phatic communion. They emphasize how it signals to others that we are friendly and open to communication. When a person says, "Hi. How are ya?" he or she is telling us, "I acknowledge your existence. I am open to communicating with you." Instructors emphasize that "the meaning is in the sound"; it is not what the person says that is important. What matters is that the person spoke in the first place.

Besides being a form of acknowledgment of the other, small talk enables people to begin to get to know each other without risking much of the self. Small talk is safe; after all, no one reveals much about him- or herself. It represents a small advertisement of what an individual might have to offer, but it is easy to terminate because there is little potential for hurt or damage to the other's self-concept.

Finally, students are asked to consider the possibility of trying to start conversations with people by skipping over small talk. One doesn't just walk up to a stranger and say, "I have something to tell you about Schopenhaur," or ask the person who he or she voted for in a recent election. Students recognize immediately that they cannot conceive of how to initiate interaction smoothly without exchanging small talk first. As Condon (1973) pointed out, "Without the small talk first there can be no 'big talk' later" (p. 46).

Students generally find the instructor's arguments about the value of small talk to be quite persuasive. When they discuss small talk, most admit their mistrust of it grew out of their inability to manage it well. They would like to skip it, know they cannot, and recognize their inability to handle it as a barrier to future relationships. They initially resist training in small talk because of their previous experience with it. When they learn about its role in human relationships, they begin to recognize it as a social activity that carries little risk.

Initiating Conversation

Once students are convinced of the value of learning to make small talk, they discover they are essentially equipped to start conversations with strangers. They learn and become skillful with many of the standard openers that people use with each other. They must be convinced that it is acceptable to use standard conversational openers and that they do not need to generate original "one liners" to initiate a conversation. However, they still need to force themselves to begin conversations with strangers.

Instructors spend a good deal of time training students to be comfortable with clichés such as making a comment or asking a question about some feature of the shared situation (e.g., the weather, the band playing, the food), greeting the other with familiar lines, and introducing oneself. Trainers ask students for examples of others' attempts to use "creative" openers and how they responded to those nonstandard opening lines. Students often identify instances where someone has tried to use a "cute" opener, and how this made for an awkward beginning, either because they did not know how to respond or because they did not react the way the person apparently had expected. Teachers emphasize that using standard openers is most effective because others know how to respond to them.

Maintaining Conversation

The reluctance of many reticent people to initiate conversation stems from their inability to keep a conversation going. They feel awkward when normal pauses occur, and they report they do not know what to do next. They seem at a loss for subjects to talk about. In essence, they have a problem with invention. In the next chapter, we discuss in detail the techniques instructors use to help students develop their ability to invent ideas and topics for conversation.

In addition to teaching specific techniques, course instructors make several important points designed to change the way trainees think about the conversational process. To maintain a successful conversation requires the efforts of all participants. Trainers emphasize this reality because reticent students seem to accept all the responsibility for keeping a conversation going and are disappointed in themselves when they cannot fill every pause. They are afraid to rely on their partner to do his or her share.

Teachers encourage trainees to use a variety of techniques in social conversation, rather than rely on one or two formulas. Some, for example, tend to overuse questions as a way to maintain conversation. They seem to want to turn the conversation into an interview, or worse, an interrogation. In response to students' occasional complaints that learning scripted techniques seems awkward and unnatural, teachers argue that over time the techniques become habits and no longer feel artificial.

Trainers make two final points about maintaining conversation. They explain that a person cannot be good at maintaining conversation without being a good listener. The techniques for sustaining a conversation require one to listen to what the other person is saying. Too often reticent people focus so much on planning what to say next, that they fail to listen. By not listening, they miss their conversation partner's cues that could lead them to the next conversational move.

Students are also urged to prepare for conversations by reading the daily newspaper and anticipating likely topics. The goal analysis procedure requires them to identify possible topics. They may find this preparation tedious because they have been taught that conversation is "spontaneous," hence, something for which one cannot prepare. However, people become effective at conversation; good conversationalists are not born. Zolten's (1982) research demonstrates how "popular" people script themselves and adapt their scripts to new situations. Conversational training requires that students master a variety of short scripts and then apply them to a variety of life situations. The classes attempt to teach them these scripts and to show them ways to compose new ones based on their own experience.

Ending Conversation

Just as they are made aware of standard, polite openers people use, students are also taught to identify standard closing lines. People end conversations by saying, "It was nice talking with you," or "I've got to go get a refill." Of all the aspects of carrying on conversation, the ending is the least problematic for students in the Reticence Program. They often are eager to end conversations because of their feelings of incompetence and discomfort. Unfortunately, they tend to let others end the conversation, rather than taking the initiative. By teaching them exit lines, they are enabled to terminate unsuccessful experiences, and move on to seek a more comfortable contact, or initiate a temporary ending to a conversation they will resume later.

One issue that trainers bring up, that does not occur to most students, is the distinction between temporary and permanent closings. "See you around," and "It's been nice talking to you" are permanent closings. They signal that there is not likely to be any future contact between the two strangers, unless they work in the same office or are in the same class, of course. Temporary closings indicate a desire for further contact. "I usually work out on Wednesday evenings between 8:00 and 9:00. I'll look for you next Wednesday. Are you planning to be here then?" is an example of a temporary closing. Another is, "There's someone over there I need to see; okay if I catch you later?"

Once teachers talk about the difference between the two types of closings, trainees often express surprise and state that they need to develop a repertoire of temporary closings. Many report they never knew how to move beyond an initial interaction toward the development of a relationship. Teachers use this curiosity to explain how to extend conversations to make dates for subsequent encounters.

Speaking With Authority Figures

One instance of conversation difficult for many trainees is talking with a person in a position of authority (e.g., teacher, boss, advisor, physician). Instructors discuss two types of situations students might face. The first is carrying on conversation with an authority figure in a social setting. For example, students may find themselves at the office holiday party, at a student-faculty reception, or standing in the checkout line with their academic advisor at a local grocery store.

The other, perhaps more common, situation they may experience is speaking to an authority for a particular purpose associated with that individual's role. For instance, a student may seek course selection assistance from an advisor, approach an employer about time off, or want to discuss a medical problem with a physician.

Trainers provide suggestions for handling both casual and intentional contact with authority figures. For casual situations, they advise students to select, when possible, conversational topics centering on what they know they have in common with the authority person (e.g., "I'm finding your course very challenging," or "I was able to get all of the courses you suggested I take"). Instructors caution that casual encounters are not the time to register a complaint or introduce serious business. Conversation about a course, for instance, should be light and neutral or positive. Students also are told to use the other techniques they have learned for maintaining conversation, and finally, to follow the lead of the authority figure. That individual is aware of his or her role and status in relation to the student and generally will take the conversational lead. All the situation requires is for the student to fall in with the topic, ask questions, and introduce a proper closing line when necessary.

For dealing with the formal contacts with authority figures, teachers present several guidelines. They encourage trainees to be clear and specific about their objectives for the contact; then to call to set up an appointment, and at that time, state the purpose of the meeting. They also urge students to prepare for the interaction so they are clear and concise in their communication. The goal-setting system is applicable here. The student can work out the script in advance, making sure everything he or she says helps achieve what he or she set out to achieve.

Students are also advised about how to introduce themselves and explain the purpose of the interaction. They are told to give "the big picture" first, for example, "I am here for advice about next semester." Then the student is told to introduce a specific question or topic, for instance, "I am not sure whether I should continue with the humanities sequence or start my science courses next semester." They are also urged to define what a satisfactory outcome would be and to continue asking until they are clear on how the situation has been resolved and what is to happen next.

Student: I am not sure whether I should continue my humanities
   courses or start my science courses.
Teacher: I think it's six of one and half a dozen of the other.
Student: You mean, I can make the choice. I am more comfort-
   able continuing the humanities sequence.
Teacher: Okay, then do it.

Once the end of the conversation is reached, the student must thank the other person for his or her time, regardless of the outcome.

The "Social Conversation Party"

The culmination of the unit on social conversation is a mock cocktail party, conducted (without alcohol) during class time. The purpose of this activity is to provide students with a relatively safe opportunity to practice their social conversation skills, particularly the new techniques they have learned. Guests are invited, including several authority figures, and light refreshments such as soft drinks and chips are served. Little time is spent on the refreshments. The focus of preparation is on "the talk."

This is an unusual party because students have an assignment to carry on conversations with at least three people. The guests do not know this, of course. Generally, the social conversation party lasts about 1 hour. Students are assigned to meet three strangers, find out their names and at least one "interesting" thing about them.

After the guests leave, the instructor leads the class in a discussion of their experiences. Each student is asked to comment on his or her conversations. For example, students talk about who they met, how they or the other initiated the conversation, what topics were introduced, and how they ended their conversations. This debriefing of the party serves several purposes. Students can review the material on social conversation, and they can share concrete examples of the techniques and issues involved in carrying on conversation. Students can also help build, through discussion, a supportive classroom environment in which they feel safe to discuss their past and future experiences and ask questions about them.

CLASS PARTICIPATION

Because participants in the Reticence Program are college students, the next unit centers on effective participation in the classroom. This material can be altered slightly to shift the focus to participation in large meetings.

The material on classroom participation is presented primarily through lecture and discussion. Teachers encourage students to use the Reticence Program course as an opportunity to practice participating in class. In addition, they discuss several aspects of effective participation: observing classroom norms, preparing to participate, and planning types of verbal participation.

Observing the Classroom Norms

Audience and situation analysis, two of the essential communication skills, come into play in the unit on class participation. Trainers explain that by carefully observing the participation norms for a particular class, students will learn to participate appropriately. Students must pay attention to how the teacher encourages or discourages participation. Are students free to ask questions or make comments at any time or does the teacher reserve particular times for participation? What kinds of participation does the teacher seem to encourage? How does he or she generally respond to participation? Particular attention is paid to these issues in the training classes. Students analyze their own participation and the participation of others. The teacher, furthermore, encourages different kinds of participation, sometimes calling for questions, sometimes encouraging students to talk to each other. When all else fails, the teacher will prepare questions, write them on 3 x 5 cards, pass them out, and make each student responsible for asking the question at the appropriate time in the class session.

By practicing in these ways, students are trained to participate in their other classes. Goal analysis trains them to observe classroom norms and show how their participation will fit the norms. They are also asked to prepare their questions in writing, so they will not hesitate when they get the opportunity to ask them. Students then report back with an evaluation of their teachers' responses to their participation. Conducting this situation analysis gives the students a sense of how to adapt their participation appropriately in a given class.

Preparing to Participate

Students in the Reticence Program often believe that other students in their courses spontaneously generate good ideas without any particular preparation. This may be true in a few instances, but most students who participate effectively in class are well prepared. They have been attending class, reading, and keeping up with the material. Their engagement with the course material and their preparation enables them to generate good questions and insightful comments. Teachers in the Reticence Program emphasize the relation of effort to success. When trainees heed the advice offered, they find they are in a better position to participate effectively and more confident about what they have to say.

Types of Verbal Participation

There are various ways that students can participate in class. Instructors discuss these ways and offer suggestions for each. Reticent students are generally most willing to participate by asking questions. However, they tend to limit themselves to asking clarifying questions, and do not typically ask more open-ended questions that go beyond the lecture material. Trainers stress the value of open-ended questions because the answers can lead to increased understanding of course content and enable students to see connections to other concepts or courses.

A second form of verbal participation trainers discuss is answering questions. Students in the Reticence Program are not likely to volunteer to answer a question in class because they fear being wrong. Instructors remind students that if they are prepared for class, they are less likely to be wrong. They also explain that not all questions have a single correct answer, and sometimes teachers ask questions because they want students to explore ideas, offer alternative perspectives, or generate new answers. Furthermore, trainers argue that it is all right to be wrong on occasion. Giving an incorrect answer is not a major catastrophe, and in fact, sometimes it is a valuable way to learn. The student should know how his or her teachers respond so they can anticipate what the response will be to their answers.

Beyond trying to persuade students why they should answer questions in class, trainers advise them to be concise when answering questions, unless it is clear that the teacher is trying to promote greater exploration of issues. In general, however, the rule of thumb is to be direct and brief in answering questions. There are usually many people in a course, so lengthy individual contributions tend to be considered as inappropriate.

A final form of verbal participation is expression of opinions. This form is typically the most difficult type of participation for reticent communicators. Expressing an opinion is risky because others may disagree and reject the opinion, and trainees fear rejection. They also do not like to be the center of attention, and offering an opinion in class can put one in the spotlight. Reticence Program instructors emphasize the need to provide support for one's opinion, to give the reasons behind it. Too many students offer unsubstantiated opinions and put themselves on the defensive when others disagree and they cannot provide needed support. Trainers advise students to formulate both an opinion and justification for it. Students can give examples, discuss experiences they have had, or cite the course reading, but they must support their views in some way. Then the discussion and disagreement can center on the evidence, and whether or not the evidence for alternative opinions is more or less persuasive than that offered by the student. Once again, offering opinions and providing supportive remarks is easier when one is well prepared for class.

General Guidelines for Class Participation

The final topic covered is a set of suggestions for improving class participation. Instructors make the following points:

- Participate early in the semester. The longer the student waits to speak out, the more conspicuous he or she tends to feel, and hence, the less likely to participate.
- Sit near the front of the classroom. Listening and staying involved in class is easier when sitting near the front of the room. Furthermore, the student does not have to speak as loudly to be heard by the teacher, an impor-

tant consideration for reticent communicators, many of whom tend to speak softly.

- Write comments and questions. There is nothing wrong with jotting down comments or questions, either when reading or during class itself. Sometimes by writing, students feel more prepared to offer their thoughts because they worry less about being at a loss for words.
- If you have a question, others probably do too. Students sometimes are concerned that they are "wasting" class time by asking a question. Trainers try to convince them that usually when one student has a question, others have the same question and are relieved when it gets asked. If a question is too individualized or requires too much time to address during class time, the teacher will generally suggest that the student stay after class or set up an appointment.

SMALL GROUP DISCUSSION

The third context incorporated into the Reticence Program is the small, task-oriented group. The fast pace and degree of verbal aggressiveness often required in such a situation make it difficult for reticent speakers. Given that there are entire courses on small group communication, instructors must focus on particular aspects of the process. They tend to center their discussion on two topics: following an orderly procedure and effective member behaviors. The focus of discussion is on problem-solving groups because the range of tasks actual groups confront is large and the material must be narrowed in some way. In this section we discuss the material covered and the teaching methods employed in this unit.

Following an Orderly Procedure

Instructors emphasize the need for groups to be systematic and orderly in their approach to problem solving. They teach students the Standard Agenda (Wood, Phillips, & Pedersen, 1986), a six-phase format for group problem solving (See Appendix L). The Standard Agenda directs groups through the processes of under-standing the charge, analyzing the problem, fact finding, identify-ing criteria and limitations on the solution(s), choosing the solution(s), and preparing and presenting the final report. We briefly describe these phases in this section. The Standard Agenda is presented in the same way it is in a regular small group communication course.

The first phase of the Standard Agenda is understanding the charge. The goal of this phase is for the group to reach a common understanding of what they are expected to produce, that is, their charge or task as assigned by a person in authority. Group members need to determine what they are supposed to do, produce, and their deadline for producing it.

The second phase is understanding and phrasing the question. Before a group can adequately solve a problem, it must reach an understanding of the problem itself. Members must spend time discussing the nature of the problem, its symptoms, causes, and implications. The group needs to reach consensus on how the problem is to be defined and whether to develop solutions to address symptoms or causes or both.

Phase 3 is the fact-finding phase of problem solving. Group members need to determine what information is needed. Then they need to collect the information, summarize it, and draw conclusions. The purpose of the fact-finding phase is to help the group better understand the problem and possible solutions to that problem.

Once groups have completed their fact-finding, they are ready for Phase 4, setting criteria and limitations. Criteria are the standards by which the group will evaluate the quality of potential solutions. Trainers remind students that they set criteria for their own behavior every time they prepare a goal analysis, and that setting criteria for a solution is essentially the same process.

Limitations are the boundaries within which the group must work. Because groups are embedded in an organizational context, they are subject to the rules and policies of that organization. When groups attempt to solve problems, they have budgetary limitations, logistical limitations (e.g., personnel, time, space), institutional limitations (i.e., organizational policies, procedures and rules), legal limitations, moral limitations, and suasory limitations (i.e., What is it possible to persuade the charging authority and relevant constituencies to accept?).

Phase 5 is discovering and selecting solutions. Once a group has identified its criteria and limitations, it is in a better position to generate and evaluate solutions. By the end of this phase, the group should have reached agreement on a solution or solutions.

The final phase of the Standard Agenda is preparing and

delivering the final report. The report must make a persuasive case for how the group has defined the nature of the problem, the criteria generated to evaluate the solution, and, of course, the proposed solution. By showing that the solution meets the criteria and, at the same time, fits within the defined limitations, the group can often persuade those in authority that the solution they propose is appropriate and likely to be effective.

The teacher provides an example or set of examples throughout the presentation of the Standard Agenda phases. For instance, he or she might present a problem, such as college students getting closed out of classes at registration, to illustrate that problems can be approached from many perspectives, and groups need to reach agreement on how they will define the problem. Trainers give examples of criteria and limitations and may ask students to generate some for a campus problem.

Effective Member Behaviors

Through a combination of lecture and discussion, trainers generate a list of behaviors exhibited by effective group members. This activity underscores the range of behaviors needed to help a group progress on both the task and interpersonal dimensions. In this section, we discuss briefly many of the types of behaviors Reticence Program teachers present to students. Not all of these behaviors involve actual verbal participation, but instructors do stress the need for students to speak out in groups. Preparing for meetings, taking minutes, and doing other tasks all represent important contributions, but group members must ask questions, state and support opinions, and challenge assumptions to be effective participants in the group process.

Helping Maintain Orderly Procedure. One important contribution members can make is to assist the group in following the Standard Agenda or whatever orderly procedure is being used. A member who sees that the group is trying to generate a solution before considering the nature of the problem can attempt to persuade the group to discuss the problem first. Moreover, if it becomes clear that the group is uncertain of what its charge is, someone can ask the group to back up and talk about what it is supposed to be doing.

Preparing for Meetings. Teachers discuss the need for members to prepare for meetings, even if that preparation involves simply thinking about ideas that might be useful to the group. This preparation is especially important for students in the Reticence Program because it tends to increase their confidence, and hence, their verbal participation. Many group members do not come to meetings prepared; the member that does is more likely to offer valuable ideas to the group.

Expressing Ideas and Opinions. Groups cannot make much progress if members do not offer ideas or state their opinions about topics and issues being discussed. Ideas are the stuff of group problem solving and decision making. Instructors urge students to express their ideas, but to recognize that some ideas will be rejected, others accepted, and still others will be modified by the group. Ideas become the "property" of the group, so individual members need not feel threatened by the group's scrutiny of those ideas they offered. Students are also taught to provide support for their opinions. Effective members are able to offer evidence or good reasons for their opinions, and hence, to persuade the group to accept or see the value of those opinions.

Taking Responsibility. Effective group members complete their share of the work and meet any other responsibilities that they incur. Teachers stress that fulfilling basic responsibilities, like attending meetings and being prepared for them, can contribute much to a group's success. Beyond that, members need to volunteer for tasks and then follow through. Members can volunteer to take minutes, make telephone calls, photocopy documents, tabulate statistics, prepare visual aids, or perform any number of other tasks.

Performing Leadership Functions. Not all groups have a designated leader, but even when a leader has been appointed or elected, other group members can perform leadership functions. For example, any member can help keep the group on track, clarify objectives, or summarize the group discussion. Teachers encourage students to observe what leadership the group needs at the time, particularly when the group has no designated leader overseeing the process.

Demonstrating Supportive Behaviors. A final set of effective member behaviors includes those showing respect and support for other members and the group as a whole. Examples of such behaviors include being attentive, showing trust, communicating disagreement tactfully, commenting on ideas rather than members, and expressing loyalty to the group. Members who participate in these ways help maintain cooperation and morale in the group as well as contribute to the development of group cohesiveness.

Teaching Methods in the Small Group Unit

In addition to the lecture and discussion format for the material on the Standard Agenda and effective member behaviors, teachers in the Reticence Program use both an in-class group activity and a group project as instructional methods. Students are divided into small groups of about five members for both group activities. For the in-class exercise, there is no particular method for arranging students into groups. Generally, they group themselves on the basis of proximity of their seats.

For the group project, completed largely outside of class, the instructor devises the groups. Typically, instructors try to compose the groups so they are mixed-gender, although this is not always possible depending on class composition. They also take into consideration the severity of the students' communication problems, avoiding placing an exceptionally reticent student in a group of moderately outgoing classmates (generally no one in the class is highly extraverted).

The in-class exercise is a decision-making task that can be accomplished by a group in about 30 to 40 minutes. Any number of tasks would work, but one that is commonly used at PSU is the scholarship exercise (see Appendix M). This type of task has been selected because what the group is supposed to accomplish is straightforward; all the information the group needs to make a decision can be provided on a handout, yet the task is complex. This activity illustrates the need for groups to develop and use a systematic procedure and develop ways for members to contribute effectively to the group's discussion.

The more extensive group project task varies from semester to semester, but often involves some aspect of the course itself. For example, groups have been given the task of designing materials and activities for teaching course units. Another task involved making recommendations for improving the way students learn about and are enrolled into the program. The projects are designed to allow students to apply the Standard Agenda; in fact, groups must give evidence of following the agenda in their final written report. For instance, they must phrase a question and discuss their understanding of the problem/charge, present evidence of fact finding, identify their criteria and limitations, and offer recommended solutions. The project is assigned during the unit on small group communication, but students have until the end of the semester to complete it. Instructors provide students with some class time to work in their groups, but most of the work is completed outside of class. All groups produce a written report; groups may opt to present an oral report to the class as an in-class public speaking goal. The group presentation is an oral version of the material in the written report.

As a result of these activities, all students have an opportunity to develop their skills in small group communication. The emphases of this unit are on understanding and following an orderly procedure (the Standard Agenda) and developing effective member behaviors. This somewhat limited coverage of the small group process is necessitated by the structure of the course and the amount of time needed for the many other topics. However, the material included is central to increasing the student's effectiveness as a communicator in the small group context.

JOB INTERVIEWING

Job interviewing was incorporated into the PSU Reticence Program because so many of the students in the program are seniors. Many delay enrolling in the regular speech communication course until their last year because of the difficulties and fears they have about speaking. Because many fear the interview situation, and many of them face job interviews in the spring of their senior year, instructors devote class time to discussing the employment interview and practicing in mock interviews. Specifically, the unit begins with material on resume writing, followed by how to prepare for and participate in an interview. Students can then choose to undergo a mock interview to practice their skills. This section describes each of these components.

Resume Writing

Trainers lecture on how to write a resume, distributing sample resumes for students to use as models for their own. Like many college students, these students generally have no experience with preparing a resume. Instructors discuss the purpose of the resume (i.e., to land an interview, not a job), the kinds of information that should or should not be included in a resume, and acceptable resume formats. All trainees prepare a resume to be evaluated by the course instructor, who provides each student with a written critique. Most report that this assignment motivates them to develop their resumes and gives them suggestions for strengthening their resumes.

Material on Job Interviewing

Material on the employment interview falls into two main categories: preparing for the interview and communicating effectively during the interview. This material is presented in a lecture/discussion format, usually during one class session.

Preparing for the Employment Interview. Teachers discuss three aspects of preparation for job interviews. The first stage of preparation is self-analysis. Students learn to think about their job and career aspirations, what kind of work they like and do not like to do. They consider their strengths and weaknesses, particularly in terms of the type of job they are seeking. Teachers suggest students think about what they are looking for in a company, a job, and a career. This kind of self-reflection is crucial for success on an employment interview because many interview questions probe these issues. The person who has given little or no thought to questions such as these will find it very difficult to provide answers, let alone well-developed, specific answers.

The second aspect of preparation instructors discuss is researching the particular organizations to which the student is applying. Students are taught to find out as much as possible about a company prior to the interview (e.g., the location, size, product and/or service lines, market share, chief competitors). This information allows the student to make an informed decision about whether he or she would want to work for a given company. Doing homework on a company also provides the background necessary to ask intelligent and fruitful questions and demonstrate interest in the company.

Instructors in the program help students in the final aspect of preparation, developing and practicing answers to common interview questions, by providing a list of typical questions (see Appendix N). They may even have students take some time to write answers to a few of the more challenging questions (e.g., "What is your greatest weakness?") and then lead a discussion of the trainees' answers. Students are encouraged to think through their answers to all of the common questions and practice saying

72

those answers aloud. The purpose is not to memorize answers, but to practice articulating them so that answering the questions in an actual interview situation is easier. Rehearsing responses also can help build student confidence and decrease anxiety about the interview, two consequences especially significant for the students in the Reticence Program.

Participating in an Interview. Thorough preparation is very important to successful performance in a job interview. Teachers also address dos and don'ts of handling the actual interview session. They stress that interviewees should answer questions directly and specifically, providing concrete examples to support claims. The student who claims to have leadership ability, for instance, should provide examples of how and when he or she has demonstrated leadership behavior. This kind of specificity is unlikely to occur if the interviewee has not thoroughly prepared.

Reticent individuals have difficulty selling themselves in the employment interview situation. They are generally unaccustomed to talking much about themselves, let alone about their positive qualities and strengths. Instructors talk about the importance of speaking positively and confidently about oneself. The best way to sell one's qualifications is to provide evidence using specific examples and experiences as discussed previously.

Reticence Program trainers tell interviewees to be active in the interview process. Students should demonstrate active listening by responding nonverbally (nodding and smiling when appropriate, maintaining eye contact), asking relevant questions, and making comments. If the interviewer does not ask a question about an important job qualification, the interviewee should mention that experience or expertise at an appropriate time.

Beyond these guidelines for communicating effectively in the interview, teachers discuss what constitutes an illegal question and how to respond when asked an inappropriate or illegal question. The primary way to deal with such a question is to counter with a question about its relevance to the job.

The Mock Interviews

Students have the opportunity to participate in a mock employment interview as one of their out-of-class goals for the course, even though the interviews take place in the classroom. On their resumes, students electing to be interviewed indicate the type of job they are seeking. The instructor collects the resumes several days in advance and distributes them to the interviewers. Interviewers are other faculty, graduate students, or staff from the campus career center, whoever the instructor is able to recruit. The interviewers are given resumes in advance so they can prepare both general and specific questions.

At the class session in which the interviews take place, the students are placed in small groups, the number depending on how many interviewers are available. Each group consists of an interviewer, one or two students who will be interviewed, and two or more students who will observe the interviews and take notes. Interviewers conduct 10- to 15-minute interviews with each student interviewee. After each interview is completed, the interviewer leads the small group in a discussion of what occurred, focusing on what each interviewee did well and how each could improve. Student observers comment on what they observed as well.

Students respond very favorably to this activity, even those who do not choose to participate as interviewees. They report that they learned by observing and listening to the interviewers' feedback. Those who participate in the interviews usually consider the experience valuable practice. They often admit they did not prepare adequate answers and, as a result, were stumped by some of the more difficult questions. Thus, all students in the program have experience writing a resume, receiving information about preparing for and handling interviews, and either observing or observing and participating in mock interviews.

PUBLIC SPEAKING

The last content area given specific attention is public speaking. Much of the content covered resembles that normally found in a public speaking course. The unique feature of the public speaking instruction in the PSU Reticence Program is the methods used to help students prepare for and actually deliver a public speech. Many of these students are absolutely convinced at the beginning of the program that they will not be able to stand up and speak in front of the class. Most of them have managed to avoid public speaking completely, or have not spoken to an audience in years. They have persuaded teachers to allow them to write a paper instead of speaking, or they simply have not shown up to speak and accepted the consequence of a failing grade for the assignment. For most, public speaking is the dreaded experience. As a result, instructors in the Reticence Program must use special methods to get students ready to speak and to actually perform.

In a regular speech course, teachers typically just assign a speech and students fulfill the assignment. In the PSU Reticence Program, some proportion of the students simply would not or could not comply to this assignment. In this section, we discuss briefly the content covered in the public speaking unit, and then explain the instructional methods used to ensure that all students are able to present a speech to the class. Over the years there have been only a negligible number of trainees who did not fulfill this requirement, illustrating the success of the methods employed.

Public Speaking Content

Most of the content in the public speaking unit concerns stages of preparing a public speech. Delivery is also taught as explained in Chapter 6. Prior to discussing speech preparation, however, instructors spend time persuading students to look at public speaking a bit differently. Many of them view speech making as very formal and threatening; they see it more as performance than communication. Although this view can be correct, to begin to develop their speech skills, students need to view speaking in a less intimidating way. Thus, the concept of public speaking as "enlarged conversation" (Winans, 1938) is emphasized.

Teachers explain this metaphor as reflecting the similarities between giving a speech and having a conversation with a group of people. If we think of public speaking as an extension of conversation, we are more likely to speak to the audience rather than at them. To accomplish this objective, instructors explain, students should use an extemporaneous style of speaking initially. Although manuscript speaking is sometimes appropriate, for the students in the Reticence Program, preparing notes and speaking from them is a better way to begin developing their speech skills. Preparing carefully, rehearsing, and talking from notes allows the speaker to adapt to audience response and to sound more conversational. Some people can sound conversational when they read, but many beginning speakers cannot.

Once this perspective on public speaking is discussed, trainers lecture on the stages of speech preparation as they would in a regular public speaking course. Choosing a speech topic, identifying the specific purpose and main point, analyzing the audience and situation, generating and organizing ideas (using structuring), incorporating forms of support, preparing notes and visual aids, and rehearsing are the stages of preparation discussed. During the three or more class sessions devoted to these topics, instructors give students brief activities to help them understand each part of the process. For instance, they may give students speech topics or have them generate ones on their own, and then ask them to write a specific speech purpose for each topic. Teachers may have students conduct an audience and situation analysis for a particular speech topic. When we describe structuring as a method for organizing ideas in Chapter 5, we include an explanation of an in-class exercise designed to help students learn to use the structures.

Thus, students have opportunities to practice various aspects of the speech preparation process. They practice both in class and out of class, since the teacher has assigned a speech for which they must prepare. Generally, the speech assignment requires students to select a topic in consultation with the teacher, develop a speech purpose, and then fully prepare about a 5- to 7-minute extemporaneous speech to be presented in class.

Several methods are used to prepare students for their in-class speeches. As mentioned in Chapter 3, seated in a circle, students briefly and informally report to the class about their first goal assignment. Teachers ask them to state what the goal was, what happened when they tried to carry it out, how well they think the goal went, and what they would do differently next time. This report occurs about the third or fourth week of the semester. When all students have said at least a few words about their goals, the teacher suggests that they all just gave their first speech. He or she tells them they all have just presented a brief impromptu speech because they spoke to the whole class for a slightly extended and uninterrupted period of time. Students give similar reports when they have completed their second goal. One purpose is to get students to speak to the whole class to prepare them for the more "official" speech they will give.

A second method used is an impromptu speech activity occurring near the end of the presentation of the material on public speaking. Students are not told about this activity because they are likely to miss class. The goal is to get every student to successfully stand up and speak for several minutes. Success of this activity requires that the teacher provide a supportive, non-threatening environment, which he or she has been building since day one of the program.

During the class period immediately following the lecture

and activity on structuring (see Chapter 5), the instructor brings a set of index cards with impromptu speech topics. The topics are light, often humorous, and simple, such as "The three best excuses for missing class," or "The worst meals served in the dining hall." Each student takes two or three index cards, and then selects a topic. Students are instructed to develop a mini-speech on the topic by drawing the structure they would use, including identifying the main points in that structure, and preparing a very brief introduction and conclusion.

As students work on their speeches, the instructor circulates among them to help as needed. The instructor wants to make sure each student has an organized mini-speech to give so that no one can say they were unprepared. One goal of the activity is to check the students' ability to work with the structuring method, thus the teacher states that when each person gives his or her speech, the audience is to listen for the structure. Teachers downplay this activity as a speech and emphasize its role in teaching structuring. They also try to make the experience seem light, relaxed, and enjoyable so students do not panic.

Students then volunteer to present their speeches. The teacher explains that they need to be in front just for the practice of speaking from the front of the room. Each speech is followed by applause. Because the topics are humorous and light, the teacher and students engage in a fair amount of joking in between speeches. For example, someone might say they think "taco dogs" should be on the list of worst meals served in the dining halls, a comment sure to elicit laughter. In other cases, a student or the instructor asks the speaker a question. These comments are to release tension and make students feel that the class has been listening to their speeches. The applause also helps demonstrate support of each speaker.

Normally, every student in the room presents a speech. After everyone has presented, the instructor can breathe a sigh of relief because it will now be much easier to get each student through the main speech assignment. Another benefit of this activity is the experience students gain in working with the structuring method and the opportunity to clarify misunderstandings about it. Furthermore, students generally enjoy the session and have a positive speech experience to build their confidence for their prepared speech. On the rare occasion when a student refuses to give the mini-speech, the instructor must work closely with that student to enable him or her to complete the speech assignment.

Another important method for getting students ready to

give a speech is the office rehearsal. Each student must rehearse his or her speech with the instructor before presenting it to the class. This tactic accomplishes several things. First, it gives each student a chance to rehearse in front of an audience to see how it feels and to find out how well he or she can explain ideas to others. Second, the instructor gives suggestions so the student can improve his or her speech prior to presenting it in class.

For many students this situation can be more difficult than speaking in front of their peers. If they can give the speech to the instructor, they can present it in class. Some students do not feel ready to present the speech to the class even after rehearsing with the teacher. In these cases, the instructor works with the student by gathering a very small audience of three to five classmates so the student can build up to a larger audience. In these rare instances, only one extra step has been needed to get the student ready for the classroom presentation.

Students sign up in advance for their speech day, and the schedule is adhered to as closely as possible. Instructors do not present oral criticism of individual speeches; instead, each speech is followed by applause and a brief question-and-answer session. After the last speech is presented on a given day, the instructor may choose to mention a positive trend in the speeches (e.g., all the speeches were clearly structured or had effective introductions). Teachers provide a written evaluation to each individual at the class period following the speech.

All students must complete one public speech in class to pass the course. Most elect, however, to complete two or more speeches because they want to acquire greater skill and achieve a higher course grade. Students can present an oral interpretation of literature (see Chapter 6) or participate in a group oral report based on the semester group project. Thus, students have a variety of opportunities to develop competence in public speaking.

CONCLUSION

The program covers five main communication situations: social conversation, class participation, small group discussion, job interviewing, and public speaking. In each unit instructors present material and include activities to help students grasp content and apply it. Some activities, such as the mock interviews, are optional, whereas others are required of all students. Beyond these in-class activities, however, students complete goals (see

Chapter 3) in any or all of these areas, depending on what they have established with the instructor in the individual conference at the beginning of the program. The general approach is to provide students with basic techniques to communicate competently in mundane, but critical social situations.

5

INVENTING AND
ORGANIZING IDEAS

Communication competence depends on having something to say. In her dissertation research, Begnal (1983) discovered that many reticent women lacked topics to talk about. Kelly, Keaten, and Begnal (1992) also found lack of topics to be a problem for both men and women in the PSU Reticence Program. "I don't know what to say," and "I can't come up with topics" are fairly common complaints in the screening interviews. Adults often make the same complaint; "Bill and I have nothing to talk about. We have nothing in common."

In essence, the ability to identify topics worth speaking about is a major component of the classical rhetorical canon of invention, and is central to communication competence (Phillips, 1991). A person speaks to attain some objective, but the arguments to support his or her point of view must be phrased so they are relevant to the listener. An important component of instruction in the PSU Reticence Program addresses the skill of invention, how to generate topics for conversation and public speaking and locate support for ideas.

A companion skill is the ability to organize thoughts so speech is coherent and orderly. Making discourse understandable to others is a major component of the classical canon of disposition. Both the ability to generate topics and the skill of organizing ideas can be taught and both are emphasized in the reticence training program. Students learn a method called *structuring*, which we describe in detail in this chapter, for the dual purpose of generating and organizing ideas for conversation, speeches, interviews, or any other communication situation.

In this chapter we describe how the two critical skills of topic selection and organization of ideas are developed through the Reticence Program. Any program of remediation should incorporate instruction in invention and disposition; the material offered here is designed to serve as a model of how this instruction can be accomplished.

INVENTION: GENERATING IDEAS

People need to talk about ideas; there simply is no way to make an interesting conversationalist or a competent public speaker out of someone who has nothing to say. This section details the methods used at PSU and in spinoff programs to teach students how to come up with topics. In addition to these methods, we encourage students to remain current with the news, books, and films because these are often the subject of conversation or the impetus for a speech topic. People who see movies, read books, and keep up with the day's events find it easier to contribute to conversations or initiate topics. The media represent the best sources for developing invention skills. Beyond being well informed, however, there are some techniques people can use to expand their repertoire of conversation topics.

Training People to Develop Repertories of Conversational Topics

If you followed an interesting conversationalist around, you would soon discover that individual has a well-developed repertoire of topics. However, good conversationalists also use some of the same topics and responses over and over again with different partners or groups. People do not need an endless supply of topics, but they do need a repertoire from which to draw and the ability to fit their remarks into the flow of interaction. In the Reticence Program, instructors use a variety of means to help students develop and utilize their repertories of topics. They train students to improve their skills in monitoring conversation and teach them techniques for maintaining conversations, as discussed in Chapter 4. Teachers also train students in techniques of structuring to generate topics, which we describe following the detailed explanation of structuring.

Becoming an Observer of Conversation. Students are urged to observe good conversations carefully. A good conversation is defined as an oral encounter when all participants seem involved by speaking or listening and seem pleased by their involvement. A simple exercise is to ask students to select someone who they think is skilled at making conversation and watch that person interact with others. In making their observations, they are advised to focus on the following:

- What kinds of topics does the person initiate?
- How are new topics introduced?
- At what point in the interaction?
- What kinds of things does the person say about the topics?
- How are transitions to new topics handled?

If the student can observe the individual on several occasions, he or she can get a better idea of how the skilled conversationalist adapts to different situations. Observers are likely to notice that, although skilled conversationalists may have a limited repertoire of topics, they are able to adjust them to the needs and interests of different listeners in a variety of situations.

Observation of people engaged in conversation also reveals consistencies in the topics people discuss in particular situations. Initially, students in the Reticence Program often fail to realize there are norms for topic choice in various contexts. What two strangers talk about when they meet for the first time at a party is fairly predictable and differs from the topics of conversation between two classmates after class has ended for the day. People who work in the same setting will tend to talk shop. Family members will discuss other family members. Friends may engage in reminiscences or make plans for future encounters.

Shy people spend so much time thinking about what they are going to say they often are not good observers or listeners. They feel there is some magical force that smites people in conversation and brings words to their lips. They need to understand that most conversations are both scripted and predictable. During class discussion and lecture, instructors encourage students to observe conversations for regularities. Invariably they come back to class saying, "You were right! People are predictable in what they talk about and with whom!"

Learning Techniques for Maintaining Conversation. Fortunately, conversations are not entirely predictable, or else we would all be bored most of the time. Students need to do more than learn that there are conversational regularities. They can benefit from learning methods to improve their skill at generating conversational topics and introducing topics into the interaction. Program instructors cover four basic techniques that can be used to keep a conversation going.

1. *Use open-ended questions.* Closed questions like, "Did you like the concert?" are not helpful in maintaining conversation because the answers to them provide little information and often require the questioner to follow with an additional question or comment. Overuse of closed questions also can make a conversation seem like an interrogation. A better question would be, "What did you like best about the concert?" Asking an open question encourages the respondent to say more because it disallows a "yes" or "no" response.

An open-ended question actually sets a brief agenda. Whatever the other person says can guide the original speaker in making a response. The more the respondent says while answering an open-ended question, the more opportunities there are for follow-up comments by the questioner. In answer to the open question about the concert, the other person might say, "The concert was great! I couldn't believe all the people dancing on their seats!" Although a brief response, it provides information for the speaker to probe or add to. For example, he or she might follow with a question, "Were there many people dancing or just a few?" or "Did you dance too?" Another option, if the questioner was also at the concert, is to offer a comment, "I haven't seen so many people dancing like that in ages," or "It was easy to dance because they played all their old tunes that we used to dance to."

2. *Answer a question and follow with a question.* Conversations can sound more like interviews when one person asks all the questions and the other simply answers. The person who answers the question can ask the same question of the partner, resulting in the common form:

Fred: Where are you from?
Beth: Albany. **How about you?**
Fred: Bellefonte.

Although this seems very simplistic, by not returning with the same question, people can contribute to a very awkward interaction:

Fred: Where are you from?
Beth: Albany.
Fred: Is there much to do there?
Beth: No.
Fred: So what's your major?

Monosyllabic answers make the respondent seem rude or uninterested. Thus, instructors teach students the technique of answering a question and asking another because it not only helps them keep conversations going, but also makes for a smoother, more comfortable interaction and projects the image of a person interested in the conversation.

3. *Use situational cues to generate topics.* Topics can always be found by examining the situation in which the interaction occurs. While at a party, people can comment on the food, drink, entertainment, music, the occasion for the party, the people there, their connection to others at the party, or the actual physical setting. They can also compare this party to other parties they have known and loved.

When carrying on conversation with a classmate before or after class, a student can discuss the course subject, the teacher, the assignments, the exams, the sequence of courses it is part of, and so forth. All situations provide some topics of conversation, although certainly some are a richer source than others.

4. *Follow up on what has been said previously.* Teachers explain that follow-up can be used to pursue a conversational line or introduce a topic when a silence has occurred and the direction the talk should take is not obvious to either person. If Sue asks Nancy what she does for a living and Nancy says, "I'm a high school teacher," Sue can follow up on that answer in any number of ways. She can ask questions about how Nancy likes teaching, what it is like to be a high school teacher, or why she chose high school instead of some other level. Within Nancy's statement are two important pieces of information, that she is a teacher and that she teaches high school. Sue can focus on either of the two bits of information. She can also introduce her own job and make comparisons.

Nearly all conversations produce unintentional, and often awkward, moments of silence. These moments occur when a topic has been exhausted and the conversation needs a change in direction. One way to make this change is to backtrack to an earlier topic. Assume that after Sue asked Nancy what she did for a living, and Nancy replied that she was a high school teacher, Nancy immediately asked Sue what she did. Assume also that the two never really developed the topic. When there is a pause later, Sue can ask, "So how did you become interested in teaching?" The conversation can then play through almost limitless iterations if both participants are interested.

In essence, students are taught not to let go of topics immediately, but to follow up on them. If each topic is pursued, even briefly, fewer topics are needed to maintain the conversation and both participants feel a higher level of involvement. A conversation is not superficial when topics are explored in some depth. This is important, given reticent students' objections to "small talk."

To teach the necessary techniques, instructors discuss them and provide opportunities for students to practice them. Students prepare for and complete out-of-class social conversation goals as described earlier, and have other opportunities in class to work on their conversational skills. At the mock cocktail party we mentioned in the previous chapter, students can practice their conversation skills by speaking with at least three others. The debriefing concentrates on the techniques used to get information about these strangers. The instructor leads the class in a discussion of their experiences: how they initiated conversations, what topics they selected for conversation, how they continued the conversation, and how they ended interactions. Students generally enjoy the activity because it gives them a chance to practice the techniques for maintaining conversation in a relatively safe environment. They also like hearing about each other's experiences.

These three methods—training students to observe conversations, providing them techniques for maintaining conversation, and teaching them the structures (discussed later)—are used in the Reticence Program to help students develop their ability to generate topics for conversation. Teachers encourage students to use these techniques, to keep abreast of current events and happenings, and to take advantage of opportunities to engage in conversation, so that they can build their repertoires of topics.

Training People to Generate Speech Topics

Training in speech performance must be directed at carryover. Once people are employed and socializing in the world, most of their presentations are directly related to their jobs or their lives. People, in vivo, have no trouble finding topics about which they must give speeches, although they do often have trouble with generating social conversation topics.

Often, the difficulty isn't with finding a speech topic but with the "spin" given to it. Speakers must learn to select a residual message (i.e., the small bit that audiences remember 24 hours afterward). They need to narrow their topics so their speeches have a clear focus.

Students, of course, participate orally in class, where they ask and answer questions about the subject matter of the course. They are frequently required to give formal reports or presentations in classes. They may have to choose a specific topic, although their range of choice is restricted by the nature of the course.

Some students find it difficult to make a specific selection of what to talk about because they do little reading or listening. They have a shortage of interesting events and information in their lives in general. The conclusion that some people avoid conversation and public speaking because they simply have nothing to say raises the possibility that shyness and communication apprehension are not psychological problems, but rather competency deficits.

For others, choosing a topic is difficult because they are anxious about the appropriateness of what they have to say. Teaching them to analyze the audience and situation is very helpful as a way to determine the appropriateness of topics.

Many individuals, however, have a fairly good storehouse of possible topics; indecision about precisely what to choose may freeze them temporarily. Instructors can provide them with guidelines to help them in the topic selection process.

Guidelines for Topic Selection. Topic choice is important because it affects both the audience's response to the speaker and the way the speaker feels about presenting the speech. Beginning speakers often choose topics they feel are unsatisfactory, and are uncomfortable delivering the presentation. Right up until the minute they speak, some of them are still questioning their topic choice. Therefore, instructors encourage students to start thinking of a topic as soon as they know they have to give a speech. Trainers stress the importance of finding a satisfactory topic and then sticking with it. Inexperienced speakers will sometimes change their topic several times after they have already started the speech preparation, and they end up not well prepared for the speech they finally choose. In addition to the advice to get an early start, teachers present three guidelines.

1. *Choose a topic about which the speaker has some knowledge.* Although choosing a topic the speaker knows may sound like common sense, the advice is valuable because many reticent students have the misconception that only creative or significant topics are appropriate. They do not know what a creative or significant topic looks like, or they know they do not have the expertise to talk about such a subject. They need to be taught not to choose a topic by running to the library, finding an article in a current magazine, and using it as the basis of the presentation. Although the topic may seem important or original, the speaker is unlikely to have either the expertise or the confidence to succeed.

Instructors urge students to identify subjects about which they already have some knowledge. Generally, topic options are not limited, although students must get instructor approval for their speech topics. This procedure is used primarily to prevent problems, such as two students presenting the same topic, which usually makes the students involved very uncomfortable. By checking topics in advance, instructors also prevent a student from selecting a topic that cannot be dealt with well in the allotted time.

To help students create a list of possible topics, instructors ask them to consider a series of questions:

- What do you do when you are not working? What activities or hobbies keep you occupied?
- What is it about your college major (or your job) that interests you?
- What kind of career are you seeking (or are in) and why does it interest you?
- What have you learned in a course that you found interesting or exciting?
- What is going on locally that grabs your attention? Nationally? Internationally?
- What is happening on campus (or in the organization) that upsets you, stimulates you, or in some way has your attention?

The purpose of this set of questions is to stimulate ideas. Most students have no difficulty generating a list of possible speech topics using this procedure.

2. *Choose a topic for which the speaker has enthusiasm.* Once students have generated lists of topics, they are instructed to consider how much interest they have in the topics. People tend to be more enthusiastic about some topics than others, and this enthusiasm can translate into greater confidence and a more dynamic delivery. Students generally do not have trouble identifying those topics that interest them the most.

Enthusiasm for a topic is also important because students need to do additional research on it and spend quite a bit of time in preparing their speech. All of us who have spoken or written on a subject in which we had little interest know how painful the preparation process can be.

It is also important to teach students how to cultivate enthusiasm when confronted with an assigned topic. Their jobs may require them to make presentations. By analyzing the importance of the presentation to their career possibilities, they can get more involved with the speech. Telling students in the class that they will get a grade for doing well on an assigned topic simulates the kind of feelings they will experience in "real life."

3. *Choose a topic that can be adapted to the audience and situation.* Teachers discuss the importance of choosing a topic that can be adapted to the speech situation, including the context and the listeners. A topic might be very interesting to the speaker, but may be too complex or involved to be developed sufficiently in the 5 to 10 minutes allotted per speaker. Furthermore, students must learn that not everyone shares their enthusiasms. They are taught to "market" their topics using the Aristotelian cliche, "The fool tells me his reasons; the wise man persuades me with my own!"

Students also have to consider the availability of space, equipment, and whether the facilities meet the needs of a particular topic. The physical conditions are especially important for a speech involving demonstration or the use of visual aids.

Teachers also advise about the appropriateness of topics because speeches are given in a classroom with an authority figure present. Although a student might have a lot of knowledge about sexual positions and be highly interested in them, a speech on four favorite sexual positions is hardly appropriate for the situation.

Students are trained to consider the listeners. How much knowledge of and interest in the topic does the audience have initially? Does the speaker have enough time to provide the audience with the necessary background before getting into the main point of the presentation? Can the speaker find a "hook" to generate interest in the topic? Students discover that it simply may not be possible to give an effective speech on a particular topic under the circumstances created by audience and context. They also discover or are told that there is no perfect topic that will instantly enthrall all listeners. Speakers can make any topic dull or interesting depending on what they say and how they say it.

Other Assistance in Topic Selection. Instructors follow standard procedures to train students in the invention of speech topics. They discuss the guidelines presented here, and ask students to generate possible speech topics. Students either write their topics and the instructor returns them with comments, or students and teachers meet to discuss the topic. Even when students are not required to meet with their instructors, many of them do because they want to check the appropriateness of their topic selection. They often want reassurance that they have made a good choice.

There are some students who are unable to make a decision about a topic on their own. They need their instructor to walk them through the guidelines. It is vital that the teacher take time to meet with those students who need the additional help. These students are usually the ones most anxious about speaking, and their inability to come up with a topic is an avoidance mechanism. "If I don't have a topic, I can't give a speech" appears to be their reasoning. In our experience with these students, every one of them has been able to decide on a topic and stick with it after the help session.

People cannot give speeches or engage in conversations unless they can invent topics. Later in this volume, we discuss training in effective delivery, but students are not ready to learn delivery skills if they have not learned ways to discover topics. Without a repertoire of ideas, there is nothing to deliver. Beyond a repertoire of ideas, however, trainees need to organize their thoughts so they can be communicated coherently. In the Reticence Program time is devoted to the process of organizing ideas, the classical canon of disposition.

DISPOSITION: ORGANIZING IDEAS

The structuring method was developed by Phillips and Zolten (1976) and first presented in their book, *Structuring Speech.* A *structure* is a visual representation of the organization of a set of ideas. In our society there are particular ways people connect ideas or arrange them, arrangements that make sense to us. There are, according to Phillips and Zolten, seven basic structures that can be used to prepare a functional written or memorized speaking outline.

The Structuring Method

Most of us were trained to use outlining as a method for arranging ideas in an organized fashion. Structuring is a method to use before an outline is generated. For beginning speakers, structuring seems to work more effectively than outlining, and it has the advantage of novelty. Many students are bored with outlining. They find it hard to understand why it should be done, and most of them write their speeches before doing the outline. Structuring is new to students and is a method that can be used in both formal and informal situations.

As the models of the structures illustrate (see Figs. 5.1-5.8), a completed structure looks more like a flowchart than an outline. Individual ideas or points are put in boxes, which are connected by lines to show the movement of the speech from idea to idea. The student learns to think of the boxes as storage units for the speaker's ideas, each containing the information needed to make that point, such as definitions, examples, or stories. Anything that does not fit in a box is extraneous to the speech. Structuring is advantageous because it helps students see where they need to eliminate information or gather more.

The seven basic structures correspond to the ways people tend to connect ideas: time, space, classification, analogy, contrast, relationship, and problem solution. In organizing a speech, for example, a student selects one of the seven structures to serve as the main structure. If the student had collected information about classical dance in the United States—the history of ballet, how modern dance developed out of ballet, and influential choreographers—he or she would have a number of different directions the speech could take, each calling for a different structure.

The main point or residual message of a speech (Phillips & Zolten, 1976) determines which structure to use. If the student wants to emphasize that modern dance is a radical departure from classical ballet, the structure to use is contrast. If the residual message is that techniques of ballet have changed over the years, a time structure would be more appropriate. Finally, the student might use a classification structure if the speech focuses on influential U.S. choreographers.

The Seven Structures.

Before using the structuring method, it is essential to understand the details of the seven types of structures. Specifically, we provide examples of when to use the various structures and some of the basic rules that apply to each. The reader is encouraged to examine *Speaking to an Audience: A Practical Method of Preparing and Performing* (Zolten & Phillips, 1985) for an additional detailed discussion.

Time. The time structure is used when ideas must occur in a particular order for them to be understood. This structure is appropriate in speaking about the history of the American family, the evolution of the modern organizational form, the sequence of events leading up to the Persian Gulf War, or the instructions for how to make gumbo. Each of these topics will only make sense to the listener if the ideas are presented in the proper order. The audience would not be able to make gumbo if steps were skipped or put in the wrong order. Figure 5.1 illustrates the use of the time structure.

The rules for using this structure are straightforward. Students are told to be sure the steps or points are in order. They are taught to provide clear transitions from step to step so the audience can follow. Finally, they are cautioned to avoid digressions that confuse the listener and are not germane to the development of the residual message.

Space. Students generally find the space structure the most difficult to understand until they happen to select a topic on their own that requires the space structure. This structure is used when the speaker wants to describe the parts that make up a whole and how those parts fit together. When a speaker is describing some real thing that exists or some concept, the space structure is the appropriate choice. For example, the speaker may wish to describe the sections of an orchestra and how they are arranged according to a specific plan. Figure 5.2 represents the structure one might use (Phillips, Kougl, & Kelly, 1985). Other examples include descriptions of an organizational chart,

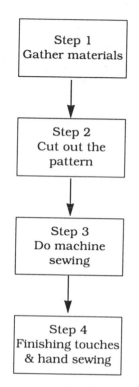

Figure 5.1. Time structure.

the components of a solar energy system, vacation spots in Connecticut, or the location of cities included in a sales region.

One of the basic rules students are taught is to use a visual representation of the thing or concept being described. They also are trained to pick a starting point in the diagram (e.g., the percussion section), and move logically through the parts (e.g., the tympani section, then the snare drums, then the brass section, etc.).

Classification. Instructors often refer to this structure as the "garbage can" because if all else fails, the student can usually arrange the ideas according to this structure. This pattern is appropriate for any topic that can be divided into types or categories. The indices of the current recession, the symptoms of alcoholism, the types of products a company manufactures, or the key issues facing dual-career couples in the 1990s are all topics best developed using a classification structure. Figure 5.3 is a sample classification structure.

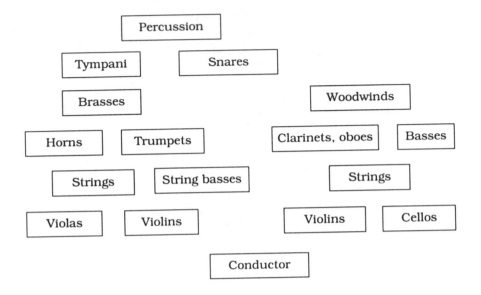

Figure 5.2. Space structure.

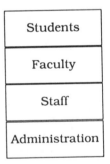

Figure 5.3. Classification structure.

Instructors discuss several rules for use of this structure. First, the categories must be mutually exclusive (Phillips & Zolten, 1976). It would be confusing to listeners if the categories overlapped. A speech about the quality of a university organized into the categories of academic programs, extracurricular activities, and sports violates the principle of mutual exclusivity. The sports and extracurricular activities categories overlap.

Second, the categories must be exhaustive; all components should be included (Phillips & Zolten, 1976). For example,
a speech on the academic programs offered at a college should
include all of the major programs. If the speaker left out all social
science programs, his or her categories would not be exhaustive.

Finally, relatively equal weight must be given to each category by spending approximately the same amount of time on
each and developing each to the same extent. For example, the
speaker should give equal weight to humanities, social sciences,
and science programs in his or her speech on what a college has
to offer.

Analogy. Figure 5.4 presents an analogy structure. This
structure is appropriate when the speaker's intent is to show the
similarities between things, people, or concepts. The analogy
structure would be used for topics such as similarities in the
campaign strategies of the 1992 presidential candidates, in the
techniques of two film directors, or between the issues involved in
two civil wars.

Students learn to make sure the points of comparison are
significant, not trivial, and to discuss the feature being compared
before moving on to the next feature. So rather than completely
describing all Bush's campaign strategies and then discussing

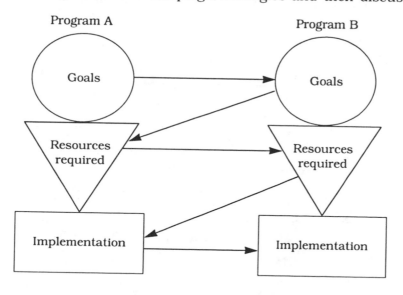

Figure 5.4. Analogy structure.

Clinton's, the speaker should discuss a particular strategy and how it is used by both candidates, then move to the next strategy.

Contrast. Once the analogy structure is explained, it is easy for students to grasp the contrast structure (see Fig. 5.5). Contrast is used when the speaker is arguing that two things are different or one is superior to the other. Examples of topics appropriate for the contrast structure include differences in the writing styles of two authors, ways in which jazz and rock music differ, and how one type of insurance is better than another. The rules for the use of the contrast structure are the same as those for analogy.

Relationship. When people talk about ideas, they often argue that two events or concepts are associated in some way. For instance, they might claim that one set of events caused another set to occur. Even if they do not specify a cause-effect relationship, they may discuss how two events or conditions seem to go together. In both conversation and public speaking, people talk about topics that could be organized using the relationship structure (see Fig. 5.6). If a speaker wanted to describe the causes of the 1992 riots in Los Angeles or the reasons why

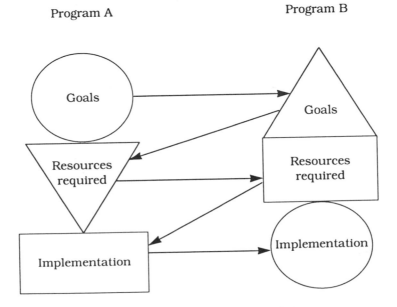

Figure 5.5. Contrast structure.

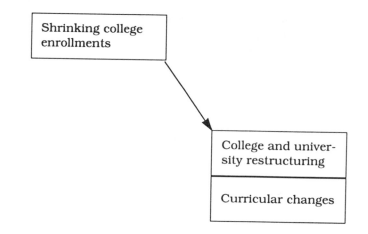

Figure 5.6. Relationship structure.

U.S. business has fallen behind some of its competitors, he or she would use the relationship structure.

Students are taught to make the relationship between events or conditions clear. If they are arguing for a cause-effect or effect-cause situation, they must clearly identify which is cause and which is effect. If they are not claiming a cause-effect relationship but merely an association between events, they need to be sure to state that. A second rule is to include plenty of supporting materials to strengthen the argument for a particular type of relationship. To use a relationship structure is to make an argument; any argument needs to be supported.

Problem Solution. The last structure students are taught is the problem-solution pattern. It is common for people to talk about problems and how they should be solved. This structure would be appropriate if a speaker's point was that tougher laws and stricter law enforcement will reduce illegal drug traffic or mandatory education programs in high schools will help stop the spread of the AIDS virus. Figure 5.7 represents a problem-solution structure.

Instructors explain four obligations the speaker has when using the problem-solution format (Phillips & Zolten, 1976). First, the burden of proof rests with the advocate of change. The speaker must justify the need for a change by giving specific reasons

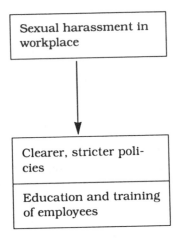

Figure 5.7. Problem-solution structure.

and evidence. Next, the speaker must present a plan designed to meet the need. Audiences rarely are satisfied when a speaker discusses a problem but offers no solution. The third obligation is for the speaker to demonstrate that the plan will actually address the need, and last, that it will not cause additional or worse problems.

Using Substructures

When a student is presenting a brief speech, the main structure may be sufficient for organizing all of the information. There are times, however, when the presentation is complex and lengthy, with too much information for only a main structure. To accommodate this situation, students are trained in the use of substructuring. For each of the main points in the boxes of the structure, the speaker needs a substructure to develop that point. The type of substructure selected depends on the information the speaker has to present and may be the same or different from the main structure. If, for instance, a student chose to speak on influential U.S. choreographers, he or she would have to use substructures to develop what to say about each of those people. If the speaker wanted to present a chronology of the choreographer's life or artistic development, the substructure would be a time structure. The student who preferred to discuss the main contributions of each choreographer would use a classification substructure. Figure 5.8 provides an example of the use of substructures.

The Grevitz Exercise

Since the 1970s, we have used an exercise to teach students the principles of forming structures as a preliminary to outlining.[1]

"The Grevitz" exercise gives the students a list of 62 random statements (Appendix O), each relevant to a central theme (residual message or speech purpose). There are linguistic cues in each statement that position it in a structural diagram from which an outline can be built (see Zolten & Phillips, 1985). The title of the presentation is: "The Composition, History, Uses, and Operation of the Grevitz." Because there is no Grevitz, there is no sociocultural bias in the exercise.

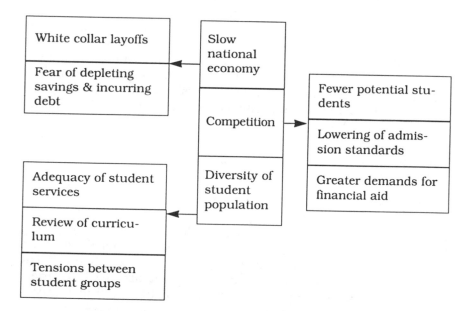

Figure 5.8. Main structure with substructures.

[1]See the *Instructors' Manual* to Zolten and Phillips (1985) for the original problem. The example presented in Appendix O is extracted from Phillips (1991), *Communication Incompetencies*, with the permission of Southern Illinois University Press.

We have used the Grevitz exercise on more than 1,000 students. The pedagogical purpose is to train the students in the structuring method before putting their notes into an outline for a public speech.

The speech title specifies an outline with four main headings. The idea is initially to find 4 statements among the 62 that represent the most general statements of the four main headings, then group the remaining 58 items under the appropriate headings in proper sequence. Once the statements are grouped, subheads become evident, generating another reordering. Statements that do not seem to fit are cast aside and later checked once the related items are put in order. The result is the generation of an outline of a speech about the Grevitz, which sounds coherent when read aloud.

Students have been able to perform this task solo with about 95% accuracy. The mean time for solution is approximately 3 hours. We have not been able to find any common feature in the 5% who do not succeed. We assume this success rate means there is sufficient logic in the statements for trainees to find the proper arrangement. To provide them with additional cues, we present them with a blank structural diagram of the composition. Their task is to place the numbers of the statements in the appropriate boxes. The boxes are labeled so that once they are filled in, they can be formed into an outline from which a speech can be presented.

Other Techniques for Teaching Structuring

Several procedures are followed by Reticence Program instructors to teach the structuring method. Teachers usually begin by explaining some of the problems students typically encounter with the use of outlining. They then present structuring as an alternative method for organizing ideas and go through the details of the seven structures and how they are used. Trainers use visual aids of the seven structures during this lecture. Students are then asked to perform the Grevitz exercise.

The Grevitz activity is usually followed by an exercise in which the teacher presents a list of residual messages and asks students to identify which structure should be used to develop each. Students rarely have difficulty with this exercise. Then the method of substructuring is explained, accompanied by a detailed example.

Additional teaching techniques are typically necessary.

The teacher gives students, who have been placed in small groups, a nonsense topic such as "peanut butter" or "frogs" and asks the groups to generate seven residual messages and draw the accompanying main structures they would use to develop each of those residual messages. Groups then display one or two of their structures and messages on the board until all seven structures with seven main points appear on the chalkboard. This activity is followed by discussion in which the instructor asks the class to evaluate the messages and the structures. Any errors are noted and corrected, although the students typically do not have difficulty with this activity. Instructors explain one difference between this exercise and the use of structuring to present an actual speech is that the groups could make up information to fit into the structure. When using the method to organize a speech, the speaker must fit the ideas into a structure and gather information where it is lacking, rather than create it.

Trainers can also put speech topics on index cards, have students select a card, and then generate ideas and the structure to develop the speech. They are given only a brief time to do this, and then they deliver the speech from the structure in a semi-impromptu fashion, as described in Chapter 4. Topics are simple and most pertain to campus life such as "The three worst meals served in the dining hall," or "How to impress your professors." Audience members are instructed to note the structure the speaker used, and after each speech is given, comment on the structure. This activity shows students how structuring can be used in public speaking situations, and illustrates how it can help organize their thoughts for more impromptu speaking such as answering a question on a job interview or speaking out at a meeting.

Students are assigned to give a public speech, using structuring. They are given plenty of time to prepare, and the assignment is similar to that given in any standard public speaking class. However, instead of turning in an outline, as required by most speech teachers, students submit a drawing of their main structure and substructures. They are required to rehearse the speech with the instructor, and at that time they bring in their structure for the teacher to check.

Students may speak extemporaneously from the detailed structure, or they may develop note cards to deliver the actual speech. Some students say they find it very easy to speak from the structure because they can see the entire speech in front of them. Others prefer note cards so they can have fewer ideas in front of them at one time.

To teach students how to employ the method for

impromptu kinds of situations, other activities are appropriate. For instance, the instructor may give trainees conversation topics to talk about or interview questions to respond to demonstrating one of the seven structures. A student may be asked what qualifications he or she has for a particular job, and he or she may use a classification structure to organize the response. Any exercise that gives students a chance to practice organizing ideas according to the seven structures is helpful.

Using Structuring to Generate Topics for Conversation

Earlier in this chapter we discussed methods to teach students to invent conversational topics. Structuring is one of the methods we mentioned. Now that structuring has been explained, we can describe its application to generating ideas for social conversation.

Students are taught to take a conversational topic and think through the seven structures to help them generate "sayables," subtopics that develop the main topic. For example, if the topic of golf is brought up, a person can use the structures to identify aspects of the sport to be developed in conversation:

- time: how golf clubs have changed in recent years
- space: the location of the best courses to play in the state
- classification: types of clubs, balls, or golf shoes
- analogy: similarities between courses or equipment brands
- contrast: differences between golf and other sports or among various clubs
- relationship—the health benefits of playing golf or how a particular technique can improve one's game
- problem solution: how to solve the problem of a hook or a slice

Obviously, individuals have to know about these subtopics to be able to talk about them, but the structures provide a set of categories for thinking about a topic and inventing sayables. One can use them to generate questions about a topic as well. Students spend time in class practicing their use of these structures. Instructors give students topics and ask them to come up with subtopics using each of the seven structures.

CONCLUSION

In this chapter we described how the processes of invention and disposition are handled in formal instruction. We explained the details of these skills and the methods by which they are taught. Students in the program must develop their invention skills to increase their conversational repertories and generate ideas for public speaking and other more planned communication situations. Students are taught to become better observers of conversation, to use several techniques for maintaining conversation, and to use the seven structures to stimulate their thinking about topics. To assist them in generating speech topics, instructors present students with several guidelines and then guide them in topic selection for their actual classroom speeches.

The trainees are also assisted in the development of their skills of disposition. They are taught the importance of organizing their ideas in all communication situations. The method of structuring is presented for arranging ideas in an orderly fashion. Instructors spend a fair amount of time explaining the method and leading students in activities to become adept at using it. Structuring is developed for use in planned communication, like public speeches, as well as for relatively unplanned speech such as answering questions or speaking out in meetings.

6

TEACHING DELIVERY

A major component of rhetoritherapy is training in delivery, refer-
ring to how people say things as opposed to what they say.
Delivery can be broken into two communication components,
paraverbal and nonverbal. *Paraverbal communication* refers to
aspects of the voice, such as pitch inflection, rate, volume, or
quality. *Nonverbal communication* refers to expressing messages
through the use of the body, such as posture, gestures, facial
expressions, and eye contact.

In the PSU Reticence Program, students receive training
in both aspects of delivery. They learn delivery skills in the classroom and are given two opportunities to practice in front of an
audience: an oral interpretation project and a public speech. In
this chapter we describe the content and techniques of the unit
on delivery. We begin with our rationale for incorporating delivery
instruction into the training program.

THE IMPORTANCE OF DELIVERY TRAINING

To be effective at oral discourse, speakers must have a message and present it so people understand both the message and the speaker. Effective speakers have personal power that gives them credibility with others. They are able to evoke emotions of their listeners and present an argument that appears reasonable and looks documented, whether it is or not. The important word here is "present" with emphasis on the last syllable. Without the ability to deliver messages in a clear, coherent, and interesting manner, attempts at communication are usually ineffective. Incompetent oral performance is more than a trivial disability. Consider the husband and wife who cannot communicate. Regard the aspiring executive who cannot lead. Study the failed politician who cannot command respect and get votes. There are a great many people well trained in preparing a game plan who are unable to execute that plan effectively.

The speech professionals in the academy, however, have generally backed off from offering instruction in performance. They teach students about the rhetorical tradition or offer various models of communication theory. There are no studies to confirm the notion that learning theory of communication has anything to do with learning how to do it. There are few studies that purport to show that formal training in public speaking actually improves performance. Our own reliance on criticism as the main means of inducing change is not documented by formal studies, although research summarized in Chapter 12 supports the effectiveness of the PSU Reticence Program. We rely mainly on anecdotal evidence from experienced teachers, and on a series of studies done by Lutz (1967), Butt (1965), and Pederson (1965) for scholarly support for the effectiveness of criticism. Yet, concepts associated with speech communication research have the potential for application to instruction.

We believe that all speech training must be accompanied by careful instruction in performance technique. By performance technique, we mean control of voice, correct pronunciation, intonation appropriate to the situation, modulation of expression calculated to catch and hold the interest of listeners, and phrasing suitable to make the information presented intelligible to an audience. Without training in delivery, most students will not become fully competent communicators. They will have training in how to prepare speech content but not in techniques of effective delivery. In the following sections we explain how delivery training is accomplished in the PSU Reticence Program.

ORAL INTERPRETATION TRAINING

One way students develop delivery skills is through oral interpretation training. Oral interpretation, short for oral interpretation of literature, is a process in which performers select, analyze, interpret, and perform selections taken from literature. In some ways, oral interpretation combines skill from both public speaking and acting. Oral interpretation is similar to acting in that performers adopt roles and are placed in dramatic situations. However, in oral interpretation, performers limit their movement to focus attention on the message (the literature) rather than the performance, similar to public speaking.

Functions of Oral Interpretation Training

Oral interpretation training in the Reticence Program serves three functions: creating an awareness of paraverbal and nonverbal components (self-monitoring), developing effective delivery skills, and discovering implementation strategies. These three functions can be summarized by three questions about delivery: What is it? (awareness), How do I do it? (development of skills), and When do I do it? (implementation strategy).

One advantage of having students give an oral interpretation before giving a public speech is that they can practice their delivery without having to generate their own content. The students can use their newly developed delivery skills to augment the words of the author. Oral interpretation training in the Reticence Program consists of two modules that precede classroom performance: skills training (lecture, discussion, and activities, lasting approximately 75 minutes), and rehearsal with the instructor.

Oral Interpretation Skills Training

The skills training module consists of mini-lectures, discussion, and activities. Typically this module takes 75 minutes of class time. Before class begins, instructors tell the trainees they will be doing some silly things, but if everyone is equally silly, no one will notice.

An effective way of starting the skills training component is with an activity entitled nonsense dialogue. This activity has several objectives: creating a warm and acceptable classroom climate; showing students the expressive power of the voice and body; and allowing students to explore, in a nonthreatening way, different aspects of their voice and body.

The nonsense dialogue exercise consists of five modes, explained later in this section: full-full, nonverbal-full, full-nonverbal, nonverbal-nonverbal, and full-full. For all five modes, the instructor asks students to work with the person sitting next to him or her. If there is an odd number of students, the instructor serves as the partner of the remaining student. Once everyone has a partner, the trainer distributes the nonsense dialogue sheet. The sheet presents the dialogue, without any punctuation that could restrict how the students read the dialogue. One dialogue trainers use is as follows:

A.	Well
B.	Well I'm here
A.	So I see
B.	Yes
A.	Well
B.	Is that all you can say
A.	What do you want me to say
B.	Nothing
A.	Nothing
B.	You don't trust me
A.	It's not that
B.	Then what
A.	Never mind
B.	Stop it
A.	What
B.	That
A.	I can't
B.	Try
A.	Is this better
B.	This is hopeless
A.	What's the matter
B.	I don't know
A.	You don't know
B.	No
A.	Tell me
B.	I can't
A.	Then go
B.	I will

The instructor asks the students to decide who will be A and who will be B for the nonsense dialogue. Once roles are assigned, students determine who A and B are (e.g., boyfriend-girlfriend, mother-daughter, colleagues, etc.) and decide on the situation (stressing creative and interesting situations). After students have created the setting, the instructor asks them to practice Mode 1, in which both students use verbal and nonverbal components.

The instructor then asks two students to read their nonsense dialogue. The students listening are asked to figure out the identity of the two people and the situation. Both are discussed after the dialogue. The instructor emphasizes that the voice and body of the performers rather than the words created the situation and characters. The instructor uses this information to stress the communicative potential of delivery.

The trainer moves on to Mode 2 of the nonsense dialogue. In Mode 2, students use the same situations and the same characters; however, the student reading part A cannot use words. The student must use nonverbal communication (e.g., gestures, facial expressions) to react to Person B. The student reading part B does not change from Mode 1. In Mode 3, Student B does not talk, but Student A can again talk. In Mode 4, both Student A and B can not talk. In Mode 5, both students can talk. The instructor should stress the integration of nonverbal and verbal components during Mode 5.

Once the students have completed the nonsense dialogue, the teacher asks the question: "As you can see, the words used in the nonsense dialogue are practically meaningless, but did anyone find that the way you read the dialogue made it meaningful?" After students respond, the trainer makes the point that the way you say things can enhance or detract from what you are saying. In fact, delivery of a message can override the verbal content of the message. The instructor then turns the discussion to how people say things.

Paraverbal Communication

Paraverbal communication refers to those components of the voice not related to content. Paraverbal communication can be broken into four components: pitch, volume, rate, and quality.

Pitch is determined by the length, tension, and thickness of a person's vocal bands. Pitch is like a musical scale. As you go up the scale you are going up in pitch. An average human voice has approximately a two-octave range (2 scales or 16 notes).

In oral interpretation, pitch can suggest the emotional arousal level of a character. More variation in pitch typically corresponds to more emotional arousal. Variation in pitch can also convey sarcasm or highlight specific words.

Volume can be thought of as the loudness or softness of a person's voice. An easy way of demonstrating differences in volume is to talk to a student at the back of the classroom (loud) and to talk to a person at the front of the classroom (soft). To make this demonstration effective, the instructor should change only the volume, keeping pitch and rate similar for both examples. The instructor might ask what the difference in volume suggests, eventually making the point that volume can indicate the level of intimacy between two people.

To have proper volume, students must learn to control exhalation. The trainer might ask students to count from 1 to 12, trying to sustain an appropriate amount of volume. If the student is using an adequate volume, he or she can hear a slight echo from the back wall of the room. Students should repeat this exercise until they can control exhalation while speaking.

Rate refers to the speed of speaking described in the following ways: words per minute, number of pauses, or duration of individual words. Rate should not exceed 150 words per minute, unless rate is intended to suggest a character. Variation in rate can suggest thinking, emotional arousal, or other states.

Quality can be thought of as the resonance of the voice. The vocal mechanism contains a set of resonating cavities. Changing the resonance pattern will change the quality of the voice. For example, if someone talks into a glass soda bottle his or her voice would sound different because an extra resonating cavity, the glass bottle, altered the quality of the voice. Some examples of voice qualities are described as follows:

- *Aspirate.* An aspirate quality is created by air passing through the vocal tract with less than normal vibration of the vocal bands. An aspirate quality sounds like a combination of whispering and talking.
- *Guttural.* A guttural quality is created by tensing the vocal bands and forcing air through them. Because of the unnatural tension on the vocal bands, the guttural quality is harmful to the vocal bands.
- *Nasal.* A person with a nasal voice quality directs the flow of air into the nasal passages. Because the breath stream flows out the nose, the phonetic distinctness of certain consonants is lost.

- *Denasal.* Opposite to nasal, a person with a denasal quality does not allow air to flow through the nasal passage. A person with a severe head cold will likely have a denasal quality. If students pinch their nose while talking, they can listen to a denasal quality.

In order to demonstrate the qualities, the instructor has two options: give examples or use videotape or a tape recorder. A discussion might follow that examines the expressive capabilities of voice quality. (A series of voice training audiotapes is available from DAS-Dialects Accents Specialists of Hollywood. These tapes can be used by students individually or as classroom demonstrations.)

At this point, the teacher summarizes the four paraverbal components. The instructor might ask students to go through the nonsense dialogue again, this time playing with variations in the four paraverbal components.

Nonverbal Communication

Nonverbal components, known as body language, can also be expressive. In oral interpretation, performers concentrate on four nonverbal components: posture, gestures, eye contact, and facial expressions. Each of these components have communicative potential. The trainer should refer to the nonsense dialogue for examples of the nonverbal components, particularly in Mode 4, in which both students were not allowed to talk.

- *Posture.* One of the ways of provoking discussion of the expressive nature of posture is for the instructor to assume different postures and have students write their impressions of the posture's meaning. Posture can suggest age, status, confidence, and many other attributes.
- *Gestures.* Gestures tend to complement or augment the attitude or message conveyed by a character. People use varying degrees of gesture. A lack of gestures might suggest a low level of energy and enthusiasm. Too many gestures can send mixed messages to an audience. Gestures can be either intentional, such as waving to a person in the distance, or unintentional, such as shrugging your shoulders.
- *Eye contact.* The instructor might ask what a lack of eye contact suggests about a character, or what an excess of eye contact might mean. For example, eye contact

can indicate a character's level of involvement in a particular situation.

- *Facial expressions.* Facial expressions, along with paraverbal components, indicate the attitudes and emotions of a character. Ekman and Friesen (1975) stated that the face can suggest at least six different emotions: happiness, sadness, surprise, fear, anger, and disgust.

Types of Oral Interpretation

There are four general types of oral interpretation: monologue, dialogue, narrative, and poetry. A *monologue* literally means "one voice." In the context of oral interpretation, a monologue is a selection, or part of a selection, in which only one character speaks to the audience (either a narrator or a person). Sources for monologues include diaries, short stories, or novels.

A *dialogue* is a performance with two voices, one character speaking to another character. In contrast to a monologue, characters in a dialogue typically do not acknowledge the audience. Instead, their complete attention is focused on either the other character or the dramatic situation.

A *narrative* can be considered as a combination of a monologue and a dialogue. A narrator speaks directly to the audience (giving a monologue) discussing characters, setting, action, and the like, and characters interact with each other to further the plot (engaging in dialogue). Narratives are most commonly found in novels.

Poetry refers to language that is given a prosodic structure (stress, foot, rhyme, stanza, etc.). Poetry can include one or more characters, and might include a narrator. Because of poetry's complex structure, it should be considered an advanced form of oral interpretation. In addition, instructors usually do not have the time to cover the fundamentals of poetry.

Once the types of oral interpretation have been discussed, the teacher might want to discuss preferences for types of interpretation. The preferred order for types of oral interpretations is dialogue, monologue, narrative, and poetry. The first preference is a dialogue. Dialogues are readily available from scene study books. In scene study books, dialogues have already been edited, saving the student editing time, and usually fit the time limits of the performance. Dialogues also allow students to perform in pairs. Although monologues are relatively easy to find, a student giving a monologue performs without a partner, a situation undesirable to some students.

Although narratives are easy to find, they require editing and presentation is demanding. In a narrative the performer assumes the part of the narrator, as well as all the characters that are in the selection. Poetry is probably the most difficult form of oral interpretation because poetry contains complex rhythms and rhyme schemes. Trainers should discourage using poetry for this assignment unless students have prior training and experience.

Preparation Process

Performing in front of an audience is likely to be an anxiety-provoking situation for most students. To help students minimize their anxious feelings, the instructor must give students step-by-step instructions for preparing for their performance. Following is a discussion of the 12 steps needed to prepare for an oral interpretation.

Step 1. Students must select a piece of literature that meets three standards: universality, individuality, and imagination. A selection of literature that is universal includes an underlying message or theme that applies to almost anyone. Individuality suggests that the way in which the author explores the theme is unique, but at the same time, is well written. The final standard is that the piece is imaginative, meaning that the piece appeals to the senses (e.g., sights, sounds, smells).

Step 2. Although the piece students select should be universal, it is important that they take their audience into account. What are the issues or messages that are of particular interest to the audience at hand? Knowing that the audience is interested in the theme of the piece might make students a bit more comfortable about performing.

Step 3. Up to this point, the criteria for selecting a piece have dealt with characteristics of the piece and the interests of audience members. In Step 3 students are asked to select a piece that they like. If students like the piece, they might put more energy into its preparation and will likely feel more comfortable presenting.

Step 4. Once students have selected their piece of literature, they need to divide the piece into component parts. Literature usually contains four segments that are based on the amount of tension created by the author: exposition (low tension), inciting force (tension starts to build), climax (tension reaches its highest level), and resolution (tension drops to a low level).

Exposition is that part of the selection when the author answers the who, what, where, and when questions. For example, in the story of "Little Red Riding Hood," the exposition informs the reader that Little Red is traveling to her grandmother's house in the woods. Inciting force is the point when something goes wrong, the "spark of conflict." In "Little Red Riding Hood," this point is Little Red's meeting with the wolf. After the spark of conflict, the tension builds to its highest point, called the climax. In Little Red Riding Hood this point occurs when the wolf, posing as her grandmother, attacks Little Red Riding Hood. In the final segment, conflict is resolved and the tension level drops. Typically the resolution immediately follows the climax. In the example, the huntsman rescues Little Red by killing the wolf.

Step 5. If a student selects a piece of literature that is over the time limits of the oral interpretation assignment, he or she can either make a new selection or edit the existing one. Students should edit based on two factors. First, they should edit in a way that brings out or strengthens the literary theme. One way of strengthening the theme is to cut subplots or secondary characters. Second, students should edit to limit the amount of exposition. Much of what is said in the exposition, can be provided to the audience in the introduction (step 11). Students need to edit, then read the piece checking for continuity, then re-edit if necessary.

Step 6. Once the piece has been selected and edited, students should start to familiarize themselves with their selection. The student should read the story slowly and visualize. Students must visualize the setting, characters, and everything involved in the piece of literature. Instructors might require students to write down the clothes that each character is wearing, the temperature, weather, and so on.

Step 7. Students might consider finding out about the author of their selection and his or her background. This step is especially important for students who have selected works of literature that are dated. Furthermore, knowledge of the author might help the student to discover the theme of the selection.

Step 8. Students should explore the denotative and connotative meanings of the piece. A dictionary makes discovering denotative meanings easy. However, connotative meanings are not so easily identified. Connotative meanings are meanings the words suggest, or overtones the words create. One way of deciphering connotation is to analyze why the author selected one word over a similar word. For example, if an author states that a character "perfumed the air" as opposed to "spoke" the connotation is quite different.

Step 9. Students must work for conceptual clarity in their delivery. In order to make the concepts in the piece clear to the audience, students should go through two steps: grouping (separating the text into thoughts), and locating the central idea within each group.

Grouping is the process of breaking the text into separate ideas. An idea can be a picture, thought, feeling, or action. To stress the importance of grouping, the instructor writes the following sentence on the board:

That that is is that that is not is not.

Students are instructed to put slash marks between the words, indicating a pause. The instructor tells the student that this set of words, when grouped correctly, will make sense. Once the students have had time to try different ways of grouping, the instructor can ask for student input. The correct grouping might look like the following:

That that is / is / that that is not / is not.

The instructor might ask the students to read the correct grouping to make sure it makes sense.

Students should be aware of two types of punctuation: grammatical and oral. Grammatical punctuation (e.g., commas, periods) makes the author's meaning clear to the reader, whereas oral punctuation (e.g., pauses) makes the author's meaning clear to the listener. Students should also know that the two types of punctuation do not always coincide. For example, observe the grammatical punctuation in the following sentence from Shakespeare's *The Taming of the Shrew*:

Why, sir, what am I, sir, that I should knock you here, sir?

If a reader were to pause at every comma, this sentence would sound choppy and unnatural. The instructor might use this sentence as an exercise to show how commas do not necessarily indicate a pause.

For example, when read, the line is punctuated: why sir/ what am I sir/ that I should knock you here sir. The slashes indicate the required pauses. This example shows how grammatical punctuation can be different from oral punctuation.

The next example shows the same idea in a different way. In the following sentence from the *Newburg Scroll*, grammatical punctuation would indicate that there are no pauses; however, when read aloud, it becomes evident that oral punctuation is needed:

> Newburg Church tries to assist in serving a luncheon for the families of church members who have died immediately following the funeral.

Without oral punctuation this sentence suggests that people dying immediately after a funeral will be served lunch. With oral punctuation the sentence might be delivered as follows:

> Newburg Church tries to assist in serving a luncheon / for the families of church members who have died / immediately following the funeral.

By using oral punctuation, the three thoughts or groups are separated and the meaning behind the sentence becomes evident.

Pauses can be separated into three types: minor (1 second), major (1 or 2 seconds), and elongated (more than 2 seconds). A reader determines which type of pause is appropriate by examining the conceptual distance between the two thoughts, the content similarity of two ideas. Recall that pauses are used to separate ideas; therefore, the farther apart two adjoining ideas are (conceptual distance) the longer the pause needed between them. For example, notice the conceptual distances between ideas in Line 1 and Line 2.

1. I am going out now. Do you want to come with me?
2. I am going out now. Did the mail come yet?

In Line 1, the conceptual distance between sentences is relatively small, because both sentences focus on going out. In Line 2, however, the conceptual distance between sentences is relatively large because the idea of going out and the mail being delivered are not that similar. Therefore, the two sentences in Line 1 might be separated by a minor pause, whereas the two sentences in Line 2 might be separated by a major pause. Students might read the two lines and discover what type of pause best suits each line. Major and minor pauses are used frequently in oral interpretation. The elongated pause, used infrequently, creates a dramatic effect (e.g., character discovery, conflict between characters).

The second way to enhance conceptual clarity is to identify and highlight central ideas. A central idea is the important word or phrase within the idea or group. One way of demonstrating the importance of the central idea is to conduct the following exercise. The teacher asks students to read the sentence "I'm going out now" in four different ways:

1. I am going out now.
2. I am going out now.
3. I am going out now.
4. I am going out now.

An underline indicates vocal emphasis. After the students have repeated the sentence, the instructor can ask them how the emphasis in Sentence 1 changes the meaning. In Sentence 1, the emphasis indicates that "I" is the important element, suggesting that the person speaking is going out rather than anyone else. In Sentence 2, stressing the word am might suggest that the person speaking is contradicting the person who just said something. For example, Sentence 2 might be a reply to the statement, "You're not going out." In Sentence 3, the person speaking is indicating that a change in location is important. In the fourth sentence, the speaker is indicating that time is the crucial issue, that she or he must leave immediately. As students can see by this simple example, isolating the central idea in a word group is important because the emphasis on key words can change the meaning of the word group.

To reinforce the idea of grouping and central ideas, instructors should select a short work and have students group the work and determine its central ideas. The instructor can either ask for input on the assignment, or read the work aloud.

Step 10. As discussed previously, the purpose of Step 9 is to develop conceptual clarity. The purpose of Step 10 is to create emotional clarity. That is to say, students learn how to communicate the emotions and sensory experiences they find in the text. Students learn how to use both *sense memory* and *emotional memory* to convey sensory experience and emotions. Both sense and emotional memory are techniques the reader uses to substitute his or her emotions and experiences for the emotions and experiences found in the literature.

The process of emotional memory takes three steps: identifying the emotional subtext, recalling similar emotional experiences, and superimposing the performer's emotional experience onto the literature. When performers identify emotional subtext, they determine the emotions that complement the literature. Identifying emotions in the literature is a difficult process because there are many interpretations, most of which are valid. Once students identify the emotional subtext, they should review their past experiences and locate a time when they felt similar emotions. Students then use their emotional experiences to bring out the emotions in the literature.

The process of sense memory follows the steps of emotional memory (identify, recall, superimpose). The only difference between sense memory and emotional memory is that students recall sensory experiences rather than emotions.

Step 11. Students should construct a brief introduction to their piece. The introduction can be separated into five parts: attention getter, title and author, significance to audience, unknown words or allusions, and situation.

In an introduction, students should start by arousing the interest or gaining the attention of their audience. Students might read a captivating excerpt from their piece of literature, or startle the audience with words or actions. Although there are many ways of gaining an audience's attention, the guideline for an effective introduction is to focus attention on the selection of literature.

After gaining the attention of the audience, students should state the title and author of the selection and explain why the piece is appropriate. Instructors should remind students that the significance to the audience was determined in Step 2. Students should also define unknown words, explain any allusions to unknown events, and set up the scene. Students should tell the audience the whos, whats, wheres, and whens, unless this information is given as exposition in the text.

Step 12. By this point, students should possess the necessary knowledge and skills to perform an oral interpretation.

The final and probably most important step is for the student to rehearse. The instructor should give the following suggestions to the students concerning rehearsal preparation:

1. Either type the piece (double-spaced) or enlarge the text using a copy machine. Larger print will make reading easier, and prevent students from losing their place. Also the enlarged text will allow students to place marks on their text.
2. Put the piece into a three-ring binder. The binder will make turning the pages simple, and prevent the problem of book pages turning while the performer is reading.
3. Mark the text. Place slashes in the text for pauses, underline key words, make notes about emotions. Marking the text will help performers to rehearse in a consistent way and will serve as a guide during the performance. Students should make a photocopy of the marked script for the instructor to use at the student-instructor rehearsal.
4. Effective delivery focuses attention on the message, not the performer. The purpose of oral interpretation is to communicate, in a dramatic way, the message or theme of a selection of literature. The performer should use delivery skills (e.g., sense and emotional memory) to enhance the theme; however, if the performer draws attention to the performance then the theme cannot be communicated effectively.
5. Be ready to perform the piece by the time it is rehearsed with the instructor. The instructor's role during rehearsal should be to help the student refine skills. If the student has not adequately practiced before the instructor rehearsal, then the rehearsal time is wasted.

Rehearsal Process

Each student must sign up for a rehearsal with his or her teacher. The rehearsal process should include the following steps: initial comments and questions from the student, performance of the selection with an introduction, feedback from the instructor, work through, and final comments and questions. The rehearsal begins with questions from the student about the performance. Many times these focus on the interpretation of the piece or specific emotions. During the initial question-and-answer period, the trainer gives optimistic comments about the student's upcoming performance to make the student feel more comfortable during the rehearsal process.

After questions and answers, the student should perform the piece for the instructor, complete with an introduction. During the performance, the teacher takes detailed notes, indicating any difficulties and marking them in the script. Recall that the instructor has been given a marked copy of the student's script.

The trainer starts the feedback session by commenting on positive aspects of the performance, such as conceptual clarity, the selection itself, or the amount of time spent rehearsing. He or she then suggests areas for improvement, focusing on the skills discussed in class. The instructor can use the following list of questions as a guide:

- Where are the changes in the level of tension? Is the spark of conflict clearly communicated through voice and body? (structural clarity—Step 4)
- Are the thoughts separated into groups? Are key words and phrases emphasized? (conceptual clarity—Step 9)
- Are the emotions in the subtext clearly communicated? Are different emotions communicated? (emotional clarity—Step 10)
- Are the sensory images clearly communicated? Is the performer using recall to enhance his or her performance? (sensory clarity—Step 10).

It is important that the teacher specifies the delivery skill that should be better developed (e.g., grouping) and identifies sections of the reading that could improve. After discussing areas for improvement, the instructor should again mention the positive aspects of the student's performance.

Once the student clearly understands the feedback, the teacher and student work through problem areas. For each problem area, the instructor should identify the delivery skills that need to be practiced. It is not necessary for the instructor to work on every trouble spot; however, it is necessary for the instructor to reinforce through examples the skills discussed in class. The rehearsal ends with any remaining questions or comments by the student.

Students generally like the oral interpretation assignment. Most students find it an enjoyable way to improve their delivery skills, in part because the audience's response is positive. The oral interpretation experience can also serve as a stepping stone to delivering a public speech, helping to prepare students for their first presentation by giving them a chance to speak in front of an audience.

PUBLIC SPEAKING

Many of the same delivery skills that students develop during oral interpretation training are used for public speaking (see Table 6.1). For example, both types of speaking require students to work for structural, conceptual, and emotional clarity.

Although there are similarities, public speaking differs from oral interpretation in some important ways: students are not suggesting a character, the level of emotional arousal and tension is much lower, and nonverbal communication is limited. Despite these differences, the objective of public speaking delivery is similar to oral interpretation: to develop a varied, yet natural, delivery. Similar to oral interpretation, students should work for clarity when giving a speech. The following is a discussion of three types of clarity and how they apply to speaking in public.

Structural Clarity

In oral interpretation training, structural clarity refers to separating exposition, inciting force, climax, and resolution. In public speaking training, structural clarity refers to separating the introduction, main points, and conclusion. Because of large conceptual distances (see Step 9 of oral interpretation preparation), major pauses are needed between the introduction and first main point, between each main point, and between the last main point and the conclusion.

Trainers should remind students that pauses can indicate a transition. Many students, when speaking, find pauses or silence to be anxiety provoking. It is important that students learn that silence has an important communicative function. To emphasize this point, the instructor might give two different points without pausing and the same two points with a pause to demonstrate the function of pausing. The instructor might also ask a student to discuss what he or she did over the past weekend, and instruct other students to listen for pauses. Students

Table 6.1. Components of Delivery for Oral Interpretation of Literature and Public Speaking.

Delivery Component	Oral Interpretation	Public Speaking
Paraverbal		
Pitch	Suggests character attributes, such as emotional arousal	Used within the natural range of the speaker
Volume	Suggests character attributes, such as intimacy	Maintained at optimal level
Rate	Suggests character attributes, such as level of thinking	Regulated by structured pausing
Quality	Differentiates or suggests certain characters	Maintain natural quality
Nonverbal		
Posture	Suggests character attributes, such as confidence	Upright, yet relaxed
Gestures	Natural gestures	Natural gestures
Facial expressions	Used to complement emotional subtext	Naturally shows attitude
Eye contact	Varies according to character type and or oral interpretation type (e.g., monologue)	Distributed evenly as with a conversation
Clarity		
Structural	Separate exposition, inciting force, climax, resolution	Separate the introduction, main points, conclusion
Conceptual	Separate thoughts and dramatic moments	Separate supporting materials
Emotional	Use of emotional and sense memory to communicate subtext	Use of emotional memory to communicate attitude

will find that people pause when they think, and thinking frequently occurs during transitions. Pausing is a natural and useful feature of communicative behavior, which students should use to enhance structural clarity.

Conceptual Clarity

Within the introduction, main points, and conclusion, there are supporting materials. Because of a relatively small conceptual distance, supporting materials should be separated by minor pauses. For example, if a student was giving a speech on vacationing in Florida, and the student's first main point was the outstanding climate, the student might support the point by stating the average number of sunny days (statistic) and follow by giving a personal experience. Because both of these supporting materials contain similar ideas (outstanding weather in Florida), the conceptual distance is small and a small pause is appropriate.

One way of teaching effective pausing is to have students look down at their note cards between supporting materials, and to have each main point on a separate card. By looking down, students pause in a natural, inconspicuous manner.

Emotional Clarity

Step 3 of the preparation process for oral interpretation is for students to pick a selection that interests them. The same process is extremely important for selecting a public speaking topic, as discussed in Chapter 5. Furthermore, students also should know why the topic interests them so they can communicate enthusiasm during their speech. Students might visualize an experience they have had regarding the topic, or recall an image that captures their enthusiasm toward the topic. For example, if a student chooses the topic of scuba diving for a speech, he or she might concentrate on the excitement of a first dive in the ocean.

The teacher should not ask students to work on vocal variety (e.g., varying pitch, volume, etc.) for a more exciting delivery because students will likely develop a mechanical and unnatural delivery. Instead, instructors should encourage students to bring out the enthusiasm that they already have for their topics. The enthusiasm a student has about a speech topic will naturally lead to vocal variety. To demonstrate this point, the instructor might ask students to list the behaviors that suggest enthusiasm. The instructor will find that enthusiasm and vocal variety are strongly correlated. Therefore, if the instructor promotes enthusiasm about the topic by the use of emotional recall, then chances are that students will develop both an interesting and natural delivery style.

Nonverbal Communication

The same four-category typology of nonverbal communication used for oral interpretation can be applied to public speaking. These four categories are posture, gestures, facial expressions, and eye contact.

Posture. When giving a public speech, students should stand up straight, maintaining a relaxed posture, and distributing their weight evenly on both feet. Students might be reminded of the expressive power of posture, which was discussed during oral interpretation training.

Gestures and Facial Expressions. The only guideline for both gestures and facial expressions is to use them naturally. Students should not be encouraged to or discouraged from using gestures and facial expressions. Instead, they should use them as they would in a conversation. In addition, students should be cautioned against holding onto the podium or fidgeting with their note cards.

Eye Contact. Instructors must stress the importance of eye contact with an audience because reticent individuals sometimes find looking at the audience difficult and refrain from doing so. The teacher should tell students that a speech is essentially a conversation with a number of people; the notion of enlarged conversation discussed earlier. To establish a conversational atmosphere and to involve audience members in the conversation, students should establish eye contact with many members of the audience. The instructor might ask how to nonverbally involve a stranger joining a social group at a party. The answer is to adjust body position to include the person, and more importantly to make eye contact with the new person when talking. The teacher should show how the group situation parallels the public speaking situation. Students should get the audience involved in the conversation (public speech) by making eye contact. They should distribute their eye contact throughout the audience, looking at each person for a couple of seconds. If a speaker makes extended eye contact with an audience member, that person will become uncomfortable. However, if the speaker does not look at the audience member long enough, that person might not feel involved in the speech.

Rehearsal Process

While rehearsing, students must concentrate on the skills they have learned. Teachers can suggest that students write notes to themselves, to remind them of effective delivery practices. For example, students might write such things as: "eye contact, pause here, remember the time when. . . . " These messages will help the student to concentrate on giving the speech.

The rehearsal process for the public speech closely parallels the rehearsal process for the oral interpretation assignment: initial comments and questions from the student, giving the speech, feedback from the instructor, work through certain spots for delivery (e.g., pausing, central idea), and final comments and questions (see the oral interpretation rehearsal process for details). The instructor can use the following list of questions as a guide for public speaking delivery:

- Are transitions between the introduction, main points, and conclusions signaled by major pauses? (structural clarity)
- Are transitions between supporting materials marked by minor pauses? (conceptual clarity)
- Does the student express his or her enthusiasm about the topic during the presentation of the speech? (emotional clarity)
- Does the student's nonverbal communication enhance or detract from the speech?

CONCLUSION

To summarize, students must develop effective delivery skills in order to increase their competence as communicators. Effective delivery establishes conceptual clarity, communicates attitudes and emotion, but does not draw attention to the communicator.

Instructors must avoid using mechanical approaches to delivery training. Instead, they should adopt delivery techniques such as grouping, highlighting central ideas, and emotional memory to enhance delivery. Trainers must stress the importance of practice when teaching delivery because understanding without practice will not improve delivery skills. With diligent practice, students can significantly improve their delivery skills and competence as communicators.

Training in oral interpretation before attempting a public speech helps students understand that they can use their voices well. A successful interpretation generally frees students from burdensome worries about how they will sound, because the successful reading has instilled confidence in the use of their own voices.

THEORETICAL AND PHILOSOPHICAL UNDERPINNINGS OF THE TRAINING APPROACH

7

THE PROBLEM OF
INEPT SOCIAL BEHAVIOR

Part I provided the details of our training approach as carried out in the PSU Reticence Program. Now we examine the assumptions underlying the pedagogical model just described. We begin by discussing the nature of the communication problems students in the Reticence Program display.

In a study of 40,000 students in California and Pennsylvania, Merriam and Friedman (1969) found a consistent 14% of elementary students, 24% of junior high students, and 12% of senior high students so unskilled at speaking, they were unable to cope with the normal communication demands of the classroom. These students could not ask or answer questions, make requests of their teachers, give oral reports, participate in classroom discussion, or make their feelings and emotions known to school personnel. They were often classified as retarded, low achievers, or willfully resistant to instruction. It is interesting to note that a population of students in a reformatory junior and senior high school mentioned in the same report showed more than 60% were inept at performing ordinary speaking tasks.

Zimbardo and colleagues (1977, 1986) conducted extensive surveys of shyness and consistently found approximately 40% of respondents claimed to have a shy "disposition." About 15% indicated they were shy in specific stressful situations, and another 40% claimed they had once been shy but had overcome it. These findings show that only a very small percentage of respondents had no personal experience with shyness. However, the definition of *shyness* used in this study was exceedingly broad, broad enough to include major politicians and famous performers.

These studies demonstrate that a substantial proportion of the population has difficulty communicating in some situations. What exactly is the problem these people experience? We cannot provide a definitive answer, but we will clarify why it is so hard to define and classify communication problems. We intend to discuss the types of problems reported by and observed in the thousands we have trained. We begin by examining several of the labels used by experts to describe people with social communication problems and try to differentiate among them. We then focus more specifically on those who designate themselves or are designated by others as reticent (Phillips, 1965) or, more recently, incompetent (Phillips, 1991).

The broad range of problems we encountered in the PSU Reticence Program provides a functional pool of people from whom we can derive categories of inept performance. Furthermore, we have treated enough people to have a sense of the problems that accompany their communication ineptitude. We discuss these problems at the end of the chapter.

WAYS TO CLASSIFY COMMUNICATION PROBLEMS

Three main concepts have been developed to describe essentially normal people who seem to withdraw from communication, particularly in novel situations or with strangers: *reticence, communication apprehension* (CA), and *shyness*. Several other terms have been used, but these three dominate the scholarly literature on the topic.

In 1965, Phillips coined the term *reticent* and introduced to the field of communication the notion that some people have difficulty communicating across a range of situations. Until that time, the field had focused almost exclusively on fear of public speaking.

Phillips' original conceptualization defined reticence as a personality-based anxiety disorder. He rejected this notion, however, and limited his view of the problem to one of inadequate communication skills, for whatever reason (Phillips, 1977, 1984a, 1986, 1991). We emphasize this most recent conceptualization of reticence.

The major characteristic of reticent persons is avoidance of social situations in which they feel inept. Reticent persons may or may not actually have deficient social skills (Phillips, 1986), but they think they do. Phillips' (1991) latest work asserts that most do. Either they have experienced social failure because of their ineptitude or other people have pointed out their deficiencies. In addition, a reticent person may or may not experience fear about speaking (Phillips, 1986). Phillips (1984a) stated that "When people *avoid communication because they believe they will lose more by talking than by remaining silent*, we refer to it as *reticence*" (p. 52; emphasis in original).

McCroskey (1984a) defined *communication apprehension* as "an individual's level of fear or anxiety associated with either real or anticipated communication with another person or persons" (p. 13). Individuals who experience high levels of CA tend to avoid and withdraw from communication (McCroskey, 1984a). Apprehension is experienced internally and may or may not produce behavioral consequences (McCroskey, 1984a). One study (Beatty, Dobos, Balfantz, & Kuwabara, 1991) even suggests that behavioral disruption might be a cause rather than a consequence of CA.

Communication apprehension may be characterized along a continuum from traitlike apprehension to situational apprehension (McCroskey, 1984a). Traitlike apprehension is seen as "a relatively enduring, personality-type orientation toward a given mode of communication across a wide variety of contexts" (McCroskey, 1984a, p. 16). People who experience traitlike CA feel anxious about communicating much of the time. They are distinguished from individuals who have generalized-context CA (McCroskey, 1984a), which refers to anxiety about communicating in a particular type of context like public speaking or meetings.

A third classification is person-group CA, defined as "a relatively enduring orientation toward communicating with a given person or group of people" (McCroskey, 1984a, p. 17). Individuals who are usually apprehensive when they communicate with their fathers, for example, illustrate person-group CA (Beatty & Dobos, 1992). Finally, there is situational apprehension, which is a statelike response to a specific situation (McCroskey, 1984a). Most people experience situational apprehension on occasion, for a variety of reasons (Daly & Buss, 1984).

According to Phillips (1984a) and McCroskey (1984a) the crucial distinction between the two concepts is that reticence refers to a skills deficit and CA refers to anxiety about communicating. Others have argued, however, that the differences between the concepts are not so clear because in both cases the individuals avoid or withdraw from communication and reticent people may also experience anxiety (Clevenger, 1984; Kelly, 1982; Miller, 1984).

The concept of *shyness* has been developed primarily by psychologists, and thus is not directly connected with communication. When used by psychologists, the term refers to a personality trait or quality of personality. Shyness is not necessarily connected with overt behavior. Thus, Zimbardo (1977) made a major point of noting that many public performers classified themselves as shy.

Shyness is also the term most people use to describe individuals who are quiet and reserved in social situations. The literature on shyness reveals a variety of definitions, most of which view shyness as a multifaceted problem encompassing the characteristics of reticence and communication apprehension (Buss, 1984; Zimbardo, 1977). Buss defined *shyness* as "discomfort, inhibition, and awkwardness in social situations, especially with people who are not familiar" (p. 39). Shyness is a problem with instrumental, emotional, and cognitive components (Buss, 1984). In this view only awkwardness points to overt behavior.

Zimbardo (1977) described *shyness* as a problem characterized by anxiety, low self-esteem, inadequate social skills (which he did not specify), and feelings of self-consciousness. Jones and Russell (1982) conceptualized *shyness* as including, "attitudes and feelings such as reticence and a lack of confidence particularly in new or unfamiliar social settings, excessive preoccupation with self in the presence of others, inadequate social skills, and disruptive anxiety and self-derogation in social settings" (p. 629). This approach defines shyness as a problem that is both behavioral and internally experienced, although the behavioral manifestations are not spelled out.

McCroskey and Richmond (1982), among the few communication scholars who studied the shyness concept, defined it as "the tendency to be timid, reserved, and most specifically, talk less" (p. 460), providing a view of shyness as a strictly behavioral problem. However, they do not provide a criterion against which to compare "talk less." Talk less than what or whom?

These three labels—*reticence, communication apprehension,* and *shyness*—encompass several types of communication problems: skill deficits, self-consciousness, anxiety, behavioral avoidance and disruption, and low self-esteem. Although the concept of CA appears to be distinct from the other two in that it is mainly internalized, the behavioral differences, if any, between shyness and reticence are not as clear. Although these three labels have been useful in generating separate lines of research, the labels have made it difficult to integrate findings. On the other hand, within the three classifications, we can find problematic but modifiable situations and behaviors to serve as a basis for training.

Kelly et al. (1992) suggested that the time is right to clarify our understanding of the nature of social communication problems. Phillips' (1991) most recent work, discussed in the next section, has begun this process by removing the psychological component from the problem and concentrating on the behavioral aspects of inept communication performance.

THE INCOMPETENCE (RETICENCE) CONSTRUCT

Since its inception as a skills-based problem (Phillips & Metzger, 1973), the construct of reticence has been quite broad, encompassing several types of individuals with related but distinct problems. As Phillips (1977, 1986) described them, reticent communicators can have problems in a wide array of skill areas as described earlier. There may be several types of individuals whose communication difficulties can be subsumed under the *reticent* label. As Kelly et al. (1992) argued, the experience of instructors in the PSU Reticence Program suggests there is merit to this idea. Instructors frequently comment about the vast differences among the trainees, both in severity and in kind of difficulties.

In his latest refinement of the reticence construct, Phillips (1991) acknowledged the difficulty of defining terms like *reticence, shyness,* or *incompetence.* Phillips (1991) originally chose the term *reticent* because of its neutral connotations, but it has lost its neutrality, so he has opted to use the phrase *communication incompetence.* As Phillips stated: "The important question is, What do shy people do that leads others to regard them as shy? Once we focus on 'doing,' we can ignore all prior designations. It is no longer important to label people as 'shy,' 'reticent,' or 'apprehensive.' Once we have identified inept behaviors, we can work on modifying them, without labeling the individual at all" (p. 49).

Phillips has both broadened his approach to communication problems and incorporated greater specificity. He has broadened his approach by presenting a theory of incompetent communication, preferring the term *incompetence* to *reticence*.
Simultaneously, he has delineated the concept by identifying the
classical canons of rhetoric (invention, disposition, style, delivery,
and memory) as the major processes that are involved in a competent act of communication. The reticent communicator may be
incompetent in one or more of these rhetorical processes (Phillips,
1991). Although this concept was a theme in earlier work (Phillips,
1977), it is articulated with greater detail in this latest treatise. In
the next section, we present a method for classifying communication incompetencies based on Phillips' (1991) system.

ONE METHOD OF CLASSIFICATION

An effective way to look at communication incompetencies is
through the five classical canons of rhetoric: invention, disposition, style, delivery, and memory. This mode of classification pre-
sumes that we can establish behavioral standards or norms and
specify core behaviors in which all students could be trained. An
approach through the canons would satisfy the curricular
requirements of a school system on any level because the
approach would provide a reputable theoretical basis, a minimum standard of performance, and a repertoire of training exercises and generally applicable techniques. To understand what
would be included in such a curriculum, we need only examine
the norms for instruction in standard speech performance courses in elementary and secondary schools and in colleges.
    Some errors people make when communicating can be
corrected easily; some cannot. Of all the possible errors a person
can make in social discourse, which are most productive to treat?
Using the canons, we can isolate some possible errors.
    The canons are an appropriate way to classify the kinds of
communication difficulties trainees typically report because they
specifically focus on behavior, and they accommodate common
problems. Most students have trouble deciding on a topic and
supporting their ideas. Much social speech is disorganized
because conversationalists get disconnected and cannot arrange
ideas in logical sequence and support them with examples.
Frequently, they have difficulty choosing appropriate language for
presenting their ideas in an interesting fashion. Many have memo-

ry problems and are unable to remember ideas or information. We have encountered students who experience some or all of these difficulties. In this section, we examine the five canons of rhetoric to further identify the types of communication problems trainees typically present when they enroll in the Reticence Program.

Errors in Invention

In the first place, speakers often do not know the possibilities of a given social situation. Some people are simply inept at adapting to the needs and interests of the people around them and need training in ways of adapting to others. They must learn to select topics; to decide what is appropriate to say, to whom, and on what occasion.

If the speaker cannot think of speech or conversational topics, he or she suffers from topical incompetence. Begnal (1983) concluded that a great many people appear to be incompetent in social situations because they have little to say. Some can talk about themselves, their problems and their narrow interests, but they are not able to adapt to what other people might find interesting.

One goal of the invention process is to select ideas that gain listeners' attention and use them to convince the listener of the speaker's point of view. The main idea is to adapt Combs and Snygg's (1959) statement:

> However capricious, irrelevant, and irrational his behavior may appear to an outsider, from his point of view at that instant his behavior is purposeful, relevant, and pertinent to the situation as he understands it. How it appears to others has no bearing upon the causes of his behavior. (p. 17)

Each person has stored in his or her mind memories of experiences, evaluations, and criteria from which to draw ideas useful in specific social situations. Much of that personal experience is repetitive. We find an idea that works in one situation and we can use it again under similar circumstances. One form of inventional disability is a scant repertoire. To be effective, a speaker must be able to predict what is on the listener's mind and act accordingly. This task requires considerable social experience to perform consistently. People skilled in social conversation are able to select their own behaviors with considerable precision. The outcome of the give and take of social conversation depends on the participants' repertoires. The problem is a matter of learning social adaptability and then finding the means to compose and deliver remarks.

Errors in Disposition of Social Discourse

However chaotic it may sometimes appear, social life is essentially orderly. It is a process of formal give and take and informal responsive dialogue. If you have something to say, it is possible to improve the way you say it by applying rules of orderly arrangement of speech.

Many of our trainees have difficulty arranging ideas in an orderly fashion. Their stories often seem to have no point. Many of them cannot give intelligible directions. They are disorganized and misunderstood. If discourse is people taking turns talking in order to develop an idea, speakers must decide on a sequence to be successful. Sequencing is not easy because most people do not listen well. They are busily composing their own remarks while the other person is talking. Consequently, they may find themselves repeating what was already said or making a point that appears to be "out in left field." If people merely make statements without any apparent relationship to what has just been said, the talk will appear inane, pointless, or at best, stilted.

Errors in arrangement are, perhaps, the most frequent of all in social discourse, and also the easiest to remedy. There are a limited number of ways ideas can be connected because the mind can only fathom a few sequences. The seven structures presented in Chapter 5 reflect common ways ideas can be logically arranged. What we must emphasize is listening. Each speaker must listen to the other and connect responses in some rational way to what he or she has just heard. People must be trained to listen first and then compose their responses.

We measure the success of discourse, in the first instance, by whether it can be understood. The second measure is whether it creates the effect the speaker desires. The error in disposition can be identified merely by asking whether the listener understands the ideas. If the words are intelligible to the listener but he or she cannot understand the speaker, there is probably an error in arrangement of ideas.

Disposition is the process by which ideas are made intelligible. The ideas the speaker thinks up during the invention process must be put in order before they are spoken. Disposition connects ideas with delivery. It is the process by which ideas are organized and directed toward a purpose. The speaker has an explicit and implicit goal in the arrangement process. The explicit goal is to get the ideas arranged in an order sensible to the listener. The implicit goal is to get the listener's assent to the speaker's ideas.

There is always competition for the auditory and intellectual attention of the listener. In order to be effective, the speaker must gain attention and keep it by transmitting an orderly message of potentially effective ideas conceived during the invention process and properly sequenced for the listener. The process includes the arrangement or deployment of supporting materials (examples and arguments) to convince the listener. We have repeatedly used the phrase "to the listener" because the interests, concerns, and capabilities of the listener determine the sequence. All ideas are arranged with the listener in mind. The speaker who arranges ideas for his or her own convenience is in error.

Errors in Style and Delivery

Selection of words and the way they are spoken represent the performance aspects of speaking and are other areas in which people often are incompetent. They tell us they cannot find the right words or have trouble thinking of words to express their ideas. Others explain that they cannot get the words out or their voices are too soft or unpleasant. Some are uncomfortable about using their hands to gesture, and still others feel their delivery is dull and unexciting. All in all many of the trainees we work with are unhappy with their spoken delivery style.

Some people have good delivery and some do not, but ordinary inadequacy is not normally considered a problem. A good vocabulary and an interesting manner, however, can be cultivated. A speaker can learn words and acquire through practice the ability to speak them fluently and in a pleasant voice. Gestures, facial expressions, and body movements can influence interest and credibility. Improved performance can result from training and formation of good habits.

Most people need training in delivery. It is not as simple as it appears. Training can help to relax the vocal mechanism; synchronize breathing and vocalization; acquire resonance; improve vocal quality; learn variety in intonation; make intonation appropriate to the ideas; synchronize gestures with speech; move appropriately; develop pleasant facial expression; gain and maintain eye contact; learn to pronounce consonants, vowels, and diphthongs; pronounce words correctly; use idioms and slang properly; select appropriate words; avoid offensive language; and sense when the listener wants to take a turn. This last skill depends on a repertoire of experience, a final area in which incompetence occurs.

Errors in Memory

If the speaker cannot receive, store, and retrieve information relevant to social speech, he or she is usually not competent to respond effectively. Response comes from memory. As we noted earlier, when we encounter a social situation, we seek the memory of a similar social situation and select the behavior that was effective at that time. Of course, if there was no successful behavior, there can be no memory of it. Very often, training requires creating situations in which the trainee can experience success in controlled situations, so that the memory of success can be transferred to real situations.

Some students who enroll in the Reticence Program report having difficulty remembering what they want to say. This lack of memory may be the major cause of their "timing" problems, that is, coming up with an appropriate comment or topic only after the opportunity to speak has passed. Some students tell us they do think of things to say, but their anxiety interferes with their ability to remember what they intended to say.

Zimbardo's (1977) research suggests that shyness, and the anxiety associated with it, can impede memory. For many, this anxiety is exacerbated by the public speaking context, which they consider to be their worst nightmare.

A major element in successful use of memory is the ability of the speaker to observe and interpret the behavior of listeners and to monitor his or her own behavior to instantly adapt to changing social situations. Training in delivery often includes specific methods of observing audience behavior and modifying discourse accordingly. The trainer-critic uses this method to train speakers for both formal and informal social situations.

Testing the Model

Kelly et al. (1992, 1994) conducted two studies to determine if there are distinguishable types of reticent communicators enrolled in the PSU Reticence Program. Using Phillips' (1991) notion that skill deficiencies can occur in any or all of the canons of rhetoric, they developed a self-report measure to assess the types of skill problems students experience. The researchers also included several items to assess whether or not the trainees feel anxious about communicating. Students were instructed to complete the items as if they were carrying on social conversation with a stranger.

In the 1994 study, the researchers collected two samples of reticent college students. In both samples, the most commonly reported problem was anxiety; however, the number of students who reported problems with anxiety in the 1994 sample (72%) was considerably larger than students in the 1993 sample who reported anxiety problems (54%). Table 7.1 shows the percentage of problems reported by respondents in the two studies, and illustrates a remarkable amount of similarity between the two samples. In fact, the average difference between the two samples for the skills dimensions was only 4 percentage points. The largest difference, 12 percentage points, between the two samples was found for delivery. Kelly et al. (1992, 1994) concluded that the skill areas that presented problems for the largest number of students in the Reticence Program included timing, delivery, and knowledge, although the greatest percentage of students reported anxiety problems in both studies.

Results of the 1994 study suggest five types of reticent communicators, and again the two samples were quite consistent. In fact, the first five types listed in the 1993 sample matched five of the types identified in the 1994 sample. The five types, each of which accounted for at least 5% of the sample, found in both samples include:

- problems reported in all areas (anxiety, knowledge, timing, organization, delivery, memory);
- problems reported in the areas of anxiety, knowledge,

Table 7.1. Percentage of Problems Reported by Respondents in Kelly et al. Studies.

Year	Anxiety (%)	Knowledge (%)	Timing (%)	Organization (%)	Delivery (%)	Memory (%)
1994	72	35	48	27	53	28
1993	54	33	44	26	41	28

timing, and delivery;
- problems reported in all areas except organization (anxiety, knowledge, timing, delivery, memory);
- problems reported with anxiety only; and
- no reported problems in any area.

The Kelly et al. studies provide empirical evidence for the usefulness of the classification system derived from the canons of rhetoric. Their research also encourages others to continue refining ways of assessing the trainees' problems so instruction can be delivered to meet their specific and individualized needs.

Problematic Types of Situations

As students discuss their communication problems with trainers, it becomes apparent that they all feel some situations are more difficult to handle than others. The situations differ from person to person, but they can be arranged hierarchically from easiest to most difficult. In this section we consider the types of communication situations that generally are problematic for reticent individuals. The reader will note that the Reticence Program provides training in all of these situations as described in Chapter 4. The five areas of incompetence based on the canons of rhetoric—invention, disposition, style, delivery, and memory—can and do occur in all types of social situations. The types of problems trainees report, then, are summarized by the grid presented in Table 7.2. In the spaces of the table are names of two hypothetical trainees (Mary and Tom) to illustrate their communication problems.

Table 7.2. Summary of Communication Problems.

	Communication Context					
	Interviews	Conversation	Meetings	Public	Authorities	Groups
Invention		Mary/Tom	Mary	Mary		Mary
Disposition	Tom		Tom	Tom	Tom	
Style	Tom	Tom		Tom	Tom	
Delivery	Mary/Tom	Mary		Mary/Tom	Tom	Mary
Memory						

Carrying on Social Conversation

For some trainees initiating and carrying on social conversation is the least difficult type of situation; for others it poses the greatest challenge. Most reticent communicators have some trouble performing competently in casual conversation, especially with strangers, because of the unstructured nature of the interaction (Pilkonis, 1977b). Unstructured situations require skill at inventing topics and phrases to speak, choosing appropriate language, and remembering and delivering those words and ideas. Students who find social conversation difficult and anxiety provoking usually describe two main problems: working up the nerve to initiate a conversation and thinking of things to say. These students seem especially concerned about their ability to make small talk, and often remark that such talk is superficial and unnecessary. They find the situation uncomfortable and try to avoid it.

Speaking to Authority Figures

Many students in the PSU Reticence Program find it very difficult to talk to people in positions of authority or to those who have higher status. They tend to avoid talking to teachers, advisors, employers, and even parents of friends, as a result. They do not ask their teachers questions after class, they do not seek help from their advisors, they rarely ask their bosses for a raise or time off, and they generally fail to carry on any informal, more personal interaction with any of these people. In later life, many of these trainees are unable to ask for help when they need it, for example, from physicians. Often, they are unable to work well with helpers when help is offered. Although status differences are a source of situational apprehension for many speakers (Daly & Buss, 1984), they are very problematic much of the time for reticent communicators. These situations tend to trigger high levels of anxiety and exacerbate problems of invention, disposition, style, delivery, and memory.

Speaking in the Classroom or at Meetings

For many trainees, asking or answering questions in class or contributing ideas at meetings is nearly as frightening as giving a public speech. Some have never volunteered a comment or answer in a class or meeting situation. Others do not answer when called on. A major problem for many of these students is the invention process; either they do not know what is appropriate to say in class or they think that what they have to say is irrelevant or not worth saying. Some have timing problems; by the time they generate a question or comment, the appropriate time for offering it has passed. Still others claim that once called on, they forget what they wanted to say or cannot find the right words.

Being Interviewed

Those who have difficulty communicating with authority figures also tend to find the interview process troublesome. Interviews can be even more unnerving because of their evaluative nature. Students are especially troubled by job interviews because they know that their suitability as employees and their communication skills are being judged. It does not occur to them that they can use the interview as an opportunity to assess the organization as a place of employment. They make themselves vulnerable to evaluation and criticism. This provokes a nervous reaction which students report interferes with their ability to think of responses or deliver them in an articulate manner. Many candidates report they cut their answers short and do not question the interviewer because of their anxiety. Often they fail to recognize that with better preparation they could circumvent most of these problems.

It is important to recognize that the "interview" occurs in a number of forms. Evaluation and criticism are constants in organizational life. Inability to withstand criticism and respond to it can handicap an employee seriously.

Working in Small Task Groups

Many trainees report difficulty communicating in small task groups. Most such groups operate in a fairly unstructured way, which poses a problem for reticent individuals. When the flow of interaction is unstructured, reticent people have a hard time thinking of remarks and speaking them before the topic changes. They lack the ability to push their way into a conversation. Once groups get going, interaction takes on the characteristics of a "free for all," so usually those whose ideas get heard are the most aggressive. Moreover, group roles and norms get established early so those who talk in the initial stages of group development generally get the floor more than those who have been quieter. Because reticent members do not talk much and are usually very quiet at the initial stages of the group process, they are even less likely to have opportunities to share their ideas when the activity level of the group is high and members must compete for the floor. When this competition factor is added to their self-doubt about the significance and relevance of their ideas, it is easy to see why so many of our trainees do not speak much in groups.

Public Speeches

Most of the students we have worked with in the Reticence Program find the public speaking situation the most difficult of all. The majority of them find it so distressing that they have consistently avoided it, regardless of the penalties. Students tell us that having to give the speech is greater punishment than anything a teacher or anyone else can inflict. Some have feigned illness and some have actually become ill at the prospect of having to give a speech. They have volunteered to write extra papers or complete other kinds of assignments to avoid the most dreaded of all situations. One survey reported that a great many people fear public speaking more than death itself. Whether this is hyperbole or not, the notion of stage fright has been around for a long time.

Of course, not all trainees have this extreme a reaction to public speaking, but the vast majority of them find it distressing and report experiencing various physical symptoms of anxiety when forced to speak in front of an audience. They worry about giving the speech from the moment they are assigned to speak until they have finished the speech and are sitting down. Many of them continue to feel nervous long after the speech is over.

Many trainees tell us that they do not know what to talk about and spend hours brooding over their topics, a problem with invention as just described. They usually do not know how to go about putting a speech together, but their main worry is that they will forget what they want to say or will be unable to get the words out. This, they are sure, will lead to disaster; they will have made fools of themselves in front of an audience. They feel so much performance pressure because they exaggerate the evaluative nature of the public speaking situation. They often experience high levels of anxiety that are manifested in a variety of ways including blushing or blotching of the face and neck, shaking hands or knees, dryness of the mouth and throat, excessive perspiration, queasiness, quavering voice, and general awkwardness of movement. In a rare case, individuals may become physically ill and/or pass out.

These, then, represent the types of situations in which errors of invention, disposition, style, delivery, and memory are manifested. Trainees sometimes report other, usually very specific, kinds of concerns such as difficulty talking to a particular person or about a given topic. These usually can be subsumed within one of the other categories. Because instruction is individualized, as described in the next chapter, students can direct their efforts toward improvement in these specific contexts.

ACCOMPANYING PROBLEMS

Most of the people who participate in training programs like the one at PSU are essentially normal individuals. Trainers occasionally encounter people whose problems seem to go beyond communication incompetence. There is no doubt that there are people with emotional disturbances characterized by avoidance of social situations, fear of speaking, and taciturnity. In these cases, however, speech is not the problem. It is a symptom. Whatever the nature of the personal distress these people feel, there is ample reason to believe that helping them acquire communication competency facilitates improvement in self-image and helps them overcome their psychological problems. In any event, solution of their psychological problems does not guarantee that they will automatically become competent speakers. In fact, improving their psychological state may help them learn, but more often, learning improves their psychological state. They may well acquire the ability to risk in social encounters only to lose their nerve once they discover that they do not have the skills necessary to perform well. As a clincher, it is much easier to teach speech than to modify personality.

The disability commonly known as stage fright is an example of a problem that is brought on by poor performance due to inadequate skills. People not trained to perform in public are required to do so. The process begins with "Show and Tell" in elementary school and continues through the various oral reports required in school and on the job. We seem to assume that speech skills are innate; that inability to perform is the sign of a handicap, social or psychological. We refuse to accept the fact that oral performance is a skill that can be taught and learned.

Many skilled psychiatrists and counselors understand

that their clients may be so disabled in oral communication that they have to get training in how to speak with their professionals. The important lesson is that the skills of effective social speaking exist apart from personality. The willingness to speak, to social-ize, to control, and to participate may be components of personal-ity. The skills of audience analysis, selection of viable topics, arrangement of ideas, word selection and deployment, delivery, and responsiveness to listener behavior can all be acquired apart from personality modification. Trainers and teachers might have to adapt to some of the foibles of their students, but it is their pedagogical problem to overcome psychological resistance and teach speech skills apart from personality training.

Instructors in the Reticence Program also encounter stu-dents who have problems with the actual production of speech, such as stuttering, lisps, and pronunciation difficulties. People with these difficulties as well as those with physiological anom-alies also need modification, but this is usually the responsibility of a specialist in communication disorders.

CONCLUSION

Students in the PSU Reticence Program are all volunteers. They generally do not have psychological problems or speech patholo-gies. They are, however, individuals who have consistently avoid-ed or withdrawn from situations in which they are incompetent and experience anxiety. Those situations can range from simple social conversation with a stranger to presenting a formal speech, and the kinds of skills they lack can be categorized by the canons of classical rhetoric: invention, disposition, style, delivery, and memory. Trainees (some 5,000 of them over a 20-year period) have told us what it was important for them to learn. Although a few spoke about seduction and power, virtually all raised issues about mundane competencies, abilities that were important in conducting everyday life successfully:

- They wanted to know how to meet new people, to open conversation, continue it, and possibly make arrange-ments to meet again.
- They reported having difficulty dealing with tradespeo-ple and professionals. They complained they could not give information successfully and claimed they had trouble asking questions.

- Most of them reported that they could not make coherent and extended reports on the job or in class. In short, they could not speak in public.
- Virtually all would explain they had problems making themselves appealing to others. This problem was particularly troublesome in job interviews. It also hampered them in making friends or participating in community activities where they were required to state their views in public.
- Very few understood the role that speech plays in the organization of society. They were not interested in learning complex theory or criticism. They wanted to master simple skills.
- Most felt that speaking was a gift some people were born with, but they also felt they could learn a magic formula to improve themselves.

Thus, our concern in the Reticence Program is with problems in performance that have the following characteristics:

- They do not fit into any of the pathological categories employed by professionals in the field of communication disorders.
- They interfere with ordinary social communication and performances generally required of the population at large.
- They are noticed by others; that is, when people who have problems display them, attention is focused on the communication performance rather than the content.
- The people who have problems are often concerned about them. They understand that their performance on the job and in their ordinary social life is, somehow, affected by these problems, but they do not seem to be able to find ways to overcome them. However, they transcend the simple and general ineptitudes that are the focus of most performance-based speech communication courses and training programs.
- Problems are rarely pervasive. That is, they are manifested in some social situations but not in others. This condition is referred to as the state-trait issue. We are not concerned with general communication disability as a manifestation of global personality disorder. These problems we refer to clinical psychologists and psychiatrists.

The question of the nature of shyness remains unanswered, but it is irrelevant to our task. For us, shyness is an abstraction. It is an evaluation made of someone's behavior, not a state of being. Frankly, we believe it is a word that should not be used. There are some psychological conditions characterized by social withdrawal. They are rare and they are amenable to treatment by a trained medical professional. Most people are occasionally withdrawn. They may be intimidated by a particular social situation; they may feel unskilled. These people are our target population. They are everyone. Concentration on performance training provides benefits to everyone, even those under professional care. There should be no apology necessary for modification of inept communication. Better communication serves us all.

8

BASIC PEDAGOGICAL PREMISES FOR PERFORMANCE MODIFICATION

To be effective, a program of instruction must fit the problem it is designed to remedy. The PSU Reticence Program is based on a set of premises about pedagogy that follow directly from our perspective on the nature of communication reticence as described in the previous chapter. Teachers and trainers who want to incorporate all or some of the instructional techniques described in Part I into an existing program or who intend to develop a new program will see the logic of particular teaching methods once they understand these premises. The purpose of this chapter is to provide that logic by discussing the overall model of instruction at the heart of the Reticence Program.

CONTEMPORIZING THE MEDICAL MODEL

The problem of incompetent speaking can be considered a clinical problem. The practice of clinical medicine is based on the establishment of taxonomies of diseases and disorders against which individual cases are measured. Once a case is classified, the treatment is virtually automatic—at the start. However, because each individual has his or her idiosyncrasies, treatment must be modulated and modified to fit the particular case.

In the same way, generalizations exist about types of communication problems. Some people can be conveniently assigned to categories, but each case still requires a particularized treatment. Let us examine the nature of medical practice to get an idea of how this system works.

A physician will identify symptoms of a problem, and then will relate these to a category that has a particular remedy. To be explicit, red rash, fever, photophobia, and spots on the tongue are signs of measles. A measles case mandates a particular treatment. Presence of a particular kind of bacteria indicates the use of a specific antibiotic, with the proviso that the patient is not allergic. On the other hand, a lump can be diagnosed as a tumor. There is a treatment of record for each type of tumor, but a biopsy is required to accurately describe the tumor. There is a vast difference between a sebaceous cyst (swollen oil gland) and a cancer. This analysis method, in essence, is how communication incompetencies are handled. Problems can be grouped into categories, but the instructor must particularize pedagogy to suit the demands of the given case.

Sometimes it is possible to prevent disease. A person suspected of having heart disease will be told to minimize risk factors (i.e., stop smoking, eat a proper diet, exercise regularly). In dealing with communication, proper training and appropriate models can guide the individual into competent performance. When students enter the Reticence Program, they already have communication problems. The instructor must not do further harm. The instruction must be tailored to the student, the consequences observed, and the training modified as necessary. An important element is to present the student with a worthy model to imitate, a teacher who can speak fluently and skillfully.

Sometimes, in medicine, it is important for the physician to identify the cause of the condition. Knowing the cause allows the physician to direct treatment at the cause rather than alleviating symptoms. Unfortunately, instructors cannot identify the causes of communication incompetency in a particular individual and so must provide immediate training addressed to the skill deficiencies the student demonstrates. If a patient has lung cancer caused by smoking, knowing the cause does not obviate the need for surgery. Similarly, if a student cannot talk in a discussion class, knowing that he or she was traumatized in a group in the fourth grade does not help.

The main question in training incompetent speakers is how to assign problems to categories that can be handled by particular kinds of training. Even though the pedagogical process fits a clinical model, treatment cannot be in a clinical setting. Classes or workshops are essential; the cost of one-to-one training is prohibitively labor intensive. Furthermore, private lessons in public behavior are a contradiction.

The medical model enables us to proceed in a nonjudgmental way. We are not treating defective people; we are treating behaviors (symptoms) that interfere with optimum performance. We do not have to take responsibility for total personality changes. Our goals are not modification of the person but of the person's performance.

Our problem is complicated because most of our students are not willing or able to identify their specific incapabilities. When a patient sees a physician, there is a tacit admission of some problem. The patient can usually point to symptoms he or she is experiencing. Many students who present themselves to the Reticence Program know only that they are uncomfortable about speaking and sometimes avoid speaking if they can. Some of them believe they could be suffering from a psychological disorder, which allows them to take diminished responsibility for their problems, and leads some to seek therapy. The program is an alternative to expensive treatment, the efficacy of which can be documented.

Our rhetorical problem is to convince our trainees that modification of particular performance behaviors enables them to perform tasks that they have been incapable of performing. We do not and cannot regard them as ill or disabled. They are deficient in their ability to perform specific communication behaviors. We have to refocus their attention from their personality deficits to specific performance techniques.

Thus, the Reticence Program relies on a combination of skills training and cognitive restructuring as noted in Chapter 1. The skills training component of the program is designed to help trainees develop general communication abilities like goal setting, organization of ideas, and audience analysis, as well as more specific competencies like initiating social conversation, offering opinions in a group meeting, and developing an effective speech conclusion. In the Introduction we discussed how students are trained to rethink the nature of the communication process and their role in it, the cognitive modification component of the

Reticence Program. Instructors must persuade students to accept the following concepts:

- People can become better communicators by developing their skills through training and practice.
- It is important to become a competent speaker and it is worth the effort.
- What happens during interaction is not completely out of their control; they can exert influence over other people and the situation.
- By developing their skills, they can feel more relaxed and confident.
- They do not need psychological treatment designed specifically to reduce anxiety about communicating.

Students must accept these premises if training is to be effective. If they do not believe they can improve, they will not commit to the change required to succeed. The cognitive restructuring that occurs is at least as important as the actual skills training.

In the following sections, we examine the major pedagogical premises underlying the training program. Specifically, we discuss five premises: the focus on behavior, building a repertoire of skills, incremental skill development, individualized instruction, and the maximization of carryover beyond the training experience.

PREMISES UNDERLYING THE PROGRAM

Behavior, Not Feelings

Students who seek help for their communication problems say they feel tense, nervous, uncomfortable, afraid, or inadequate. They often refer to physiological sensations like shaking and trembling that accompany these feelings. As discussed in Chapter 3, we insist that students focus on behavior and, to the extent they can, advise them to ignore the feelings.

The rationale for this emphasis on behavior is really quite simple. It is easier to change what people do than how they feel. Furthermore, it is not clear that modifying feelings will produce changes in behavior. Changing feelings may make it easier to modify behavior, but the two are not automatically connected. Feelings will not change if the person does what he or she has always done. Even if we could motivate people to feel more confident and less nervous, these new feelings would dissipate if our trainees were unable to improve their public social performance.

An assumption underlying the Reticence Program is that feelings of confidence and reduced anxiety will come as the individual becomes a more competent speaker. Most of us were not good public speakers the first time we stepped up to the podium, just as many of us were not relaxed when we got behind the wheel of a car to learn to drive. As people become more skillful at any task, their confidence increases and they are less anxious. Even when they become anxious at the prospect of performing, they know they have the skills to behave competently, and this realization allows them to accept their nervousness as natural rather than as a threat to their performance ability.

Building a Repertoire of Skills

When students enter the Reticence Program, they have varying levels of competency at performing social behaviors. Because for many of them, novel situations generate apprehension, they have a tendency to avoid exposing themselves to new communication contexts (Duran & Kelly, 1989). One of the unfortunate consequences of avoidance is their failure to build a repertoire of skills and behaviors to draw on in future situations. For example, many trainees report they have been so successful in avoiding public speaking, that they have never actually given a speech. As a result, they have no idea how to prepare for a speech situation or how to cope with normal audience response.

An important premise of the program is that trainees must learn skills that can be used in all contexts, as well as skills and techniques specific to personal situations. They must have the opportunity to practice both sets of skills in a variety of settings. By demonstrating that they can be successful, they can begin to build a repertoire of behaviors from which to draw in both new and familiar interactions. In the Introduction, we discussed five key skills central to successful speaking in all situations: goal analysis, audience and situation analysis, organization of ideas, delivery, and self-evaluation. The chapters in Part I presented the content and techniques for training people in these skills. The program helps students develop these five, not by telling them exactly what to do, but by requiring them to learn methods for approaching each skill area. The methods allow room for personal experimentation with application of general principles. This flexibility encourages development of a repertoire.

For instance, as described in Chapter 3, students are taught goal setting and are required to set their own goals, choose their own criteria for success, and develop their own plans for goal implementation. There are many choices students make in this process. They can make new choices for each goal. As a result, the student learns the general method of goal analysis and acquires techniques that become part of a personal repertoire. The same process applies to the skill of organizing ideas. Trainees learn the structuring method and then experiment with the seven structures so they can develop a repertoire of ways to arrange ideas.

Because the program also examines specific contexts, such as social conversation and class participation, trainees are taught techniques and skills unique to each type of situation along with general principles of effective speaking. Students are not told exactly what to say or do, but instead are motivated to develop techniques for identifying possibilities in situations. For example, teachers help students learn general ways of initiating conversation. They learn standard social forms and questions they can apply to specific situations to tailor social clichés to meet their own needs. In the process they develop their personal repertoires.

The building of repertoires of general and specific skills is an important part of the instructional program. Our assumption, based on years of working with students in the Reticence Program, is that successful speakers have these five skills and can adapt to situations. To be deemed successful in the program, students must leave with a repertoire they believe is adequate to meet present and anticipated needs.

Incremental Skill Development

A third pedagogical premise is that trainees must develop skills incrementally. The process is one of layering skill upon skill, technique upon technique, until a repertoire develops. The first processes are so fundamental they are automatic for most of us, for example, simply saying, "Hello, How are you?"

There are two reasons for the incremental approach. First, trainees come to us after years of forming bad communication habits, avoidance, and withdrawal from communication. They are mostly disorganized when they speak, and many have acquired genuine skill in avoiding any kind of face-to-face talk. Clearly, it is impossible for them to change their entire style of communicating in a brief period of time. They must gradually change their habits.

The second reason underlying incremental skill development is that students need to have a history of successful experiences to motivate them toward continued improvement. Many of them come to us demoralized and feeling at a loss about how to become better communicators. Asking too much of them too early is likely to do more harm than good by convincing them that they are doomed to fail. They need successful experiences, however simple, on which to build. We ask them to take small steps in areas where the probability of success is high. How exactly do we do this?

As described in the goal analysis section of Chapter 3, we ask students to begin by selecting communication goals that are not too difficult for them. Trainees are taught the goal analysis method and are asked to pick one communication goal in the situation of their choice. For instance, a student might select a goal such as, "I will have a 3- to 5-minute conversation with a classmate before English class starts," or "I will initiate a conversation with a stranger at the party on Saturday night." These are small goals that trainees almost certainly can accomplish. The instructors teach them skills, like audience and situation analysis, and techniques for maintaining social conversation. Students individually prepare a formal goal analysis, and their instructors go over their plans with them and suggest modifications and alternatives. They practice the skills of social conversation in the classroom, and then they are given the green light to attempt their goals.

Successful goal accomplishment is almost guaranteed. The goals are small, realistic and not too demanding. The student has prepared fully for the situation and has practiced. He or she has developed behavioral criteria for success. After the trainee completes his or her goal, he or she evaluates success in terms of individual behavior. The standards the student set were realistic and doable, thus they were within reach. Each trainee achieves his or her goals, has a successful experience, and begins to develop confidence that other goals are within his or her grasp.

The rest of the program provides students with new skills and new opportunities to communicate. They move from easier, smaller goals to more challenging, demanding ones. By the time they face difficult goals, they have built up a pool of successes that instills confidence and reduces anxiety. Public speaking assignments are saved for the end, so students can approach them with a proven record of success.

Individualized Instruction

What is difficult or easy, small or demanding varies from individual to individual. Public speaking is usually more feared and more challenging than social conversation. Group instruction forces us to make some generalizations, but the program is built on the assumption that instruction must be individualized. As much as possible, the program is tailored to meet each person's needs. The next sections describe how this goal is achieved.

Joint Identification of Skill Areas. As described in more detail in Chapter 2, the process of identifying trainee communication problems is a combination of self-reporting and teacher observation. Students talk about and write about their weaknesses and strengths. Instructors use prompts to get more information about what skills the student hopes to improve, what he or she would like to do better as a result of taking the program. This cataloguing is done on a case by case basis in a conference. Instructors keep a written record of the skill areas each individual selects for work, and this list is modified, as needed, by the student during the training.

This procedure allows for individualized instruction because not everyone works on the same skill areas. All students are exposed to the entire range of skill areas discussed in class or reading material, but they choose to spend time out of class developing skill areas of their choice.

Trainee Selection of Goals. A second way instruction is tailored to meet individual needs is through goal selection. Preparing for, completing, and evaluating goal accomplishment is the primary activity of the program. With very few exceptions, students select the specific goals they complete, the pace for completing them, the number of goals they attempt, and the completion order. Some students achieve a large number of goals, whereas others complete the minimum required by the syllabus. Some students work quickly, whereas others take more time to prepare for each goal.

It is fairly simple for the instructor to discover common features in the various goals. These form the target for general classroom instruction, with adaptations made in private conference. There are few exceptions to the policy of allowing students to control the goals they complete. They must, for instance, meet deadlines. A second limitation on flexibility is the minimum number of goals students must complete to receive course credit. In addition, minimums are linked to levels of grade achievement, with a greater number of goals required for higher course grades. Finally, at PSU where the Reticence Program is an option of a required speech communication course, trainees are required to do at least one in-class public speech to meet college standards.

Maximizing Carryover of Skills

A final premise that guides instruction is that carryover of skills is essential. We want students to continue to improve as communicators after the course is over. Students should not confine their improvement to the classroom; they should take with them methods that will enable them to perform in unfamiliar situations outside the classroom. To facilitate this process, the instructional program is designed to maximize skill carryover. This objective is accomplished in two primary ways: through assignments in goal setting and by teaching general skills useful in all communication contexts.

The goal-setting assignments take students outside of the classroom to try out new communication skills and techniques. Because they must attempt to accomplish their goals outside the training setting, students learn to use the skills in their real worlds. They approach the bank clerk, they discuss problems with their parents, they meet someone at a party, and they ask questions in classes. All of these goals provide trainees with opportunities to develop their skills in actual, rather than simulated situations. Moreover, students are encouraged to select personal, meaningful goals. Instructors tell them, "Identify something that you need or want to do that you have been unable to do, and select that for a goal." The goals, thus, are integrated into the ongoing lives of the trainees, which undoubtedly maximizes their ability to transfer those skills beyond the classroom.

New training methods are available to assist in this process. Visualization, for example, emphasizes the ability of the trainee to imagine him or herself performing skillfully in a particular situation (Ayers, 1988; Ayers & Hopf, 1985, 1987, 1989, 1990, 1992). Training through virtual reality systems on the computer inserts the student into a simulated reality in order to practice for a life situation. Both of these methods have met with initial success. Virtual reality training has been particularly useful in medical education, and visualization has had good early results in psychotherapy as well as in alleviating public speaking anxiety. Instructors should watch for developments in these areas.

The other way the goal assignments promote retention of skills and techniques is through the self-evaluation process. After completing each goal, students are required to assess their own behavior and identify ways that they could improve. This process encourages skill carryover by teaching students to be their own critics. Criticism is an important component of the training program (see Chapter 9). If trainees effectively criticize their communication behaviors, they have less need for a trainer. Students can then become more independent.

The second primary way the instructional program maximizes skill carryover is through the inclusion of general skills that are useful across contexts. Students are not taught what to say; instead, they are taught how to identify "sayables" from which they can choose to meet the needs of a personal situation. They are not taught the social norms for particular situations; rather, they learn how to analyze situations to determine what social norms are operating in a given case.

As described earlier, students have the opportunity to develop their skills in a variety of contexts so they can observe their general applicability. In essence, the students are taught to be adaptable, to analyze situations, and choose behaviors appropriate for the situation, the audience, and their goals. The more they develop adaptability, the more skill carryover is maximized.

The basic pedagogical premises of the Reticence Program can be summarized as follows:

- Students are trained to focus on their behavior rather than their feelings in specific interaction situations. It seems easier to alter behaviors than it is to engender feelings of confidence. Trainees tend to feel better, more relaxed and confident, as they improve their skills. The primary mechanism for training students to emphasize their behavior is the goal analysis procedure.
- The program is designed to help trainees develop a repertoire of general and specific communication skills. This development is central to the program because so many of the individuals we work with avoid completely or remain quiet in situations that make them uncomfortable. The unfortunate consequence is that they do not develop a repertoire of behaviors from which they can draw.
- Skills must be developed incrementally so that trainees can have successful experiences that encourage them to continue working to improve. By beginning with man-

ageable, relatively easy goals, students can build success on success until they feel confident to approach
more difficult situations.

- Instruction must be individualized because the people
  who enroll in the program are not all alike. They have
  varying skill levels and fears, and must be trained from
  where they are initially. Students report on their own
  strengths and weaknesses as speakers, and discuss
  those with their instructors. They select their own goals
  and work at their own pace. By incorporating individualized instruction into the group setting, many more
  people can be helped than could be reached through
  one-on-one counseling.
- A major objective of the program is to enable students to
  generalize what they have learned to their world outside
  the classroom. They need to demonstrate their skills in
  their everyday lives as well as learn methods that enable
  them to continue improving after the program ends.
  This objective is accomplished by having students complete goals outside of the classroom, and by teaching
  them methods and skills rather than giving them specific conversation topics or opening lines.

RESISTANCE TO INSTRUCTION

It is not a "piece of cake" to do the kind of teaching necessary to
programs like the one at PSU. Instructors often encounter resistance from trainees, some of it strong. Students resist in a number of ways. In order to understand how they resist, we should
understand what they resist.

Modification of speech behavior is a theoretically simple
process. It operates on these fundamental principles:

- Responsiveness increases with reinforced practice. The
  most productive way to use the classroom is to devise
  assignments that will enable the students to practice
  productive and useful behaviors.
- The more you stimulate students, the more they will
  respond. Whatever they are asked to do should appear
  useful to them and be interesting in its own right. If students do not see how they are going to use an activity in
  their own lives, they will acquiesce to what is going on

in order to stay out of trouble, but they will not really participate. They must participate in order to learn.

- If you do not ask for enough, you will not get enough. Higher levels of drive increase both the rate and limits of behavior change. Exercises must get progressively more challenging and the teacher must expect more from the student with each attempt. The student must understand this rule.

- Attitude is important. The teacher must consistently persuade that what is going on is important. Full compliance is essential to success. Rewards must be given at once. When the student does something that deserves a reward, it should be given immediately in the form of a kind word and a good grade. The student should never be kept in suspense about how well he or she is doing, but necessary criticism should be given in private. Every effort must be made to protect the student's ego.

- Timing is important. The teacher should not ask for too much at the outset. A few goals, all of which can be met, are better than many goals and some failures. However, training should be adapted, wherever possible, to the students' needs. As they ask for more work, it should be available. Furthermore, training sessions should be limited and there should be time between sessions for the students to internalize what they have learned and practice it in their own lives. They should have time to report on what they have accomplished outside the class.

- Distractions should be minimized. Time should not be used for irrelevant exercises. Neither should much time be given to personal counseling. Students with serious problems should be referred to professionals.

- Attention should be on the schedule. Sometimes it is possible to make a propitious intervention with one student, but taking time with one student may impede the progress of the class. Consequently, every effort should be made to stay on track.

- Consideration of individual differences is important. Attention must be paid to personal needs. If the student cannot physically perform the assignments, the teacher should make alternative plans. Sometimes the student can clearly perform the behavior but does not believe that he or she has done it. With those students, private persuasion may be necessary. Most students, however, have goals in common. Discovery and pursuit of these common goals supports the efficacy of general classroom training.

- Care should be taken to avoid discouraging students. Frustration and excess threat can undo everything that has been accomplished. Instructors must carefully modulate encouragement and criticism. Students rapidly catch on to false praise and feel patronized by excessive enthusiasm. The student who finished early should never feel smug. By the same token, the student must never feel it is impossible to finish.

- Sometimes unproductive behavior must be extinguished. A very simple example illustrates this point. Students often use a vernacular in their daily social life that is inappropriate in formal situations. One way to change this habit is to forbid using these phrases and penalize for infractions. Rule setting should be done early so phrases such as, "like, I mean, y'know," can be ruled out. Enforcing rules will focus concentration on personal performance and compel students to plan remarks. An even more effective procedure is to specify acceptable behavior at the beginning and rule everything else out. Thus, directions are limited to what should be done.

The goals of behavioral-based training are very simple. The students are to acquire a new behavior. The teacher's job is to facilitate performance of that behavior. An undesirable behavior must be eliminated by substituting a desirable one.

There are some obvious limitations on this kind of training. There is little leeway for student interpretation. The whole notion of creative behavior must be ruled out, at least for this class. This stipulation is not meant as an attack on creativity, but rather as a recognition that all behavior in this environment is creative. Creativity is a given, and with proper assignments, each behavior is a creative advance on previous behavior.

Standard Resistances

Some reticent speakers resist training the same way some patients resist therapy. It is not clear, however, what resisters are resisting. Some may be frightened by changes in their self-image because of the way they speak. Others may recognize a need to change their behavior but feel change is impossible. They may not want to risk another failure. Still others may feel a need to renege on the therapeutic alliance because of the way they feel about the instructor.

Resistances can be acknowledged, but they must be dealt with tactically. The trainer usually has neither the time nor expertise to use psychoanalysis to discover the reasons for the resistances. Strategy, however, is very important. A pocket of resisters can destroy a classroom as can a single resister.

Constant challenge is the main tactic for overcoming resistance. However, accusing the student publicly places him or her in a defensive position. If the teacher rules out resistance at the outset, the resister must display considerable tenacity to continue it. The syllabus must be followed, performance required, practice supervised, and no excuses accepted. The student must either perform or fail the course. The cost of failure in this milieu provides impetus for the trainee to overcome resistance.

There are specific techniques that can be directed against the main resistances in the given case. We discuss nine major patterns of resistance: denial, suspicion, rationalization, transference, refusal to participate, self-fulfilling prophecy, programmatic activity, fighting criticism, and narcissism.

Denial. Rhetorical competency cannot be denied. Competence can be confirmed by others and can effect them. People can hear it, pay attention to it, be moved or informed by it, learn from it; they respond to it in affirming and rewarding ways. It has discernible components. It is well organized, replete with interesting narratives and examples, phrased in attention-getting language, and delivered in a versatile and expressive voice.

A great many inept speakers often refuse to recognize major accomplishments and may even deny their small gains. Sometimes their preoccupation with their own feelings blinds them to the fact they have succeeded in performing some social task. It is more comfortable to retain the old feelings of rejection. To avoid acknowledging success, they may deny what they have done, report it inaccurately, or most often purposely misunderstand it. Sometimes they simply lie about how they feel.

Incompetent speakers must deal with their feelings about themselves. They may flinch when they are confronted with criticism about their social performance, but they have only two alternatives. Confront the criticism and modify their behavior, or find a way out.

The most effective way to counteract denial is to offer

direct evidence of success. However, student speakers can often snatch defeat from the jaws of victory by ignoring what they have done. It is sometimes more comfortable to lose than win. When this practice is the case, the instructor can become the enemy. Once the teacher is cast as adversary, the student no longer feels any responsibility to change. What the student really needs is the discipline of performance training. Teachers generally do not respond well to rejection, but the ability to withstand student rejection and still enforce course requirements is essential to overcoming denial.

Suspicion of Skill. Many reticent people are suspicious of skilled conversationalists. Their suspicion carries over into their attitude toward their own acquisition of technique. They claim they do not want to become like that "slick talker!" For some reason, they do not seem to flinch at learning writing skills, but many seem to believe planning and rehearsal in speaking is equivalent to manipulation. Students are willing to accept the idea that they need to prepare for a formal speech, but they seem hostile to the idea of developing a repertoire of conversational options for skill at social discourse.

Because social discourse carries shared responsibility, incompetent speakers must learn to ascribe credit and blame properly. They often tend to blame themselves for failure or pass the blame to others. Some believe skillful speakers take advantage of them, and they fear they will never learn to perform well in social situations.

Teaching and practicing basic rules of etiquette is an effective way to allay suspicions. Students must be trained to be polite while listening and to share responsibility for gaining and keeping attention. The rules of fair play and taking turns, the basic strategies of conversation can be learned. It is hard to be suspicious of people who play fair. By building trust within the class, students learn to be more trusting and accepting of the behavior of others outside the class.

Students must learn that sometimes it is impossible to get attention. Listeners have the right to be preoccupied, interested in something else, or simply unwilling to get involved, and when this situation is the case, nothing a speaker can do will be successful. Learning these principles helps students identify what is happening in social conversation.

Rationalization. Reticent speakers sometimes resist training by giving rationalizations for their communication difficulties.

Some of them say that they simply can never change because they have always been shy and fearful of communicating. Others argue that they will never have to give a speech or speak out in classes once they graduate, so there is no real reason to change. Still another rationalization is that they are good listeners and more people should learn to listen. They may be right in saying more people need to improve their listening skills, but good listening is not enough. To be a competent communicator requires speaking.

It is important to teach them to use their rationalizations as analysis. By understanding that the other person may be a poor listener, for example, students can legitimately explain what happens in conversation and devise strategies for future encounters. There is no point in permitting them to dream the impossible dream and seek to achieve unattainable social goals. Most rationalizations are addressed by the content on communication principles (see Chapter 1). Teachers explain that communication skills are learned and we are all capable of improving. They also discuss the idea that communication is a primary way we exert influence, so we need to be effective speakers even if we do not expect to do much public speaking. Students often do not realize that many jobs require some form of public presentation, another reason why they should develop their skills.

Transference. Transference is the most dangerous of the resistances. Although students often improve rapidly once they commit to training, virtually all of them go through a period when they believe their accomplishments are entirely due to their teacher. They admire their instructor so much, they seek ways to spend time with him or her. They want to report their successes and be congratulated. If the teacher gives in and listens to their personal accounts, they may take advantage and give their autobiographies. However, they will also use the personal relationship as an excuse for evading performance.

This attachment can be captivating for instructors. They are tempted to capitalize on their charisma and slip into a model of countertransference where they come to depend on student dependency. It is especially important that the teacher maintain a dispassionate demeanor merely by concentrating on helping the student get through the syllabus.

Transference is best defeated by avoiding countertransference. When the teacher becomes dependent on student adulation as just described, his or her usefulness as a performance trainer comes to an end. To prevent countertransference, the teacher's attention must be focused on how the student behaves rather than on who the student is. In turn, the student must concentrate on behavior rather than his or her feelings about behavior.

Refusal to Participate. Incompetent speakers often claim they can speak well enough, if they want to, but they simply do not want to very often. Denial of personal ineffectiveness is quite logical. Public scores are not kept on social victories and losses. When someone suffers a social failure, he or she need not face it. The person can walk away and deny that the incident happened. The explanation takes the form of a rationalization (see previous discussion), another form of resistance. Once having denied the problem, there is no longer a reason to try to solve it.

Most students often resist participating at all. First class sessions of the Reticence Program are markedly silent. Students file in and sit apart from one another. If the light is off, no one will turn it on. Most will avoid eye contact with the instructor in the hope they will not be asked to respond to questions. Instructors are hard pressed to find volunteers.

A more subtle resistance is when students claim, "I could have gotten the job, but I didn't really try for it." "She would have accepted my invitation, but I didn't really ask her." Sometimes they use tentative language, "You may not want to consider me for the job because I really lack the qualifications" or "You probably won't want to go with me." Often, they hang back and wait for the other person to make a request. At social gatherings, they may approach a group, hang around the edges and say nothing. If they do not get into the conversation, they can withdraw and tell themselves they did not want to participate anyway.

As for most forms of resistance, the antidote to participation failure is simply enforcement of the course requirements. Goal setting is a tactical device that demands activity. Enforcement precludes evasion. Those students who advocate spontaneity are told to avoid it because unplanned situations provide a perfect excuse for nonparticipation. When a person is reluctant to participate in a classroom exercise, however, the grade provides strong motivation to participate. He or she can rationalize, "I really wouldn't do this, but I must in order to get the grade." It actually does not matter how the teacher gets them to perform. Once they perform, they are often hooked.

Initial engagement is most effectively done by direct questioning as described in Chapter 2 when we discussed the first session of the Reticence Program. Teachers must have a standard protocol, almost like a television talk show host. What is your name? Where are you from? What is your major? What do you hope to do when you graduate? What do you do for fun on the weekend? Each student is quizzed separately, and the teacher uses the index card of information the student provides. The first ones questioned may be monosyllabic in their responses. Near the end of the exercise, some may begin to open up. Others may evade the issue with nonresponsive answers. The trainer adheres to the protocol, asking the same questions of each student. Observing they have a common problem often provides students with motivation to respond.

Self-Fulfilling Prophecy. Students will often express a self-fulfilling prophecy of ineptitude. They sometimes are quite capable of talking themselves into failure. They believe they cannot carry on a successful conversation so they avoid having conversations. By not conversing, they do not develop communication skills and they often end up alone. If they cannot avoid conversation, they may play a passive role because they believe they cannot possibly succeed. In both cases, the reticent person's belief leads him or her to unproductive behavior that brings about failure. The failure affirms the original prophecy.

The most effective way to counter self-fulfilling prophecies is to compel students to predict a successful outcome. Goal-setting procedures and rehearsal help to convince students that they are prepared for any contingency and they can do what they plan to do. Sometimes role-playing ineffective behavior shows them they have command.

Compulsive Activity. One sign of rhetorical incompetency is a tendency to repeat phrases, clichés, monosyllabic responses, vocalized pauses, and banal utterances. Part of the incompetency is just dullness. Many incompetent speakers seem devoid of information. They have trouble adapting because they, literally, have nothing to say. It is almost as if they convinced themselves that because they cannot speak well they need not have anything to talk about.

In ordinary conversation they use only familiar topics. They have phrases they repeat over and over. By mastering a few social routines, they convince themselves they have complied with the requirements of social situations and excuse themselves from broadening their repertoire. Teachers can deal with this problem by guiding speakers to select goals they would not otherwise seek. Broadening their repertoire makes it less necessary for them to rely on formulas.

Hostility to Criticism. Another form of resistance is hostility to criticism. Students are usually very edgy about taking criticism. They regard comments made about their own talk as personal attacks. Often, they will preempt criticism by criticizing themselves and challenging their teachers to do something about their problems. Each time the teacher offers them a technique or system, they respond with extended recitations of the ineffective remedies they have previously tried. Criticism well administered is the life blood of teaching performance behavior, as we discuss in detail in Chapter 9. The teacher must counter any attempt students make to avoid it!

Narcissism. It is amazing how narcissistic we all can be. We have learned to concentrate on ourselves because of the possibility of social failure. We seem to believe that other people pay a good deal more attention to us than is actually the case. In fact, we notice only a few details about the people around us. We are only concerned when we directly engage them.

Incompetent speakers are especially sensitive to what others think of them. They believe others evaluate them in advance. Because inept communicators tend to be hypersensitive to social evaluation, they keep out of situations they cannot handle or resort to inappropriate methods to take control of them. This protective mechanism keeps them from making a legitimate effort to participate socially in order to achieve interpersonal goals.

For some, their excessive concern with self generates an approach-avoidance paradox. When instruction starts, they are attracted to participation because they believe it could be helpful. Once they become involved, their fear of evaluation keeps them from seeing their personal gain and prevents them from conceding that they have improved.

CONCLUSION

In this chapter we outlined the major premises underlying the program of instruction for training reticent communicators. These premises evolved from early experience with the Reticence Program at PSU, were solidified in the early 1970s, and are the core of the program in the 1990s. All instructors are trained to follow the standard syllabus for the course to ensure adherence to its principles. Teachers encounter various forms of resistance from some students and need to be able to identify and counter their resistance if the training is to be effective.

9

CRITICISM AND PERFORMANCE IMPROVEMENT*

Throughout our lives, criticism is used to teach us appropriate behaviors. We learn, at our parents' knee (or over it), that criticism is an effective way to modify behavior. Our parents use it to teach us to brush our teeth and avoid hot stoves. School discipline is based on an in loco parentis model, in which the teacher replaces the parent. Later, on the job, the boss replaces both teacher and parent. Good grades and a large paycheck are rewards for good behavior.

Our friends also criticize us by responding to our behavior. Friends modify each other's behavior by using criticism. In fact, relationships can be described in part as mutual adaptations to criticism. Criticism is used by psychotherapists and physicians, football coaches and music teachers, art instructors and public speaking teachers. Those who use it claim that it calls

*Based on Chapter 10 of Gerald M. Phillips, *Communication Incompetencies*. Carbondale: Southern Illinois University, 1991. Used with permission of the publisher.

attention to flaws and poor behavior, and when properly applied leads to improvement.

Criticism is commonly used to refer to acts by teachers that are directed toward improving student behavior. If we examine the definitions of criticism several options emerge:

- The act of passing judgment as to the merits of anything.
- The act of passing severe judgment; censure; fault-finding.
- The act of analyzing or evaluating and judging the merit of a literary or artistic work, musical performance, art exhibit, dramatic production, etc.
- A critical comment, article, essay, or critique.
- Any of various methods of study of texts or documents for the purpose of dating or reconstructing them.
- Investigation of a text or literary document.

Of the possibilities, we are concerned with passing judgment, and in this case, about communication behaviors. Judging students' behavior carries an obligation to provide correctives exactly as in parental discipline. In that sense, the orderly relationship between the student who wants to improve oral performance and his or her teacher is parental. The teacher passes judgment on what the student does and tells him or her how to improve it. What an editor does for an author, a speech teacher does for a student speaker.

The first responsibility of the pedagogical critic is to discover incompetent behaviors and point them out, strategically, to the student. The process becomes a negotiation. The student must initially be convinced that the performance is incompetent. This implies that the teacher can identify competence and can offer methods to help the student improve. Students cannot be expected to make repairs even if and when they acknowledge repairs are needed. They must be shown what to repair and how to repair it. They need time to practice their modified behaviors. Thus, the process demands that the teacher apply all the available means of persuasion. The student must be convinced there is a need for a change, given a specific mode of change, and shown that the change is within his or her range of behavior.

The program of instruction described in this book relies on the effective use of criticism to train individuals as more competent speakers. Trainers criticize only those aspects of the students' communication for which they can offer methods or suggestions for improvement. In this chapter, we describe the process of criticism as it is used in the PSU Reticence Program.

THE REQUIREMENTS OF CRITICISM

Performance criticism is based on an implicit contract or thera-peutic alliance between the trainer and the student. Criticism works when critics know the corrective process and the person being criticized is willing to cooperate. This therapeutic alliance is essential to performance modification. The teacher and student enter into an agreement that entitles one (the teacher) to modify the performance behavior of the other. This agreement is pat-terned after the one between physician and patient. Success cus-tomarily depends on the extent to which the person criticized is willing to follow the critic's advice. This is why peer criticism often does not work. There must be mutual respect, absence of malice on both sides, and especially, confidence on the part of the student that the critic has the ability to help. The student chooses to modify behavior if, and only if, he or she concurs with the critic's judgment. If, on the other hand, he or she fears the consequences of the judgments of others, like peers, little can come from criticism except pain.

When students volunteer to participate in communication training, normally they are willing to change. In a required pro-gram or class the teacher must motivate the student to change by demonstrating that a change would bring social advantages. The trainer and the student must agree on the changes. The teacher cannot change everything about the student; he or she must be sure the proposed change is within both the physical and psychological capability of the student.

The student must recognize there is a price to be paid for change, that is, his or her personality may change. If the student has always been quiet in social situations and has been seen as shy by family and friends, his or her changed behavior will evoke new responses from others. Eventually, family and friends will stop saying he or she is shy, which may alter the student's self-perceptions. When a student changes his or her behavior and self-perceptions, and others see the changes and respond in new ways, one can argue the student's personality has been changed in the process. Furthermore, students need to understand that the change process is time limited and he or she cannot depend on the teacher permanently.

The critic of oral performance focuses primarily on errors in invention, organization, and delivery. These errors include, but are not confined to, unclear ideas; weak organization of ideas; poor documentation; faulty sentence structure and poor word choice, diction, and related matters of delivery; inappropriate use of body and facial expression; and various problems with speech content such as inappropriate topic choice for the audience, lack of a clear message, or insufficient forms of support for claims.

Critics customarily compare performance to standards derived from theory and experience. A critic expects speech to make sense in a given situation. Errors of the types discussed in Chapter 8 are usually obvious. If the speech is disorderly, for example, there is usually an error. The standard corrective is to suggest ways and means of making the presentation more orderly. The critic decides what an acceptable act should look like, compares the observed behavior to the standard, and offers the trainee advice designed to adjust behavior until the results conform, in the critic's eyes, to the standards. The difficulty is in convincing the student that he or she has made an error, that the error is correctable, and that the recommended procedures can correct the error.

LABELING AND CRITICISM

In the Reticence Program, teachers avoid labels such as *shyness* because they are of no critical value. They are the equivalent of name-calling. The critic must have concrete behaviors in mind that led to the global generalization. Once there are specific behaviors to modify, the label *shy* is irrelevant. Pointing out, for example, that the student does not maintain eye contact with others is more helpful because there are exercises that are useful to train the student to look at an audience. Telling a student he or she blushes is not useful because there are no known remedies for it.

Students often use labels for their feelings. They say they are tense, nervous, or anxious, for instance. As argued in Chapter 3, feelings cannot be modified directly, although a change in behavior often leads to a change in feelings. If the student says he or she feels anxious, the critic's question is, "How does that make you act?" Communication is an event to which feelings are attached, but performance modification through criticism must focus on events.

In fact, we have had very few cases in the Reticence Program where emotion like anxiety seriously interfered with the process of instruction. Most students learn to focus on their behavior through the goal setting process described in Chapter 3.

Goal setting is the means to establish a therapeutic relationship. In the process, trainer and trainee agree on how the trainee will meet minimum standards for a particular performance.

MODIFICATION OF BEHAVIOR

The process of changing behavior is constrained by the trainee's ability. Limits on performance are imposed by genetics and by education and acculturation, but competency can be achieved. The teacher as critic assesses competence by observing behavior. Each time people do something they have never done before, they add to their repertoire and are regarded as competent to do it again. However, we cannot simply conclude that because people have not been seen performing an act, they are not able or will not be able to do it. The trainer/critic must assume that a new behavior is possible if it is normal for other similar people to behave that way. The idea is to motivate the student to produce the desired behavior in class. Once successful, the student can be confident that he or she is capable of performing the behavior in a life situation.

Modifying human social behavior requires pedagogical technique. Although the results of any pedagogical method cannot be predicted with any degree of scientific certainty, precedent offers a powerful argument. Criticism operates on a basis of hypothesis and test. The teacher hypothesizes that a specific technique will bring about the desired result. Presumably, this conclusion is reached after substantial experience with the technique and with the agreement of the student. The technique is then applied and the result noted. It may not be possible to devise universally effective teaching methods, but there are enough alternatives to allow for a kind of "hacking" as we attempt to find techniques useful and appropriate in each case.

Criticism in education is almost always conducted in public, usually in a classroom. Assignments for the whole class are made publicly. This practice is very different from the typical clinical situation, where the therapist works with clients on an individual basis. Any public criticism is a potential embarrassment, so teachers in the Reticence Program do not give individualized, oral criticism in the classroom. Instead, with the class as a whole, instructors identify an error common to most and focus attention on the error.

As discussed in Chapter 8, teachers in the Reticence Program provide individual attention and instruction to students.

Teachers recognize, for example, that defective organization is a category of behavior problems, but different students have different organizational problems. The public discussion about problems with organization of ideas opens the opportunity for the private discussion that will follow. Students need to associate with the general issue and be motivated to receive information about their particular case.

When teachers make suggestions, they do not give guarantees about outcomes. Suggestions do not always work, and the student has to know that failure is sometimes the fault of the teacher or the suggestions, and sometimes they may have to shoulder the blame.

Instructors must keep in mind that students internalize criticism. People label their own social performance, and they are labeled by others, although the evaluations from others are usually not explicit. We assign values to the labels we and others affix to us. Usually, if a person labels his or her performance positively, he or she will defend the status quo regardless of how intensely the teacher/critic argues for modification. When students agree that their behavior is poor or ineffective, they may choose to modify it in order to modify the judgments made about it (and them). However, it is difficult to get anyone to admit he or she does anything wrong.

There are two main ways students respond to denigration. Some accept the negative label and behave in line with its predictions. Studies by Warren (1982) and others, demonstrate that people labeled *insane* by court decree are perfectly willing to act insane. Shy people are quite willing to act as shy people are supposed to act. Labels are powerful defining forces.

Others use labels as motivations to change. When they are categorized by family, friends, or teachers as *shy* or *incompetent*, they try to prove others wrong. These students embrace criticism that helps them change their behavior.

The contract between the teacher and student must make clear what form criticism will take, when and how it will be administered, and how the student is expected to respond to it. If there is no fundamental agreement about the process, it simply will not work. Much administration of criticism is governed by a tacit agreement between teacher and student to leave each other alone. Teacher is allowed to criticize; student is allowed to nod obligingly and ignore what is said. The agreement to accept criticism should be sincere and should include a commitment to action.

How constructively the student responds to the criticism depends on how viable the alternatives are that the teacher provides. To be viable, an alternative has to be within the range of the student's behavior. This condition poses a paradox because we do not know whether a person can do a particular act unless and until he or she does it. That is why, as noted earlier, the teacher must assume the student is capable because the behavior has been possible for other students in similar cases.

A student may be willing simply to put up with his or her own ineptitude. There is little the teacher can do about that attitude. He or she can cajole, persuade, con, and threaten, but it is still the student's choice.

SOCIAL BEHAVIOR AND THE CLASSICAL CONCEPTION OF CRITICISM

We have argued that criticism only works when the student agrees to it and the teacher has tested remedies. Social exchange is also a process of exchanging criticism; people often change their behavior to obtain the approval of those they see as important. Each party to a friendship has the privilege of deciding how to negotiate behavior change. What is missing in friendships and other personal relationships is a trainer who can provide the methods and procedures for change. In the classroom, the teacher can present models of standard social behaviors and train students to emulate them, although application to particular relationships takes place outside the classroom.

In social dialogue, each person evaluates the behavior of the other, decides whether that behavior signals approval or disapproval, and chooses a response accordingly. A speaker hypothesizes that a given action will evoke a desired response. He or she acts, examines the response, decides again, and then acts again, and so on. Competent speakers can, up to a point, control their own responses and predict with reasonable accuracy the responses of most others. Control means they can consciously select which actions to perform and then perform them as planned. Predict means they can anticipate the reactions of listeners with reasonable accuracy. To sustain a relationship both parties must continue those behaviors that are rewarded and either discontinue or modify those that are not.

In teaching social behavior, the best the teacher can do is train students to perform in social settings shared by others. It is difficult to criticize students' existing private relationships and certainly not within the province of a speech teacher to do so. On the other hand, the teacher may require performance and criticism of social behavior in the classroom.

Imitation is an important element of training in social behavior as well as all communication situations. Quintilian, famous Roman orator and teacher, believed that students should find models to imitate. Because our communication skills are, initially, learned through imitation, first of our parents and teachers, then of our peers and heroes, the selection of whom to imitate is important. We must choose role models we can feasibly imitate. The teacher can help the student select models to imitate and performable acts, guiding him or her away from unattainable goals. It also goes without saying that the instructor must perform well to serve as a model of competent communication. Otherwise, the student will instantly raise the question, "Why doesn't the teacher take his or her own criticism?"

There is an unfortunate tendency for teachers to ascribe student failure to the willful rejection of criticism. "I told him what to do, why didn't he do it?" Rarely is the critic faulted for delivering criticism ineptly. Given a therapeutic contract, the crucial issue is whether the student is capable of following the teacher's directions. It is easy to tell the student to "talk louder" or "use better evidence," but it is more difficult to provide methods and procedures the student can use.

When the critic gives wrong advice or suggests that the student do something he or she is unable to do, the therapeutic agreement is likely to fall apart. When the critic fails, the student gives up. Thus, the teacher must make his or her limitations clear. If the teacher makes it clear at the outset that his or her advice is a hypothesis that must be tested, the student might be more willing to adopt a tentative posture in deciding what to do. When the teacher tries to be infallible, criticism is greeted with resistance or apathy. Once the performer learns that the critic can make errors, it no longer seems sensible to attempt to follow advice.

The teacher must rely on the student's honesty in reporting on how behaviors carry over into life situations. Criticism administered in the classroom is wasteful unless the student can find a way to use it outside the classroom. The goal analysis process is designed to assist the student in applying the criticism to situations outside the classroom.

The successful critic depends on a body of information drawn from real and vicarious experience as well as from research. The critic looks at specific questions that apply to every social circumstance in which discourse plays a role. These questions form a pool of possibilities from which the critic can draw advice for specific circumstances. Following are some useful lists of these questions.

Situation. What is the nature of this situation? The critic looks for flaws in students' assessment of situations; that is, talking to strangers as if they were family, telling jokes at a funeral, or other obvious inappropriate behaviors. To do an effective job, the critic must know a good deal about social norms, phatic communion, and clichés and be able to demonstrate to the student when and how to use them.

What is the relationship between the speaker and the other people present? The critic looks for presumptions like asking to borrow money too early or areas of omission like failing to introduce oneself to strangers. Again, the critic must rely on social etiquette for standards on which to base the criticism.

Goals. What are the speaker's personal goals, and which can legitimately be sought in this situation? Which goals are most likely to be accomplished? The critic looks for goal-directed behaviors. For example, the speaker wants to arrange a date but does nothing to specify time and place, responding only to what the other person suggests or demands. The critic looks for lack of focus or commitment to a clearly defined objective. Often, the critic discovers students are not able to articulate social goals either because they have none, or because they have them but do not have conscious control over them, or because they think it unethical to have social goals. The critic can provide the student with goal-setting formats like the goal analysis procedure described in Chapter 3.

Audience. To whom should the speaker appeal? Who is the most likely person or persons to help accomplish the goal? Is speech adapted to the specific audience? The critic watches for alienating or irrelevant appeals, direct confrontation, or self-centered demands. As explained in Chapter 3, students must learn audience analysis techniques to adapt their communication to the particular audience. However, students must understand that although some generalizations can be made (e.g., Catholics tend to oppose abortion; Jews probably will not eat pork in public; many elderly people have aches and pains), they must try to avoid stereotyping and pay attention to behavior in context.

Exchange. Given what the critic knows about people in general and the people present in particular, what can the speaker offer the listeners in exchange for their support? The critic looks for demands rather than inducements to exchange. The idea of exchange is sometimes difficult for students to accept. They like to think that people should like them for themselves. Consequently, inept speakers tend to demand attention and compliance and usually do not get it. When they discover they are not getting what they want, they tend to withdraw. Cognitive restructuring can be used to sensitize students to the realities of social exchange. Rehearsal and role-play can be used to test their ability to adapt to others.

Constraints. What constraints are imposed by the norms of this situation? The critic notes improprieties like the speaker who talks too little or too much, fails to acknowledge important people, or violates social taboos. The idea of propriety has dropped into disfavor in recent decades, but is very important. Social situations are governed by norms for appropriate behavior, and competent communicators can identify and adapt to norms. For example, the host must be acknowledged, the food praised, introductions performed in traditional ways (e.g., handshakes), and the proper small talk exchanged before moving on to more substantive and pleasant matters. However outmoded the concept may seem, the idea that etiquette was invented for the protection of social participants is very important. Also, etiquette is orderly. Although compliance with social regulations may seem artificial, it makes communication more predictable and comfortable to participants.

CRITICISM BASED ON THE CANONS

In using criticism to help students improve their social behavior, most speech teachers automatically use the rhetorical canons as headings for their criticism. They may criticize selection and adaptation of topic (invention), organization of information (disposition), use of language (style), the act of speaking (delivery), and utilization of the repertoire (memory). The canons were discussed in detail in Chapter 7. In this section we are concerned with how the teacher refers to them in providing criticism.

Invention

Invention is the most difficult of the canons to manage because all the critic can evaluate is the results of thinking, that is, the discourse itself. Invention is the discovery and creation of ideas, and that is the responsibility of the entire educational system. Speech teachers, however, can offer students some sensible, heuristic questions that may help them discover topics to discuss.

Does the content of the discourse give evidence that the speaker planned? A speaker must give a reason for speaking that appears rational to the critic in light of the speech situation. Does the speaker seem realistic about identifying circumstances in which speaking is desirable and essential?

Can the student set realistic goals for communication? If the speaker does not specify attainable goals or adapt his or her ideas to potential listeners, the student needs training in goal setting, topic selection, and adaptation to audience and situation.

The critic can also look for lack of content. In social conversation a person can have nothing to say, but choose to talk anyway. A boring person may be socially inept and need instruction in techniques of invention. A great many speech teachers pick up the challenge to help speakers generate topics. They urge students to read, watch television, and listen to others. The hypothesis appears reasonable; the more people read, the more they have to talk about.

Organization

There are simple rules and standards for making discourse intelligible. There are various formats for organizing compositions, paragraphs, and sentences. In social conversation, each person must respond to the changing situation. In formal speaking, formal patterns can be used, which can range from debate outlines to complex designs based on Toulmin's (1958) organization pattern. The structuring method described in Chapter 5 is adapted from the work of Sondel (1958) and offers the categories of space, time, classification, analogy, contrast, relationship, and problem solution. The critic looks for lack of coherence as evidence of incompetence at disposition.

Can the speaker get ideas arranged in coherent fashion? The critic evaluates the extent to which speech is orderly. Most textbooks devote considerable space to instruction in outlining; many teachers devote a great deal of time criticizing speech organization. Despite outline instruction given in virtually every speech class, students are still bewildered about how to produce the outline and what to do with it once they produce it. We find many students writing their speeches, then writing the outline and submitting it to meet the requirements of an assignment. To avoid problems with outlining, the alternative of structuring was incorporated into the Reticence Program.

A structure should be used to develop a set of performance notes. The instructor must coach students in how to develop notes from the structure because students do not necessarily know how to do this. The teacher can direct criticism at the ability of the student to produce notes from the structure and then to speak from those notes.

Not all speaking is extemporaneous, however, because some situations demand the precise timing and language use of a manuscript speech. For instance, a televised speech has time requirements that must be met. Teleprompters and ghost-written scripts guide the presentations. Learning to speak extemporaneously is still a valuable skill, but teachers should teach students to write speeches and how to read expressively. The critic can focus on the orderly presentation of ideas whether the speech is manuscript or extemporaneous.

In social conversation speakers also need to organize their ideas. How well do the speaker's remarks fit within the flow of conversation? When the speaker narrates events, does the order of ideas make sense to the listener? The critic addresses these questions when evaluating the organization of social conversation.

Style

In the simplest sense, style refers to selection of words to be spoken. An actor is provided with words, whereas a speaker must select his or her own words. In evaluating speech style, the critic must assess the appropriateness of the speaker's language for the audience and situation. Is the speaker excessively formal in a casual situation? Does the speaker use language that is too technical, specialized, or colloquial for the situation or the listeners? Do language choices fit the content of the ideas being expressed?

Judgments of style are not easily separated from personal preferences of the critic because there is no standard definition of a good style and it is impossible to separate style from content. For example, examine a job interview scenario. The interviewer uses a set of questions, but rarely does an interviewer have a formal set of standards by which to evaluate the answers. Each case is evaluated, but the basis for the evaluation is rarely clear to the interviewee. The interviewer responds to the style with which answers are delivered and to the content of those answers, but he or she probably cannot determine the extent to which style and content influenced his or her judgment of the interviewee. Every speech teacher has confronted the question of "How much of the grade is on content and how much is on delivery?" In the Reticence Program, teachers direct criticism to both content and style but tend to favor content and organization in determining the actual speech grade.

Delivery

Delivery is the most obvious aspect of social discourse to criticize and relatively straightforward to modify. Again the critic assesses the appropriateness of delivery to the situation and audience. Does the speaker speak loudly enough or too loudly for the room? Does the speaker's level of animation match the occasion for the speech? Does the speaker appear artificial and insincere? Does the speaker have enough vocal variety to maintain attention and convey ideas clearly?

As any good actor knows, it is very difficult to connect delivery with personal feelings. Thus, delivery cannot be taught well without attention to content, organization, and style. Furthermore, versatile delivery is necessary to adapt to a variety of social situations, so the critic evaluates the student's skill at altering delivery to fit the situation.

Teachers need to be careful not to become too preoccupied with delivery. When this happens, training can become excessively mechanical. The experience of the elocutionists of the early 20th century indicates that emphasis on vocal delivery may subvert training in the other canons, but delivery training cannot be ignored.

Memory

Can the speaker reasonably assess reactions to his or her presentation and draw from memory appropriate responses? Responding appropriately is the hardest skill of all for students to learn. Because the student is thinking of what he or she is saying, keeping track of what the listener is doing calls for a kind of split attention. The student must modify style and delivery to meet audience needs, without necessarily changing ideas.

Of all the techniques of speaking, use of memory depends most on experience, but the teacher must continually call the student's attention to the importance of watching the listener. Speech teachers often use the cliché eye contact, but rarely do they make it clear why eye contact must be maintained.

A WORKING CATALOG OF CRITICISMS

In the two previous sections we discussed areas in which critics can make speech assessments. Following is a list of key critical questions for teachers that synthesize our discussion of criticism:

- Does the speaker have a clear purpose in speaking? If the speaker is not able to identify good reasons for speaking or appears to select reasons inappropriate to his or her personal goals, the critic must pressure the student to provide a reason for speaking to articulate a social goal for the discourse.
- Has the speaker selected an audience appropriate for the goal? Just because a person has a goal to accomplish does not mean all listeners are able to help him or her achieve that goal. The critic should assess the speaker's choice of audience.
- Does the speaker have something to say? If the speaker cannot think of things to say, says nothing, says inappropriate things, or repeats clichés, the critic can help the student by exposing him or her to reading, viewing, and listening experiences and demonstrating how these can be used to generate topics in conversation and formal discourse.
- Does the speaker focus his or her talk? If the speaker makes inappropriate appeals or presents flawed, irrational, or ineffective argumentation, the critic can train him or her in the process of retrieving (or gathering) information relevant to the speaker's goal or topic.
- Is the speaker well organized? If the speaker appears incoherent or the listeners' response indicates incoherence, he or she must be trained in orderly composition.
- Is the speaker's language clear and appropriate? If the speaker uses trite or confusing language, or language

inappropriate for the listeners or occasion, he or she needs coaching in language choice and analysis of audience and situation.

- Can the speaker execute the game plan? If the speaker does not deliver well, the critic must identify the specific delivery problems. The speaker may speak too loudly or too softly, too rapidly or too slowly, he or she may hesitate, use vocalized pauses, or speak in a monotone.
- Does the speaker have and use a repertoire of successful behaviors? If the speaker is not able to apply past experience, cannot remember what worked and what did not, the teacher may have to attempt to provide training in an effective memory system. This process would include engineering a few successful experiences from which the student could draw.
- Does the speaker pay attention to the audience? If the speaker ignores or responds inaccurately to listener responses, he or she must be trained to notice responses. Most inept speakers simply do not observe their listener and consequently are unaware of feedback.

CRITICISM OF SOCIAL BEHAVIOR

The questions just presented are applicable to any communication situation, but they do not capture all aspects of social conversation. An additional set of guidelines is necessary. We need to answer questions like, "What makes people feel as they do in social situations?" "What do people hope to gain from socialization?" "Are there skills or 'tricks' that make for successful socialization?"

There are some concepts that are useful to critics in helping students understand discourse in social situations:

Gist. Gist refers to getting the sense of something. Words are not simple codes. People do not get a one-to-one correspondence between word and thing. Words offer meaning and feeling at the same time. Because people have an idiosyncratic view of the world, they never understand us as we understand ourselves, nor do they understand what we say as we want it understood. We talk to them, hoping they will get the gist of what we have in mind. In social discourse, we exchange talk, trying to develop a common gist.

Although we have little or no control over the way people understand our words, we have considerable control over what we say. We try to control our own talk so that it is easy for others to get the gist of what we say. The critic's focus should be on helping the student exchange talk in ways that focus attention on his or her goals.

Social Clichés. Although every situation is unique in some respects, social situations have enough in common so that by learning a simple repertoire of behaviors, we can cope with virtually every situation we encounter. The teacher's job is to help the student acquire such a repertoire. Part of it is included in the phrase "good manners," part in the phrase "phatic communion," the simple give and take everyone in a social group uses on a day-to-day basis (Malinowski, 1923). The critic can assess the student's ability to engage in small talk and follow the accepted norms for social behavior.

Physiology. The body plays a role in shaping social experience. As we examine each given case, that is, the behavior of an individual in a social milieu, we must keep in mind that his or her internal feelings exert some influence over goal setting as well as selection and execution of behavior.

Freud defined *pleasure* as "the absence of pain." Humans are not usually aware of parts of their body unless those parts are malfunctioning. Malfunctions that call attention to themselves are important constraints on social behavior. We can apply these concepts to a defense of "dual perspective"; that is, however different our feelings might be from those of anyone and everyone else, they are sufficiently similar that we can find words to express discomfort, pain, anxiety, and fear.

It is important to understand that our words cannot thwart another person's intentions. Others are as focused on their own needs as we are on ours. Consequently, we do not always succeed, not because of our ineptitude but because of circumstances. If a potential listener is otherwise preoccupied with his or her own pain, there is no way to break through. We must surrender to their inattention and select another goal, perhaps another person. The critic must be aware the failure is sometimes the fault of circumstances or the other person. It is not always easy to recognize when this is the case, so the critic needs to alert the student to the possibility that he or she is not always at fault when communication is ineffective. In the Reticence Program, the student is trained through the goal analysis process to consider various sources of failure and how to deal with them.

The Unexpected. Although social conversation is often predictable because of social norms, unexpected events can and do occur. It is part of our rhetorical approach to train people to respond to alternative responses. In any given case, there is a most likely response and we seek it, but we equip our students with repertories to enable them to react to alternatives. The critic of social communication can evaluate how well the student adapts to the unexpected. Students who react poorly need to learn to anticipate possible outcomes and prepare alternative responses.

In the final analysis, what we, as critics, try to do is ascertain how the speaker views the social situation so we can assess the effectiveness of the behaviors he or she has chosen in order to deal with it. We need to assess so we can assign credit and blame appropriately to find the most effective pedagogy. If the causes of failure lie entirely in the circumstances, then it is pointless to blame the individual. It is, in short, hopeless to try to cope with the impossible. Our triage notion, inherent in our medical model, demands that we deal first with the simplest and most common problems and provide ways people can deal with their own exceptions.

A FINAL NOTE

For the teacher of performance skills, criticism is not one tool. It is the only tool. To be a skillful teacher means cultivating the skill of criticism. As critics, we are concerned with what we see a person do and we measure competency by what we see. We can only take into account overt behavior or reports that can be verified through observation of overt behavior. The pedagogical model presented in this book addresses correction of overt behavior in social situations.

We do not deny that emotions are influential, and we have provided a means for considering their impacts on individuals. We argue, however, that because their effects are idiosyncratic and because it is easier to change behavior, the training approach we use is directed at behavior. The teacher as critic evaluates the student's communication behavior and suggests specific ways to improve his or her behavior. The process is delicate because the potential exists to harm the student, but we have described a procedure for criticism designed to maximize student improvement and reduce the possibility of causing harm or distress.

ADAPTATIONS OF THE TRAINING APPROACH

10

GENERAL CLASSROOM TECHNIQUES

To this point we focused on describing a program to train reticent people in communication skills. We assumed that instructors want to institute a special program like the one offered at PSU, but we know it is not always possible to establish a reticence program. Time and resource limitations mean that teachers who want to help reticent students may need other options. Specifically, many teachers may have to work within their regular classrooms and curricula to help students overcome reticence. In this chapter we advocate that teachers should adopt teaching strategies to reduce the effects of reticence in the classroom. Instructors can select activities and assignments that minimize the debilitating effects of reticence and apply them in the ordinary classroom. They can also conduct classes in ways that support the efforts of all students to communicate and that establish the classroom as a safe place to experiment with and develop communication skills. Even those teachers who are able to set up a special program can use the strategies presented here in their other classes.

This chapter examines ways of reducing the effects of communication reticence, covering the relationship between communication reticence and academic achievement; classroom characteristics of reticents; ways of mediating communication reticence in the classroom; and ways of reducing communication reticence during oral assignments, especially public speaking. We drew upon communication research and our experience in the PSU Reticence Program in developing the material for this chapter. The first two topics acquaint the reader with how reticence is played out in the traditional classroom and how it can affect a student's academic achievement.

Before we begin the discussion, we should clarify our terminology. As noted in Chapter 7, a wide variety of constructs have been advanced to explain the avoidance of communication. Examples of these constructs include *reticence* (Phillips, 1968, 1984a, 1991), *communication apprehension* (McCroskey, 1970, 1977b, 1984a), *unwillingness to communicate* (Burgoon, 1976a), *unassertiveness* (Adler, 1977; Lazarus, 1973), and *shyness* (Buss, 1984; Zimbardo, 1977, 1982). In order to select all the published research relevant to our topic, in this chapter we adopted the term *communication reticence*, which refers to the collection of predispositions related to communication anxiety, avoidance, fear, reticence, and negative evaluation (Burgoon & Hale, 1983). We, therefore, are using the term very broadly, rather than adhering to Phillips' (1991) more precise definition of reticence as a problem of deficient communication skills.

COMMUNICATION RETICENCE AND THE CLASSROOM

Researchers estimate that approximately 20% of the population suffers from communication reticence (Richmond & McCroskey, 1992). Many children in elementary, middle, and high schools experience communication reticence to some degree (Garrison & Garrison, 1979); however, children in the primary grades (K-3) typically are less reticent than children in higher grade levels (McCroskey et al., 1981).

Although research suggests that communication apprehension is a widespread problem, the severity of the problem is not understood until one looks at the effects of communication reticence in the classroom. For example, a significant body of research indicates that communication reticence severely affects academic achievement. Just as people often misjudge a reticent individual as we said at the outset, teachers sometimes ascribe student silence to a lack of intelligence or lack of class preparation rather than to a lack of communication competence.

Academic Achievement

Research indicates that reticent students are more likely to have a lower overall grade point average than nonreticents (McCroskey, 1977a; McCroskey, Booth-Butterfield, & Payne, 1989; McCroskey & Payne, 1986), and are more likely to score lower on academic achievement tests, such as mathematics, language, and reading (Comadena & Prusank, 1988). In addition, reticent students are more likely to receive lower performance evaluations in a public speaking course (Powers & Smythe, 1980; Scott & Wheeless, 1977). Hurt, Preiss, and Davis (1976) found that reticents are more likely to receive lower grades than nonreticents when the class size is fewer than 30 and when high levels of interpersonal involvement are required by the instructor, suggesting that reticents might suffer academically when interactive learning is the dominant instructional strategy.

Communication reticence also can affect whether or not students enter college. For example, reticents are less likely than nonreticents to attend college (Monroe & Borzi, 1988), and those reticents who do attend college are more likely than nonreticents to drop out of school (McCroskey et al., 1989; Mehrley, 1984).

Besides lower achievement in the classroom, McCroskey and Daly (1976) found that teachers expect reticents to be less successful academically than nonreticents. In their study, they asked elementary teachers to estimate the success of one of two hypothetical students, based on a brief description of the student. The first student, classified as reticent, was described as follows:

> Jimmy T. was born in this community and has lived here all his life. His parents own and operate a local business. Jimmy is a very quiet child who seldom volunteers to participate in class. In fact, some days I hardly know he is in class, since he sits in the back of the room. However, his attendance is very good except when he is scheduled to make a presentation before the class. He seems to prefer to work alone rather than with a group. His written work is almost always turned in on time. I have found it hard to get to know Jimmy because he is

so reticent with me. His previous teachers have also com-
mented about what a nice, quiet boy Jimmy is. (McCroskey &
Daly, 1976, p. 68)

The nonreticent student was described as follows:

Billy G. was born in this community and has lived here all his
life. His parents own and operate a local business. Billy is a
very outgoing child who participates extensively in class. You
always know that Billy is present, because he sits right in
front of the room. His attendance is very good. Billy seems to
enjoy making presentations to the class and working on
group projects. His written work is almost always turned in
on time. I have found it very easy to get to know Billy because
he likes to talk with me. His previous teachers have also com-
mented about what a nice, outgoing boy Billy is. (McCroskey
& Daly, 1976, pp. 68-69)

The two students have similar backgrounds and both are
hard working. The only difference between them is their reaction
to communication. Jimmy avoids communicating, whereas Billy
enjoys it. Based solely on these differences, teachers estimated
that Billy would perform better than Jimmy in many areas: overall achievement, success in future education, relationships with
other students, reading, and social studies. In short, this study
showed that teachers expect reticent students to be less academically successful.

In a similar study, Schaller and Comadena (1988) found
that both elementary and middle school teachers possess significantly different achievement expectations for reticent and nonreticent children. They also found that teachers did not have significantly different expectations for reticent males and reticent
females.

The implication of lower teacher expectations is critical.
Research shows that teachers' perceptions significantly influence
the success or failure of a student (Beez, 1968; Dusek, 1975;
Rosenthal & Jacobson, 1968). Therefore, if teachers expect reticent students to be less academically successful (McCroskey &
Daly, 1976; Schaller & Comadena, 1988), reticents are likely to
be less successful than nonreticents. As discussed previously,
research indicates that reticent students' academic performance
is poorer than that of nonreticent students. However, we do not
know the degree to which teachers' expectations influence academic success of reticent students.

In short, research strongly indicates that communication reticence negatively affects the academic achievement of students. Research also suggests, however, that the intelligence of reticents is no different from that of nonreticents (Bashore, 1971; Davis, 1977; McCroskey, Daly, & Sorensen, 1976). Therefore, other factors, such as teacher expectations, must be the link between communication reticence and academic achievement. Another possible factor is the communicative behavior that characterizes reticence. Because reticents tend to avoid verbal interaction, and most learning is verbal (Carroll, 1964), reticent students do not fully participate in the learning process, which negatively affects their achievement. The next section discusses the classroom behavior of reticent students.

Classroom Interaction

Researchers have found that reticents behave in ways that reduce communicative involvement. For example, a substantial body of research indicates that reticents speak less frequently than nonreticents, and when reticents speak, their messages are shorter in duration (Burgoon, 1976a, 1976b; Cheek & Buss, 1981; Jordan & Powers, 1978; Lerea, 1956; Lustig, 1980; Lustig & Grove, 1975; McCroskey, 1976; McKinney, 1982; Mortensen & Arnston, 1974; Murray, 1971; Paivio & Lambert, 1959).

Some research indicates that reticents differ from nonreticents in their use of language. Conville (1974) found that reticent communicators use language characterized as nonimmediate. Nonimmediacy is defined as the "degree of indirect reference employed by a communicator when speaking of himself or some thing or person other than himself" (Conville, 1974, p. 1108). For example, the nonimmediate communicator typically does not use present tense, and might use the self-reference "we" as opposed to "I." Freimuth (1976) also found that the language of reticents is less comprehensible than that of nonreticents.

Researchers also identified behavioral characteristics of reticents in the classroom. Phillips, Butt, and Metzger (1974) identified 10 attributes that might identify the reticent individual:

1. Student does not voluntarily make contributions in class; does not raise hand; does not add information.
2. Student seems shaky during oral recitations, asserts that he or she came prepared but the words did not seem to come out right.

3. Student talks about symptoms when called on to recite: rapid heartbeat, headache, butterflies in the stomach, nausea.
4. Student has attempted to recite or perform orally and has quit because of fear or apprehension.
5. Student seems unable to communicate with you during a conference or other times when the two of you have tried to talk alone.
6. Student seems to have some communication problem that does not quite fall into the purview of the speech correctionist.
7. Student seems to be excessively quiet; does not participate in oral interaction with his or her peers.
8. Student seems unnaturally apologetic when ideas are challenged; backs off, seems to change ideas to accommodate antagonist.
9. Student has shown resistance when written assignments were to be presented orally: classroom reports, book reviews, etc.
10. Parents have said the student does not communicate well with them.

In addition to both classroom and verbal behavior, reticence is associated with particular nonverbal behaviors. Specifically, researchers discovered that reticents exhibit some or many of the following classes of nonverbal behaviors (Burgoon & Koper, 1984; Burgoon, Pfau, Birk, & Manusov, 1987):

1. *Negative forms of arousal.* Reticents display tension in their posture and body-blocking, cover their faces.
2. *Rigidity and stiffness.* Reticents are less likely to gesture, turn their heads, and exhibit random movement.
3. *Lack of expressiveness.* Reticents have less gestural animation, and less vocal potency (loudness, tempo, and intensity).
4. *Lack of immediacy and involvement.* Reticents give less eye contact, head nodding, facial pleasantness, and direct orientation.

In addition to verbal and nonverbal behavior, reticent students typically have a preference for certain class formats. For example, reticents prefer lecture to discussion, partially because lecture does not impose a penalty on students who are quiet (McCroskey & Anderson, 1976). Despite classroom format, research shows that reticents most likely will not ask questions or offer comments even when they are confused about the subject matter (Bowers et al., 1986; Neer, 1987).

Because reticent students avoid participating in class, it is logical to conclude that reticents prefer seating arrangements that discourage interaction. Research tends to confirm this conclusion. McCroskey and Sheahan (1976) found that reticents avoid seats that typically permit greater frequency of participation, whereas nonreticents prefer such seats. McCroskey and Vetta (1978) found that reticent students prefer traditional seating (rows), whereas nonreticents preferred a U-shaped seating pattern that optimizes the potential for interaction.

S. Booth-Butterfield (1988) found that when reticents anticipate interaction, retention of information significantly decreases. In his study, all participants attended a lecture; however, half the students were told that after the lecture they would explain the lecture material to a stranger from another class. Results indicated that reticents had poorer recall than nonreticents when interaction was anticipated. When interaction was not anticipated, reticents and nonreticents did not significantly differ in recall. This study suggests rather strongly that the attitude of reticents toward speaking directly affects their ability to function intellectually.

To summarize, reticents differ from other students in their communicative behavior. Once teachers are sensitized to reticent behavior and how reticence influences academic achievement, they can choose to structure their classes to lessen the debilitating effects of communication reticence. The next section presents strategies teachers can use to accomplish this.

MEDIATING RETICENCE IN THE CLASSROOM

Research paints a clear picture of reticent communicators in the classroom. They avoid interacting in an environment that demands interaction, and, usually, suffer academically. To reduce the effects of reticence, teachers can try to develop a supportive communication climate and select activities that benefit reticent and nonreticent students alike.

Supportive Communication Climate

A supportive classroom climate is characterized by spontaneous and open communication (Rosenfeld, 1983). The following eight statements from Rosenfeld characterize such a climate:

1. My teacher helps me understand the reasons for his/her opinions.
2. My teacher is straightforward and honest.
3. My teacher makes me feel he/she is interested in the problems I face.
4. My teacher focuses his/her attention on the problems which have to be solved.
5. My teacher can see the subject we're studying as we see it.
6. My teacher can change subjects as questions are asked.
7. My teacher makes me feel he/she understands me.
8. My teacher treats us as equals with him/her. (p. 170)

These statements suggest that a supportive climate requires a teacher to be both empathic (statements 3, 5, 6, 7), and approachable (statements 1, 2, 8).

Establishing Empathy. Instructors should communicate understanding of student problems and concerns (e.g., about the subject matter) to set up an empathic relationship. Once a good relationship is established, students will be less defensive and more likely to communicate freely (Rosenfeld, 1983). Teachers can find out about students' concerns by starting informal conversations before class starts (Kougl, 1980). Once student concerns surface, the teacher might discuss them with the class or modify instruction. However, teachers should avoid identifying the student who voiced the concern. Otherwise, student input might cease.

Approachability. The language a teacher uses can either encourage or discourage students from approaching him or her. If a teacher uses unfamiliar language, the student is likely to perceive the instructor as unapproachable (Berger & Bradac, 1982), decreasing the likelihood of establishing a supportive climate. This finding does not mean that instructors should always restrict their vocabulary; however, it does mean that language should be used to communicate ideas rather than claim status. Research also indicates that students are more comfortable in classrooms where status is irrelevant (Bowers, et al., 1986).

In addition to teachers being empathic and approachable, there are other ways of establishing a supportive communication climate. For example, the instructor should reinforce and reward communication (S. Booth-Butterfield, 1988; McCroskey, 1980) and avoid punishing students for communicating. If students are disruptive, then the instructor must let them know that disruptive behavior is not acceptable, while communication on the topic at hand should be encouraged (McCroskey, 1980).

The instructor can encourage communication and informal interaction by using small group discussions or by placing students in small groups for specific assignments. Using the small group as an interaction context encourages people to respond rather than forcing them to respond (Kougl, 1980). Neer and Hudson (1981) found that reticent students favor small group discussion more than nonreticent students. Perhaps reticent students view the small group as less threatening than the larger class, and thus feel freer to speak out in the group.

Responding to Student Questions

To ensure a supportive classroom environment, instructors must skillfully respond to student questions by looking for the merit in each question. Asking a question is a risk-taking behavior that should be rewarded by some form of verbal acknowledgment (Ortiz, 1988). Teachers also must be sensitive to the first question asked in class. Frequently the way the instructor handles the first question will set the tone for future questions.

Because reticents avoid asking questions (Bowers et al., 1986), teachers might consider using a classroom activity that promotes questions. One possibility is to use the incomplete sentence model (Simon, Howe, & Kirshchenbaum, 1972). When a teacher suspects that students are confused about course content, the teacher asks students to complete the following sentences:

"I wonder . . ."
"I wish I knew . . ."
"I'd do better in this course if . . ."

Adler (1980) identified two reasons why the incomplete sentence method benefits the reticent student: The incomplete sentence model invites questions, which reduces the trauma of asking an uninvited question; and reticent students will realize that other students have questions similar to their own.

Selecting Classroom Activities

Because classroom activities typically center on communication, teachers must remember the plight of the reticent student. When selecting activities, teachers might evaluate each one in terms of how it helps the reticent student. Adler (1980) proposed seven criteria for effective activities that integrate strategies of reticence management:

1. *Relevant to the subject matter.* Because time and resources are limited, activities must help students to understand the course content.
2. *Stimulate emotional involvement.* Activities should challenge the student; however, the activity should not produce more anxiety than the reticent student can manage.
3. *Maximize student involvement.* Activities should involve all students in the class. If an activity can be completed by a group of students in the class, the verbal students will likely participate and the reticent students will watch or withdraw. Therefore, activities must be structured so all students must participate.
4. *Promote interest and reward.* Activities should challenge the intellect of both the reticent and nonreticent students. Furthermore, activities should promote genuine student interest.
5. *Provide structure.* Activities should contain a structure that allows for valid responses. Vague questions such as "What do you think?" should be replaced with structured questions such as, "Which position do you favor: a, b, or c?"
6. *Avoid negative evaluation.* Activities should be structured so responses are not judged as right or wrong. Instead, activities should promote the sharing of ideas and opinions, which will subsequently increase the confidence of the students.
7. *Relate to student's background.* Because of the correlation between relevance of the subject matter and student interest, the goal of the instructor should be to bridge the gap between the subject matter and the background of the students.

Flexible Seating Assignments

As discussed in the section on classroom interaction, research indicates that the location of a seat in the classroom is strongly associated with levels of interaction. In other words, some seats are in low interaction areas, others are in high interaction areas. If reticent students are placed in a high interaction seat, they will likely feel pressured to communicate, which might impede their concentration and learning (McCroskey, 1980). Therefore, teachers might allow students to select their own seats or choose the seats carefully.

Structuring Assignments

M. Booth-Butterfield (1986) suggested that when teachers give assignments, two versions should be made available to students: structure-added; and structure-reduced. The structure-added description should be given to reticent students, to enhance classroom performance (M. Booth-Butterfield, 1986; Pilkonis, 1977b). The structure-reduced description should be given to nonreticents because too structured an assignment might stifle their performance. M. Booth-Butterfield gave the following example of a dyadic exercise in interpersonal communication, listing possible topics students should discuss with each other:

> *Structure-Added Version*
> When people meet each other for the first time . . .
> People are happiest when . . .
> When someone is in a relationship, they should . . .
> Most people dislike —— in others.
> Dealing with emotions is . . .
> When people are alone they . . .
> Facing new situations can be . . .
> Conflict in a relationship . . .
> Most people don't understand . . .
> A lot of people want —— in life.
> People usually fear . . .
> Most people I know look forward to . . .
> Relationship commitment is . . .
>
> *Structure-Reduced Version*
> Emotions
> First impressions

Happiness and goals in life
Relationship expectations
Relationship conflict
Fears and dislikes (p. 344)

As for group assignments, M. Booth-Butterfield (1986) suggested that groups be given structured examples. Groups then can select which qualities of the examples to incorporate in their assignment.

Booth-Butterfield gave the following suggestions and warnings for using the structure-added assignment:

- The components of the structured assignment are optional and nonreticents should not be penalized for not including them.
- The two assignment descriptions (added and reduced structure) must be equivalent in content.
- Structure-added assignment descriptions should promote thinking rather than following directions.
- Because of the different assignment descriptions, the teacher should be prepared for different types of presentations.

Avoid Grading Participation

Instructors must distinguish between reticent students and apathetic students. Both types of students participate infrequently; however, their reasons for not participating are quite different. As we established earlier, reticent students typically avoid participating in class because they fear communication or lack skills. Apathetic students do not participate because they are not motivated to interact. If a teacher assumes that any student who does not participate is apathetic, then many reticent students will be penalized unfairly. Evaluation must be based on knowledge and skills, rather than on participation (McCroskey, 1980). That means all students should have at least one alternative to oral response through which they can demonstrate their knowledge and skills.

Provide Alternate Response Formats

Teachers might consider response formats other than public communication (Burgoon, 1976b). For example, teachers might ask students to write their responses to a question on file cards. Once students have written their responses, the file cards are passed to the teacher who then shuffles the cards to conceal students' identities. The teacher can then comment on some or all of the responses. In another format students would create questions, which are then passed to other students to answer (Hittleman, 1988). Students can then discuss responses with each other without using the public arena.

Developing Communication Routines

Teachers might develop communication routines that facilitate question and answer sessions (Hittleman, 1988). A routine might indicate the student's progress toward answering a question: "I have an answer," "I am looking for or thinking about my answer," and "I do not have an answer and am having difficulty developing one." For example, an elementary school teacher might give students a multicolored block. Students would face the green side forward when they have an answer, the yellow side when they are looking, and the red side when they do not know how to find an answer. Teachers in upper grade levels might use a notebook instead of a block. When students have an answer, they might put an open notebook face down; when students are looking for or formulating an answer, they would keep the book face up; when students do not know how to formulate an answer, they might close the notebook. Whatever the signal system, instructors can develop routines for student participation.

The previous section gave suggestions for reducing the effects of reticence during classroom discussions and activities. The next section discusses ways teachers might reduce the effects of communication reticence during oral performances.

MEDIATING RETICENCE ABOUT ORAL PERFORMANCE

Many suggestions previously included, such as establishing a supportive climate, can help to reduce the effects of reticence associated with oral performance. Before selecting ways of mediating reticence about oral performance, however, teachers should consider whether oral performance is a necessary part of the grading process, or if other alternatives might be more appropriate. McCroskey (1980) stated that teachers seldom need to use oral performance as a way to grade students. Unfortunately, when reticent students are required to demonstrate their learning through oral performance, their apprehension toward oral performance might be mistaken for low achievement. McCroskey recommended, circumstances permitting, that teachers give the students the choice between oral and written forms of evaluation. We disagree with McCroskey's recommendation because we believe students, reticent or not, need to develop their communication skills. Rather than giving students a choice between written and oral assignments, teachers should structure speaking assignments carefully and be clear about the grading criteria. It is especially important for instructors to follow the advice for giving criticism we detailed in Chapter 9. Helping students perform competently is preferable to allowing them to avoid oral communication.

Structuring Performance Assignments

As discussed previously, adding structure to assignments can reduce the effects of communication reticence in dyads and small groups. Adding structure also can help reticent students to prepare for and carry out oral performance. Teachers should develop structure-added and structure-reduced assignments. M. Booth-Butterfield (1986, p. 345) gave the following examples of structure-reduced and structure-added assignments for a public speech.

Structure-Reduced Public Speech Assignment. The speech must:

1. have current impact
2. cite two outside sources
3. be 3-6 minutes long
4. effectively employ chronological or topical organization.

Structure-Added Public Speech Assignment.

1. The speech must have current impact
   a. appeared in the media in the past 2 years
   b. may be a local problem, (or state, national, or international)
   c. should not be "trivial," but may be creative
   d. may be a lifestyle trend
   e. may be a business concern
   f. may have health implications
2. The speech must cite two sources

      a. may be library-based, interviews, personal
         experence if qualified, family business, new TV show
      b. may be different sources or same type
      c. may include pertinent details about source (date,
         author, qualification, background)
      d. may not include use of dictionary
3. It must be 3 to 6 minutes
      a. three when you practice it, may be shorter when you
         actually perform
      b. include optional note cards with nonessential detail
         to use if you have time
4. The speech must have effective organization
      a. two-three major ideas about your topic
      b. transitions between major points such as (my
         second point, . . . in contrast we see, . . . finally, . . .
         another area of interest. . .)
      c. introduction with thesis and preview
      d. introduction of three to four sentences; conclusion of
         three to four sentences
      e. introduction and conclusion using the same theme
         (Begin with an example and go back to it at the end.)

Oral performance assignments, other than public speaking, can be handled in a similar way. Teachers can provide additional structure for those students who need it; however, teachers should review the warnings discussed in the section on structuring dyad and group activities.

Delivery Training

When giving oral presentations, reticent students tend to avoid thinking about delivery, instead focusing their attention on internal factors (Daly & Lawrence, 1985), topics, supporting materials, or structure (M. Booth-Butterfield, 1986; Daly, Vangelisti, Neel, & Cavanaugh, 1987). When reticents do think about delivery, they have a tendency to worry about how much they gesture or the number of times they say "um." Teachers should consider teaching delivery, incorporating techniques described in Chapter 6. Delivery training might help students to concentrate on their presentation and will likely reduce anxiety associated with public speaking (Neer & Kircher, 1989). Instructors should teach students how to manage paraverbal (e.g., pitch, volume, rate) and nonverbal (e.g., eye contact, posture, gestures) aspects of delivery.

Instructional Formats

Neer, Hudson, and Warren (1982) tested whether certain instructional methods would reduce communication reticence associated with public speaking. Specifically, they examined grading options, speech preparation procedures, speaking order options, topic selection procedures, and administration procedures. The results suggest that reticence toward public speaking is primarily associated with the evaluation process. In particular, students fear being the center of attention. They also fear instructor evaluation, especially when the evaluation immediately follows their speech. Furthermore, students are apprehensive about being compared to other students (Neer et al., 1982).

Given the findings of Neer et al., teachers might consider addressing student fears of evaluation. For example, teachers might discuss the importance of feedback as essential to learning. However, teachers should examine their system of feedback and the impact it might have on students, particularly those who are reticent.

Providing Feedback

The way a teacher structures feedback can have a significant impact on reticent students. If allowed to generate their own feedback, reticent students are more likely than nonreticents to evaluate themselves negatively (M. Booth-Butterfield, 1989). If the instructor gives descriptive and timely feedback, reticents will not interpret feedback more negatively than nonreticents. Although seemingly ironic, giving feedback to reticent students will lessen negative perceptions.

Another way of giving feedback involves using video feedback. Although some might think of video feedback as a way of providing objective and detailed information, teachers must realize that video feedback is not objective because it is interpreted by the student who receives it (Johnson, 1981; Trower & Kiely, 1983). If teachers do not carefully structure the video feedback process, the effects might be detrimental, especially to the reticent individual (Trower & Kiely, 1983). The possible detrimental effects of video feedback should be considered because some scholars suggest that video feedback is no more effective than verbal feedback (Brenes & Cooklin, 1983; Brown, 1980; Hanser & Furman, 1980; Padgett, 1983; Thelen & Lasoski, 1980). If a teacher decides to use video feedback for an oral performance assignment, Kinzer (1985) suggested the following guidelines:

- Edit out inappropriate behavior if video feedback is used for self-modeling.
- Prepare students for the videotaping process. Preparation should include what to expect and what to watch.
- Discuss the student's performance immediately after watching the videotape.
- Use videotaped exercises to reduce the novelty of being on camera. Students can then focus on performance rather than appearance.

Developmental Sequencing

Teachers can consider using a developmental sequence toward oral performance so they build toward the final performance. Students might share their ideas with audiences other than the class as a whole. For example, teachers might use the following sequence:

> Students discuss their presentation with a friend in the classroom.
> Students give their presentation to a small gathering of classmates.
> Students give their presentation to the whole class.

At each step, the instructor gives feedback to shape and reinforce the student's communicative behavior. By the time a student talks to the whole class, he or she has received extensive and detailed feedback. Teachers might also consider stopping at step two. Presentations can be given to a small group of students rather than to the entire class, which might lessen the negative aspects of the public speaking context (M. Booth-Butterfield, 1989).

Personalized System of Instruction (PSI)

One way of reducing apprehension in the classroom is to adopt a teaching strategy entitled the personalized system of instruction (PSI). Unfortunately, PSI requires considerable restructuring when applied to higher education. Despite these limitations, this system is included in this chapter because some components of PSI might be helpful to teachers of all grade levels. PSI is characterized by the following seven components (Sherman & Ruskin, 1978):

1. *Mastery learning.* Mastery learning is a teaching approach in which students must achieve a certain level of competence before proceeding to the next level. For example, mastery learning requires students to demonstrate competence in giving an informative speech before they are allowed to give a persuasive speech or in preparing a thesis statement before writing an outline.

2. *Immediate feedback.* For mastery learning to occur students must be given immediate feedback. If students do not receive immediate feedback their overall learning will likely suffer (Calhoun, 1973).

3. *Sequential units.* Course materials should be presented in small units, otherwise students might experience unnecessary difficulty in mastering the units. Research shows that smaller units are related to both increased student performance (O'Neill, Johnston, Walters, & Rasheed, 1975; Semb, 1974) and better study habits (Nelson & Bennett, 1973).

4. *Self-pacing.* Students in a PSI program determine the pace at which they will learn the course content. Students also decide when they will take quizzes.

5. *Written word.* At the beginning of the class, students are given the handouts, study guides, and workbooks that constitute the course content. Because the students have complete and immediate access to all course content, they are encouraged to become independent of the teacher in their learning.

6. *Lectures to motivate.* Because students have the content at the beginning of the course, teachers do not need to give lectures that disseminate information. Instead, the purpose of the lecture in PSI is to motivate the students.

7. *Student proctors.* Students who have already taken the class act as tutors and guides by answering questions, helping students to assess progress, generating enthusiasm, and monitoring tests. The use of student proctors is the most important component of PSI (Keller & Sherman, 1982).

Sherman and Ruskin (1978) stated that PSI adheres to three critical features of effective instruction: the presentation of information materials, tasks, or problems appropriate to the current knowledge and skills of the student; frequent opportunities to test comprehension of the information presented; and immediate confirmation regarding the adequacy of the student's responses.

Research indicates that using PSI reduces reticence associated with public speaking. Buerkel-Rothfuss and Yerby (1982) compared levels of reticence of students in a PSI public speaking class to students in a traditional public speaking class. Results show that students in the PSI public speaking class reported both lower levels of reticence and increased learning outcomes. Gray, Buerkel-Rothfuss, and Yerby (1986) also found that students in a PSI public speaking course reported less reticence about speaking than did students in a traditional public speaking course. Despite its promise, teachers must assess the advantages and limitations of the PSI. For further details on PSI see Keller and Sherman (1974) or Sherman and Ruskin (1978).

CONCLUSION

Communication reticence negatively affects student achievement. Reticent students avoid communicating with their classmates and their teachers, which subsequently diminishes achievement. However, if teachers make the effort to establish a supportive classroom communication climate and carefully select and structure classroom activities, the effects of reticence can be reduced. Although the suggestions included in this chapter are hardly exhaustive, they may promote new ways of interacting with reticent students in the classroom. For those teachers who are not able to institute a reticence program like the one offered at PSU, the only option they may have is to employ teaching strategies to help students overcome reticence in the ordinary classroom context.

11

MODIFYING THE PROGRAM FOR A WORKSHOP FORMAT

As discussed in chapter 10, it is not always possible to institute a reticence program like the one developed at PSU. The Reticence Program that serves as the pedagogical model for this book was developed at a university so it follows the typical 15-week semester model characteristic of academic instruction. This, however, is not the only context in which the program can operate. Just as teachers can incorporate techniques into their regular classes to help reticent students, trainers can easily modify the program to suit workshop formats in other settings. Several variations of these workshops have been offered for volunteers in communities and workplaces. The program can also be adapted to the needs of elementary and secondary school students. In this chapter, we describe a workshop model that can be used in a variety of contexts to help individuals improve their oral communication. We also suggest special considerations for adapting the material for a workshop format.

A MODEL COMMUNICATION WORKSHOP

The overcoming shyness workshop described in this section was developed as a noncredit program for a local organization that offers brief courses on a variety of topics ranging from cooking to psychological self-help. These workshops are open to adults in the community and are offered through the year. The workshop is described in detail here, including its goals and format, considerations for advertising, and an overview of its content and activities.

Goals and Format

The workshop is open to anyone in the community who feels he or she might profit from it. The participants are self-referred, so we take them at face value. The overall objective of the workshop is to take the trainees through an abbreviated version of the Reticence Program while maintaining the essence of the training approach. This abbreviated program has the five following goals:

> *Goal 1*: Introduce trainees to basic principles of communication as they are covered in the Reticence Program. Trainees usually have no background in communication and subscribe to many of the same erroneous beliefs about the process as college students who enroll in the Reticence Program. Trainers need to persuade these participants to view communication as a process they can control.
> *Goal 2*: Teach and have participants apply the goal analysis procedure. Applying goal analysis is a primary objective of the workshop because goal-setting skills are at the heart of the Reticence Program. Much of the progress trainees make depends on their knowledge and use of goal analysis.
> *Goal 3*: Have participants select a communication goal, employ goal analysis, complete the goal, and report on it. The most effective way to ensure that trainees understand goal setting is to ask them to complete a goal assignment, just as students do in the full program. To accomplish this task the workshop must be spread out over several days. The crucial issue is making sure a goal is selected and performed, and an oral report given.
> *Goal 4*: Teach trainees the concept of audience and situation analysis and introduce them to methods for per-

forming them. These are essential skills that trainees must develop before they are introduced to performance skills.

Goal 5: Help participants develop their understanding of social conversation and provide an opportunity to practice basic techniques. Social conversation is the central focus of the workshop because it is the problem most frequently reported by workshop participants.

Most organizations sponsoring this type of workshop also offer public speaking as a separate component because of time constraints. Those that are concerned with public speaking are either transferred to an alternative program or asked to go through the social conversation emphasis and then attempt public speaking.

The workshop has been offered in both a 3- and 4-week format, with consecutive sessions. Optimum is an 8-hour program administered 2 hours at a time over 4 weeks, although some effect can be achieved through programs as short as 6 hours administered on a Saturday.

The more time available, the more effective the workshop can be, but most adult trainees do not have sufficient time for extended training and are more willing to enroll in shorter programs. If more time is available, it can be used for exercises and rehearsal. The most important consideration for deciding on duration is to make sure participants can complete one full iteration of the goal analysis process.

The number of workshop participants should be restricted to between 10 and 20 people. If there are fewer than 10, it is difficult to create the feel of a diverse population and people become so comfortable with one another that the sense of realism disappears. The inevitable dropouts will reduce the size of the workshop to the point where the instructor must give individual instruction. Some people drop out because they are not motivated enough, some because the tension is too great for them to handle, and a few simply because they do not have the time. In groups of more than 20, it is difficult for the trainer to give any individual attention.

Most of the people who enroll for adult workshops regard themselves as shy and complain about being tense in social conversation. They report problems similar to those instructors see in the college version of the program. Some trainees have moderate trouble communicating, although a minority report fairly severe problems. All are a little apprehensive about the workshop, but most are motivated to improve themselves, although levels of motivation vary. Because there is insufficient time to give the nurturing some of the participants need, the workshop must be directed to the demographic majority.

Equipment and facility needs for this workshop are modest. The room should be comfortable, with movable chairs that can be arranged in one large circle, small circles for group activities, and classroom style for lectures if the trainer so desires. The trainer needs either a blackboard or flip chart to outline key lecture/discussion points. Participants need paper and pens, as well as whatever handouts the instructor chooses to provide (see later).

The sessions are run with a combination of lecture/discussion and communication activities, just as in the full-length version of the program. This combination is necessary not only to maintain the attention of these volunteers and keep them coming back for all the sessions, but also to give them opportunities to get to know others like themselves and practice their communication skills. Details of each session are provided later in this section.

Advertising the Workshop

In this section we deal with the content of workshop advertisements, not their placement or cost. There are two issues involved in advertising the workshop: attracting the appropriate participants and describing it accurately. These issues are interconnected in that the content of the ads will draw certain people to the workshop and discourage others from enrolling.

The kinds of problems reported by workshop participants should match those for which this particular treatment approach was developed. These trainees, like our college students, should have problems with social communication, particularly in terms of skill deficiencies in any or all of the rhetorical subprocesses already described (i.e., invention, disposition, style, memory, delivery). The workshop is not designed for remediation of psychological disturbances or speech production problems (e.g., stuttering, lisping, or other articulation difficulties), or stage fright.

The target audience for the advertising is individuals who lack competence in one or more communication skill areas, resulting in difficulty speaking in one or more contexts, especially social conversation. These individuals, like the college students in the Reticence Program, may or may not be anxious about talking as well.

As we have explained, at the university where the original program was developed, the course instructors have a chance to rule out people whose problems seem to warrant some other type of treatment. Generally, workshop trainers do not have this opportunity. They must depend on self-selection. It becomes crucial, then, that any advertising of the workshop attract appropriate candidates. Otherwise, people's time and money may be wasted and unsuitable participants may distract the trainer or other trainees from the training agenda.

After experimenting with various descriptions of the workshop, the authors recommend an announcement such as the following:

> Workshop on Overcoming Shyness: Feel awkward and at a loss for words when carrying on conversation with strangers? Find yourself avoiding social situations so you do not have to make small talk? Then this workshop is for you. The workshop is designed to help you improve your skills as a communicator, especially your social conversation skills. You will learn a method called "goal setting," which is a three-part procedure to prepare for and handle communication situations more effectively. You will also have opportunities in the workshop to practice and discuss your skills as a communicator.

Note that although the word *shyness* is in the title of the workshop, it is not used in the description. We are somewhat reluctant to use the term *shy* because of our commitment to avoiding labels that may create new problems or exacerbate existing ones. A person who has not previously appropriated the term personally may accept the label and take on accompanying negative responses and behaviors. We believe this to be an unlikely event given that the workshop situation described here is completely voluntary. More likely, those drawn to a workshop on overcoming shyness are people who already feel they are shy and/or have difficulty talking to strangers. This situation is in contrast to that of a college sophomore who must take a speech course to graduate and who may have no self-perception (accurate or otherwise) of experiencing shyness.

Whatever the specific wording of the ads, the workshop developer must be careful to write copy that attracts participants with the appropriate problems. The advertisements need to present an accurate description of what will happen in the workshop. It is, at the very least, a bit risky for people to enroll in a program to overcome shyness and improve themselves as communicators. If nothing else, trainees risk some minor embarrassment.

An honest depiction of the training program can help prevent potential problems as well as generate appropriate expectations. For example, if there are no clear statements in the ads that the program focuses on skill development, participants may expect treatment for communication anxiety. Ad copy, like the sample we provided, that emphasizes improvement of communication skills will encourage those who enroll to focus on changing their behavior and improving their skills. At the same time, it is likely to discourage those who seek medical or psychological treatment.

Workshop Content and Activities

In this section we elaborate on the specific workshop content and activities, providing agendas for both three- and four-session versions. The same material is included in both versions; the chief difference is in the time devoted to topics and the number of activities. Trainers who apply this model will undoubtedly discover they must deviate somewhat from the outline we propose because of trainee needs or interests.

As our initial description of the workshop implied, content revolves around four main topics: communication principles, goal analysis, audience and situation analysis, and the social conversation process. In earlier sections of this book, we presented detailed explanations of the material covered and activities employed in training to these four topics. Here we provide brief descriptions and refer the reader to the appropriate sections where the ideas were fully developed.

Communication principles. As described in Chapter 1, trainers in the Reticence Program spend time very early in the course discussing the process of communication. Specifically, they try to persuade trainees to accept certain principles of communication. Those principles, presented in Chapter 1, focus on the role of communication in human relationships, the need to assess audiences and situations to select appropriate behaviors from one's repertoire, the notion that we can control only our own behavior and must engage in persuasion with others, the concept of exchange as the basis of relating to others, the relationship between communication behaviors and our personalities, the belief that communication skills can be learned, the idea that communication is the primary means by which we exert influence, and finally, the issue of the naturalness of feelings of nervousness and discomfort when speaking.

Just as they do in the Reticence Program, workshop trainers arrange participants in small groups to complete a forced choice exercise. Trainees are given a sheet (see Appendix G) listing several statements about the communication process. As a group they are to decide the extent of their agreement or disagreement with each statement. The purpose is to stimulate discussion of the principles as well as encourage participants to talk.

Goal analysis. We include goal analysis in the workshop because of its centrality to the pedagogical model underlying the Reticence Program. In the workshop, trainers present the material in a manner identical to that described in Chapter 3. First, instructors lecture on the need for and three components of the goal analysis process. They distribute handouts with the goal preparation sheet, a sample goal analysis, and the goal report format sheet (see Chapter 3, Appendices H, I, J). If there is time, trainers might give participants a handout on which they can practice rewriting goal statements to make them more realistic and less fuzzy (See Appendix P).

Once trainees understand goal analysis and the steps in the process, instructors ask each person to select a goal, write a goal analysis, carry out the goal, and be prepared to report on it at the final session. Specifically, the trainer gives them the assignment of writing a goal analysis for a goal of their choice, due at the next workshop session. The trainer takes time, usually during the break plus some additional time, to meet with each individual to help him or her select a first goal. This process is elaborated later when we discuss the self-assessment activity. When students turn in the goal analysis papers, the instructor gives them a written response, including suggestions for improvement and approval to go ahead with the goal. At the final session, trainees turn in a goal report and discuss their experiences in the same fashion as students in the Reticence Program (see Chapter 3, pp. 44-45).

Audience and situation analysis. Trainers discuss the importance of the skills of audience and situation analysis, and engage participants in a lecture/discussion of the features of situations and audiences that communicators must take into account (see Chapter 3, especially pp. 47-53). The participants are divided into small groups to do an audience and situation analysis activity designed to give them practice at completing an analysis for a particular communication goal and context (see Chapter 3 and Appendix K).

Social conversation. Trainers discuss the importance of small talk and lead participants in a discussion of how to initiate, maintain, and end conversations (Chapter 4, pp. 57-59). Then trainees are given the chance to mingle with each other to practice their skills, similar to the social conversation "party" described on page 61. Trainers also debrief participants after they have had an opportunity to interact, leading them in a discussion of their experiences and the techniques they used to carry on conversation.

Additional components of the workshop. There are two other important elements of the workshop. First is the introductory "warm-up" activity. The trainer distributes index cards and asks each participant to record his or her name, city or town of residence, occupation, place of employment, and leisure-time activities or hobbies. Once these have been collected, the instructor uses them to meet each person and engage him or her in a brief conversation. This activity assists participants in getting to know each other, helps them relax and feel more comfortable in the workshop, builds a sense of esprit de corps, and enables the trainer to make an initial assessment of the severity of the communication problems trainees possess.

Second, because there is no screening interview or self-as-communicator paper, trainers include a self-assessment procedure in the workshop. Trainees complete a self-assessment form (see Appendix Q) early in the first session. The form asks them to talk about their strengths and weaknesses as communicators and what they hope to gain from their participation in the workshop. The instructor collects these forms and reads them while the trainees are involved in their first small group discussion task, the forced-choice problem regarding basic principles of communication. The self-assessment helps the instructor prepare to discuss a possible goal assignment with each individual.

Workshop Formats

The four-session format. The agendas for the four sessions (2 hours each) are as follows:

Session 1 includes
Introduction: The trainer introduces him- or herself and describes his or her background and qualifications.
Goals of the workshop: The trainer explains that the

workshop is an abbreviated version of the PSU Reticence Program and describes its goals.

Warm-up activity: Participants complete the index cards and the trainer leads the introductions of the participants (Step 1).

Self-assessment: Trainees fill out the self-assessment form; the trainer collects the forms.

Forced-choice exercise/communication principles: The trainer engages in a brief discussion of the definition of communication and then divides the trainees into small groups to complete the forced-choice exercise. While participants are engaged in that task, the trainer reviews the self-assessment forms. Then he or she leads the group in a discussion of the communication principles illustrated in the forced-choice activity.

Break: Participants take a break for refreshments. Depending on time, this may occur before or after the debriefing of the forced-choice exercise.

Conferences: The instructor meets with each trainee to discuss his or her self-assessment and to offer advice about a goal for the goal assignment.

Why are we here?: The wrap-up discussion summarizes what the program is designed to do, how it approaches the issue of anxiety or nervousness about speaking, and the necessity of improving one's competence as a communicator.

Session 2 includes:

Goal analysis: The trainer takes the group through the goal analysis process, distributing handouts, and giving the instructions for the goal process. Trainees are asked to write a goal analysis and bring it to the next session.

Audience and situation analysis: The instructor presents the material on this process.

Break: As described in Session 1.

Audience and situation analysis activity: The instructor divides the group into small groups to complete the activity, then leads a debriefing session.

Session 3 is made up of the following steps:

Collect goal analysis papers: The trainer collects the papers and evaluates them when trainees are engaged in activities.

Social conversation material: The instructor presents the material on social conversation.

Social conversation party: The participants have an opportunity to meet and talk to each other and are assigned to talk to at least three people. During this period the trainer assesses the goal analysis papers and writes comments on them.

Debriefing: The trainer leads the debriefing of the "party," distributes goal analysis papers, and instructs trainees to carry out the actual goal before next session and write a goal report.

Session 4 is as follows:

Goal reports: The trainer arranges the group in a circle and asks each person to talk about the goal he or she has completed (what it was; what they did; how successful he or she was). This is an opportunity for the instructor to bring up new points or review ones already discussed during previous sessions.

Break: As described in Session 1.

Improvement plans: The trainer leads the participants in a discussion of where they go next, how they can build on what they have learned to continue improving. Participants try to map out plans for their own improvement. Writing or speaking about their plans can accomplish this planning goal.

Workshop evaluation: The trainer asks trainees to provide a written assessment of the workshop.

The three-session format. Only experienced trainers should use this format because it requires finesse with timing and targeting of key points. Trainers who have significant experience running this workshop have a much better sense of timing, what to expect, and what points need highlighting.

Session 1 includes the following nine steps:

Introduction: The trainer introduces him- or herself and describes his or her background and qualifications.

Goals of the workshop: The trainer explains that the workshop is an abbreviated version of the PSU Reticence Program and describes its goals.

Warm-up activity: Participants complete the index cards and the trainer leads the brief introductions of the participants (see Step 1)..

Self-assessment: Trainees fill out the self-assessment form; the trainer collects the forms.

Forced-choice exercise/communication principles: The trainer defines communication and then divides the trainees into small groups to complete the forced-choice exercise. While participants are engaged in that task, the trainer reviews the self-assessment forms. After the activity has been completed, the trainer leads the group in a discussion of the communication principles it illustrates. This discussion must be fairly brief to allow time for the material on goal analysis.

Break: Participants take a break for refreshments either before or after the debriefing of the forced-choice exercise, depending on time.

Conferences: The instructor meets with each trainee to discuss his or her self-assessment and to offer advice about a goal for the goal assignment.

Goal analysis: The trainer teaches goal analysis and gives instructions for the goal assignment. Participants are asked to write a goal analysis for the next session.

Why are we here?: This is a brief, wrap-up discussion of what the program is designed to do, how it approaches the issue of anxiety or nervousness about speaking, and the necessity of improving one's competence as a communicator.

Session 2 is as follows:

Goal analysis papers: The trainer collects the goal analysis papers to assess while the trainees are involved in a group activity.

Audience and situation analysis: The instructor presents the material on this process.

Break: As described in Session 1.

Audience and situation analysis activity: The instructor divides the group into small groups to complete the activity, then leads a debriefing session. During this time, he or she evaluates the goal analysis papers by writing comments on them.

Social conversation material: The instructor presents the material on social conversation.

Debriefing: The trainer requests that each participant carry out the planned goal and write a goal report for the next session. He or she returns the goal analysis papers with comments to the trainees.

Session 3, the final session, would be as follows:

Social conversation party: The participants have an opportunity to meet and talk to each other, and are assigned to talk to at least three people.

Debriefing: The trainer leads the debriefing of the "party."

Goal reports: The trainer arranges the group in a circle and asks each person to talk about the goal he or she completed (what it was; what they did; how successful he or she was). This is an opportunity for the instructor to bring up new points or review those already discussed during previous sessions.

Improvement plans: If there is time, the trainer leads the participants in a discussion of where they go next and how they can build on what they have learned to continue improving. Participants try to map out plans for their own improvement. Writing or speaking about their plans can help accomplish this goal.

Workshop evaluation: The trainer asks trainees to provide a written assessment of the workshop.

The 1-day workshop. Conducting a one-session workshop requires singular skills on the part of the trainer. All activities must be compressed into a short period of time; breaks must be shorter. If attempting this kind of workshop, it is important to provide internal summaries of each component throughout the day. Such activities as the "party" must be severely cut in length and it is virtually impossible to have participants complete a goal. Because trainees do not have the opportunity to do the full goal setting process, we do not recommend the 1-day format unless there is no other option.

APPLYING THE WORKSHOP MODEL

The workshop just described was designed as a voluntary offering to members of the local community. The basic format of this workshop can also be adapted for a high school group or a business organization. The content and activities of the workshop remain the same. In this section we look at some special considerations the planner or trainer should take into account in organizing such workshops.

Modifying the Workshop for High Schools

One of the authors of this book offered a version of the workshop in a high school setting. Students had no trouble handling the concepts or the activities and assignments. Several issues arose, however, that workshop planners need to consider.

Scheduling. The schedules of many high school students are designed without much free time during school hours, thus workshop planners are confronted with a scheduling problem. If the workshop is offered during a particular period two problems arise. First, some students who need and would like to enroll may have schedule conflicts. This difficulty can be overcome by offering the workshop every year at various times so all or nearly all students have the opportunity to enroll. The second problem is that periods are generally too short to complete the workshop session, so the trainer needs at least two consecutive periods per session, which drastically increases the number of students with scheduling conflicts.

Due to the difficulties of scheduling the workshop during the school day, planners may want to offer the workshop during after-school activity hours. The obvious drawbacks to this alternative include further scheduling conflicts (students may be involved in a sport, club, or after-school job) and less interest on the part of the target population. Bus schedules may also interfere. Only the most motivated will be likely to enroll in the workshop, which is advantageous in that those students are most likely to benefit from participation. The author who offered the workshop in a high school ran into these scheduling problems and elected the after-school option. The audience for the workshop was indeed small but highly motivated. Because fewer than 10 students enrolled, each person received individual attention. However, other students may have wanted to take the workshop but could not because of after-school obligations.

Motivation and rewards. Even students who really want to improve their communication skills can lose their motivation, especially when the workshop must be held after school. Workshop planners need to investigate possible motivators such as course credit, extra credit to be awarded in a regular course, or relieving students who participate of particular duties or obligations, for example, excusing them from an equivalent number of study hall hours. If there is some reward or incentive for students to participate in the workshop, they are more likely to maintain their motivation level. Motivation is particularly important because participants need to complete at least one goal assignment on their own time outside of the workshop. We consider the completion of one or more goals essential to the students' improvement of their communication skills.

Confidentiality. Because the typical high school student is concerned about what peers think and wants to fit in, it is very important that workshop planners be sensitive to issues of anonymity and confidentiality. They need to advertise the workshop, enroll students, and schedule the sessions so that students do not feel conspicuous and can retain their anonymity. Ad copy must be written with some sensitivity toward these concerns, so that students who can benefit from the workshop are encouraged to do so and do not suffer unnecessary humiliation. There must be a private place for students to participate in screening interviews or talk to trainers and sign up for the program. The workshop itself must be held in a location within the school that affords maximum privacy.

Trainers should not inform regular classroom teachers of a student's participation in the workshop unless the teacher is offering extra credit or some other incentive. When it is necessary to inform a student's teacher or teachers, the trainer or workshop planner needs to talk to those teachers about respecting the student's confidentiality.

Advertising the workshop. Finally, workshop planners must decide how to inform students about the workshop. The typical mechanisms like posters, student newspaper (if one exists), or the public address system may work. However, it may be more effective to make copies of a handout (See Appendix F) similar to the one used at PSU (with necessary modifications), and ask teachers to distribute them in classes and say a few words about the program. Another mechanism for getting word out about the workshop is through the various personnel from whom students often seek help such as guidance counselors, school nurses, or psychologists. Workshop planners can inform these individuals about the program and brief them on what to say to describe it to students.

Modifying the Workshop for Businesses

The same issues confronting workshop planners in high schools loom large for those who want to offer communication training for employees in business organizations. In this section we look at the particular manifestations of those issues in the workplace.

Scheduling. Large organizations with in-house training programs have already addressed the issue of when to schedule employees for training sessions. The mechanisms currently in place in such companies should be used to schedule this workshop.

When there is no in-house training program and the organization relies on outside consultants and trainers, workshop planners have two options. Workshops can be scheduled on company time or off hours. If possible, it is best to schedule the workshop during the normal work day because being paid for their time can increase employees' motivation. This plan should only be used, however, if employees are not "on call," having to run out of the workshop to answer calls or deal with work issues. When it is necessary to schedule the workshop on off hours, such as a Saturday morning or a weekday evening, employees should be paid for their time or offered some other incentive.

Motivation and rewards. Employers can force employees to participant by making it a job requirement. This plan does not necessarily translate into motivating employees to improve their communication skills. When possible workshop planners should offer trainees some sort of incentives to participate fully in the workshop. In addition to financial compensation for their time, other options can include increased chance for promotion, merit raises, certificates/plaques upon completing the workshop, or less tangible rewards such as praise and higher marks on the next performance appraisal.

The extent to which incentives must be offered depends on how employees are recruited to take the workshop (discussed later). If they are volunteers, rewards may be minimized because they already have at least some internal motivation to improve themselves. If they are required to attend the workshop, more incentives will be needed to motivate trainees to actually try to improve their communication.

Confidentiality. In situations in which training of all types is an ongoing part of an employee's experience, confidentiality may not be an issue. When such training is routine, it is not likely that participation in a workshop will generate much attention. When training is infrequent or essentially nonexistent, issues of confidentiality become important. Casting the workshop as "remedial" or for "shy types" is likely to cause embarrassment among employees who might otherwise volunteer. Generally, if trainees are volunteers, the workshop can be advertised, and volunteers should be able to sign up in some unobtrusive manner. As in the high school, a private place is required where employees can discuss the workshop with trainers or planners. When trainees are not volunteers, maintaining confidentiality is even more essential so that participants are not labeled pejoratively by coworkers or supervisors. Notification of the required training must be done privately, and arrangements made for the employee to undergo the training without calling a great deal of attention to it.

Usually only the immediate supervisor should be informed of the employee's participation in training. Others should be notified only if it is necessary, such as to dispense rewards. The location of the training should also be as private as possible. The guiding principle is to try to prevent or minimize labeling and embarrassment because the people who most need the workshop tend to fear negative evaluation and become easily embarrassed.

Advertising and/or enrolling trainees. There are two ways to recruit trainees for the workshop. One is to ask supervisors to identify likely candidates and then require them to take the workshop. In this case, advertising is clearly unnecessary. We generally advise against this approach (as discussed in Chapter 2) for two reasons. First, we are concerned about the ethics of approaching people and telling them that they have a problem that warrants treatment. They are being asked to change their communication behavior, which is so closely tied to their sense of self. This situation strikes us as delicate and potentially risky. Second, people who are forced to participate in communication training may simply comply, rather than exerting the effort needed to make any real changes in their behavior. If being singled out for specific training is a routine part of life in an organization, this second issue may not be as pertinent.

The other way to recruit trainees is to advertise the workshop and allow employees to volunteer. All of the advice about advertising presented thus far is applicable. The ad copy should be accurate and should target the appropriate individuals. The trainer should be available to answer questions and discuss the workshop with those who question its suitability for them.

EFFECTIVENESS OF THE WORKSHOPS

Participants generally have responded very positively to the workshops offered in community organizations and in the high school. Comments on the workshop evaluation forms emphasize the relevance and usefulness of the material. Participants rate the goal analysis procedure as a practical tool they can continue to use after the workshop ends. Many of them find comfort in discovering others like themselves and learning they can become better communicators. Trainees initially express surprise that there are specific techniques they can use to maintain conversation but are delighted that techniques are available and easy to use. The workshop succeeds in exploding some of the myths about communication many participants believed.

No systematic evaluation of the workshop model has been done, but it is needed to more fully assess how well the model works. We also have not yet conducted the workshop for employees in a business organization so we cannot comment on how successful such a workshop would be. However, given the effectiveness of the pedagogical model presented here and the community and high school workshops, we have confidence that employees would find the workshop useful.

SUMMARY

Although much of this book describes a pedagogical model developed in the university classroom environment, this chapter presents a workshop version of that model. One of the authors has offered this workshop in both the high school and community, using both a three- and four-session format. This chapter provides the details of that workshop so that trainers can use it in community, educational, and business organizations. The workshop, however modified by trainers, must retain the essential aspects of the Reticence Program described in this book. It must use a communication skills approach based on the goal-setting method. It should be individualized to whatever extent is possible and should encourage participants to focus on analyzing audiences and situations to select behaviors that are appropriate and effective.

IV

EVALUATION OF THE TRAINING APPROACH

12

SUPPORTIVE RESEARCH
AND EVALUATION

In this volume we presented a pedagogical model for teaching reticent individuals communication skills. We provided detailed
information about implementing a program like the one offered at
PSU where the model was developed, and discussed the theoretical principles and assumptions underlying the model. Our focus
in this chapter is on the effectiveness of this program for reticent
communicators as well as other treatment approaches that have
been developed. We discuss various ways of treating communication problems and the research that has tested their effectiveness
and the effectiveness of the PSU Reticence Program. We include
other treatment approaches in this chapter to provide comparisons with the approach we detailed in this book.

Glaser (1981) developed a three-category typology of treatment models that serves as the organizational frame for this
chapter. The categories include: methods for treating skills
deficits (the PSU rhetoritherapy program as described in this

book and other skills-training methods), methods that reduce conditioned anxiety (systematic desensitization, flooding), and methods that treat negative cognitive appraisal (rational emotive therapy, cognitive restructuring, standard visualization, performance visualization, positively biased interaction). We discuss each of the three models along with the assumptions each approach makes about the causes of communication avoidance.

Because there have been numerous studies assessing the effectiveness of the three treatment models (Allen, Hunter, & Donohue, 1989), a thorough review of each study exceeds the scope of this chapter. Instead, we describe the treatment models and provide a brief summary of the prominent research regarding the effectiveness of each one.

SKILLS DEFICIT MODEL

The skills deficit model assumes that people avoid communication situations because they do not possess adequate interaction skills (Phillips, 1968, 1977, 1984b, 1991). Because of a lack of interaction skills, the individual learns that communication results in negative consequences, producing increased levels of anxiety and further avoidance of communication situations. These events form the following causal chain:

Lack of $\longrightarrow$ Negative $\longrightarrow$ High $\longrightarrow$ Discomfort $\longrightarrow$ Avoidance
skills   consequences   anxiety   behavior

In order to break the causal chain, the unskilled individual must be taught important social skills. When the individual has satisfactorily learned these skills, he or she will find that communicating can yield positive consequences, leading to lowered anxiety and increased likelihood of more frequent communication.

Skills training (ST) has been used to treat many different communication problems (Glaser, 1981; Kelly, 1984). The usual approach is for trainees to learn and apply social skills. One challenge of a social skills-training program is to determine which skills should be learned in order to communicate effectively. Examining the literature reveals little agreement on skills to include in a skills-training program. Glaser suggested that these programs consist of one or more of the following components:

Direct Instruction and Coaching: An instructor identifies the specific behaviors that comprise a particular skill. Students are taught how to perform the behavior, and the instructor gives feedback concerning their performance of the behavior.

Modeling: Students observe others performing some communication behavior through videotape, role-playing, or field study, and, in doing so, learn to identify skilled behavior. Once students can identify skilled behavior, they can integrate the behavior into their communication practices.

Goal Setting: Students learn to set reasonable rather than idealistic communication goals. By identifying reasonable communication goals, students increase the likelihood that they will reach their goals, thus increasing their chance for success.

Covert Rehearsal: Students visualize communication behaviors, exploring the approach that is most effective for their personal needs. Visualization focuses on what to say and how to say it.

Behavioral Rehearsal: Through the use of role-play techniques, students practice specific communication behaviors. Students receive feedback from an instructor about their performance in the role play.

Self-monitoring: Students are taught to assess their use of certain communicative behaviors. In their assessment, students might discover a lack of use, or the overuse, of particular communication behaviors, and, therefore, alter their behavior.

Some or all of these six skills components can be found in most social skills-training programs. A variety of these treatment programs is discussed here, along with the specific skills taught in each program.

Research on the PSU Reticence Program

The PSU Reticence Program, which utilizes rhetoritherapy, is a skills deficit treatment (Muir, 1964; Phillips, 1968, 1977, 1986). Since the late 1970s, several studies assessed the effectiveness of this approach. These studies employed a variety of data-gathering methods including, questionnaires, self-evaluation papers, standardized measures, and observation. The overwhelming majority of the rhetoritherapy studies examined students enrolled in the PSU Reticence Program. Following is a review of the studies that assessed the effectiveness of rhetoritherapy.

Metzger (1974) was the first scholar to evaluate the effectiveness of the rhetoritherapy program. She studied a group of students from their entry into the Reticence Program until 1 year after they had completed the program. She used three separate sources of data to draw her conclusions: observations by the course instructor, self-reports from the students, and evaluations of outside observers. All three measures indicated that students improved in their communication skills after participating in the rhetoritherapy program. Furthermore, the students who showed the greatest degree of improvement were those who were able to apply rhetorical principles such as goal setting and audience and situation analysis.

Whereas Metzger (1974) studied the effects of rhetoritherapy for up to 1 year after training, Oerkvitz (1975) studied its effectiveness for periods of 1 or more years after the students had completed the program. A questionnaire was sent to those who had completed the Penn State program. Of the 347 questionnaires sent, 154 were returned. The results indicated that approximately 65% of the respondents felt the course material continued to influence their communicative behavior. Oerkvitz also found that, at the time students completed the course, 75% indicated they had improved as a result of the rhetoritherapy program. This result confirms, in part, the findings of Metzger.

Domenig (1978) compared the self-as-communicator papers of those in the rhetoritherapy program to those of students in regular speech classes at PSU. She found that students in the Reticence Program rated their performance as more competent than speech class students at the end of the semester.

McKinney (1980) was the first to use standardized measures to assess the effectiveness of the PSU rhetoritherapy program. He used the Personal Report of Communication Apprehension (McCroskey, 1970), the Unwillingness-to-Communicate scale (Burgoon, 1976a), the Speech Communication 200 Reticence scale (Phillips, 1977), and the Stanford Shyness Survey (Pilkonis, 1977a). McKinney compared the self-reports of three groups: students enrolled in the Reticence Program, students enrolled in a public speaking course, and students enrolled in a group discussion course. McKinney found that students in the rhetoritherapy program initially indicated more reticence than students in the other classes in all contexts except for public speaking. More importantly, he found that students in the Reticence Program reported greater decreases in reticence than students in the other classes.

Kelly et al. (1990) were the first to utilize a pretest-posttest control group design to test the effectiveness of rhetoritherapy. Previous studies, for the most part, used a one or two group pretest-posttest design, without a control group. Without a control group, it is extremely difficult to determine if the independent variable (rhetoritherapy vs. no treatment) was the cause of posttest differences. It is quite possible that other factors, such as maturation, testing, statistical regression, and so on, caused the posttest differences (Babbie, 1992).

Similar to McKinney (1980), Kelly et al. (1990) used standardized self-report measures; however, Kelly et al. used the Personal Report of Communication Apprehension-24 (McCroskey, 1982), the SHY scale (McCroskey et al., 1981), and Social Reticence scale (Jones & Russell, 1982). Students in a rhetoritherapy program modeled after the PSU program, students in a regular public speaking course, and students in an introductory sociology course completed the measures at the beginning and end of the semester. Results indicated that those in the rhetoritherapy program reported a greater reduction of social reticence (as measured by the Social Reticence scale) than those in the other courses. However, on the other measures, both the rhetoritherapy group and the speech class group differed from the control group but did not significantly differ from each other. In short, this study produced mixed results concerning the effectiveness of rhetoritherapy.

Because of the mixed results found in Kelly et al. (1990), Kelly and Keaten (1992) retested the effectiveness of rhetoritherapy, this time using students in the PSU Reticence Program as participants. Although Kelly and Keaten (1992) used the same experimental design as Kelly et al., Kelly and Keaten used a statistical procedure to form equivalent experimental groups.

The use of equivalent experimental groups is an important issue. In a pretest-posttest control group design, both the experimental and control group should be equivalent before any manipulation or treatment begins. If the experimental and control groups are not equivalent, then changes in the dependent variable (communication apprehension, shyness, etc.) might be the result of differences between the groups rather than the result of the treatment variable (rhetoritherapy or no treatment).

A common way of creating equivalent experimental groups is to assign subjects randomly to either a treatment group (rhetoritherapy) or a control group (no treatment). Random

assignment of subjects in the Kelly and Keaten (1992) study presented ethical problems because students enroll in the
rhetoritherapy program based on their individual communication
needs. Randomly taking some students from the rhetoritherapy
program and putting them into a control group for the sole purpose of experimentation is unethical. Giving students the opportunity to choose whether or not they participate in a research
experiment is fundamental to the ethical guidelines of communication research (Frey, Botan, Friedman, & Kreps, 1991). Another
way of creating equivalent experimental groups would be to use a
waiting list control group; however, delaying admission into the
rhetoritherapy program for research purposes also might be considered unethical.

Instead of moving students from one course to another, or
delaying admission into the Reticence Program, Kelly and Keaten
(1992) used a statistical procedure to select students for their
study. Students who scored one or more standard deviation units
above the population mean on a self-report communication
apprehension measure (the PRCA-24) were selected for study.
Using this method meant students in the experimental and control groups who were selected would have roughly equivalent
apprehension levels, and, more importantly, any ethical violations would be avoided. The results of the study indicated that
the Reticence Program was more effective in reducing self-reported shyness and communication apprehension than either a performance-based speaking course or a control group. The results
were quite consistent across the three dependent measures
(PRCA-24, SHY scale, and Social Reticence scale).

Similar to Oerkvitz (1975), Kelly (1992) assessed the long-
term effects of rhetoritherapy by mailing a questionnaire to people who had participated in the PSU Reticence Program. Of the
100 questionnaires that were returned (a return rate of 64%),
91% of respondents reported they had improved their communication skills by the end of the program and 87% reported continuing positive benefits. Respondents reported greater confidence,
less fear of communication, improvement in their communication
skills, and more control over behavior in communication situations as results of the program.

These studies taken as a whole suggest that rhetoritherapy is an effective way of reducing self-reported reticence, shyness,
and communication apprehension. Although the results from the
early studies must be taken with caution because of methodologi-
cal limitations (Glaser, 1981), the later studies strongly indicate
that the rhetoritherapy program at PSU is effective.

A substantial limitation of the studies just reviewed is that only one (Metzger, 1974) examined changes in behavior. The primary focus of rhetoritherapy is on the development of communication skills (Phillips, 1968, 1977, 1986); however, the majority of studies assessed the effectiveness of rhetoritherapy by comparing pretest to posttest scores on a measure of self-reported shyness or communication apprehension. Therefore, further research must be conducted to assess the extent to which rhetoritherapy modifies behavior.

Research on Other Skills-Training Programs

Research has been done on the effectiveness of several other skills-training programs designed to teach social interaction skills. The research on two of these programs is reviewed in this section.

Glaser, Biglan, and Dow (1983) tested the effectiveness of ST on comfort, behavior, and impact on others. Subjects were randomly assigned to one of two groups, skills training or self-monitor delay. Glaser et al. developed a program that taught subjects five interpersonal behaviors: complimenting, expressing agreement, asking questions, describing experiences similar to those of another person, and expressing opinions. Trainees selected for ST underwent a series of steps including direct instruction, modeling, self-monitoring, and covert rehearsal. Glaser et al. found that their skills-training program, in comparison to a self-monitor group, produced greater improvements in subjects' comfort, social behavior, and impact on others. Furthermore, these improvements, due to ST, were long lasting.

Another skills-training program, based on human relations training, was developed and tested by Alden and Cappe (1986). After reviewing the research literature on shyness and other related constructs, Alden and Cappe proposed four goals for ST: increase social monitoring skills, develop strategies for initiating intimate relationships, develop a social philosophy that stresses respect and sensitivity, and redirect self-focused attention to task-relevant information.

To accomplish these goals, Alden and Cappe developed a program based on four skills from the field of human relations training:

- Active listening: Participants learn how to listen for an underlying message, and display verbal and nonverbal behaviors that give positive feedback to the person speaking.

- Empathic responding: Participants learn how to discover the feelings underneath messages, as well as how to relate their understanding of the person's feelings.
- Communicating respect: Participants learn how to acknowledge differing opinions, and express contrary opinions without discounting the other person's opinion.
- Self-disclosure: Participants learn how to match the level of intimacy established by their conversational partner.

These four skills are actually learned in Phase 3 of the four-phase program. The first phase involves learning how to relax. In the second phase, participants are asked to identify the social situations in which they experience communication difficulties, and to rank these situations from least troubling to most troubling. The third phase consists of learning the four social skills already described. In the fourth and final phase, participants are asked to practice their newly developed communication skills in real-life situations.

Alden and Cappe (1986) found that subjects in their skills-training program reported several significant improvements including: increased participation in social activities, increased participation in more diverse social activities, feeling more comfortable in social activities, and feeling more satisfaction with social activities.

Reducing Public Speaking Anxiety

Besides treating interpersonal communication difficulties, ST has been used to reduce anxiety associated with public speaking. One early investigation of the effects of ST on speaking anxiety was conducted by Weissberg and Lamb (1977). They compared ST (outlining, rehearsal, limited delivery training) to both systematic desensitization (SD) and cognitive modification (CM) with SD. Although the results suggested that all three treatments reduced public speaking anxiety, only ST and CM significantly reduced behavioral correlates of anxiety. However, ST was not as effective as SD or CM in reducing general anxiety.

Fremouw and Zitter (1978) were also interested in comparing the effectiveness of treatment approaches. Specifically, they compared ST to cognitive modification-relaxation. The social

skills-training program of Fremouw and Zitter was more extensive than that of Weissberg and Lamb (1977), consisting of
speech organization; delivery training including rate, volume,
pitch, posture, eye contact, and gestures; and feedback sessions.

The results of their study indicated that ST was more
effective than CM in reducing self-reported speech anxiety; however, both were effective in reducing behavioral manifestations of
speech anxiety. Fremouw and Zitter (1978) also found that
although participants decreased their level of public speaking
anxiety, they did not improve in other communication situations.

Stacks and Stone (1984) investigated the effects of three
types of speech communication courses on public speaking anxiety. Specifically, they looked at courses in public speaking, group
discussion, and interpersonal communication. All three courses
required students to give an oral presentation. Results of the
study indicate that all three courses reduced communication
apprehension. However, these results must be taken with caution
because Stacks and Stone did not use a control group and, therefore, did not take into account statistical regression and other
sources of internal invalidity (Babbie, 1992).

Neer and Kircher (1989) tested whether or not the teaching of delivery skills was an effective way of reducing public
speaking anxiety. They compared two treatment groups: specific
delivery instruction and general delivery instruction. Subjects in
the specific delivery instruction group spent three class sessions
discussing delivery, including both paraverbal (pausing, inflection, emphasis, rate, and volume), and nonverbal skills (eye contact, gestures, facial expressions, and posture). In addition to a
discussion of delivery, subjects in the specific delivery instruction
group evaluated the delivery of videotaped models.

Subjects in the general delivery instruction group spent
one class discussing the role of delivery in public speaking.
Results of the study indicated that high apprehension students
benefited from specific delivery instruction.

The majority of studies testing whether or not ST reduces
public speaking anxiety did not measure individual skill acquisition. Without a measure of skills, it is impossible to say that ST
was responsible for reductions in public speaking anxiety. An
alternative explanation for reductions in anxiety might be that
subjects were repeatedly exposed to the public speaking situation, which served to neutralize their anxious response (a technique called *flooding*, discussed later).

Other Uses of ST

ST by peers. Fremouw and Harmatz (1975) found that a social skills program taught by peers also was effective in reducing speech anxiety. In their study, a student with high speech anxiety learned how to implement a skills-training program to speech anxious peers. Booth (1990) found that peer counselors trained in social skills can effectively reduce the level of shyness of college students.

Oral interpretation training. Researchers have assessed whether or not training in oral interpretation reduces public speaking problems (Mino, 1982; Rekert & Begnal, 1990; Zolten & Mino, 1981). Zolten and Mino found that subjects reacted positively to training in oral interpretation. However, in a study by Mino, subjects with oral interpretation training were not judged to be more skilled public speakers than subjects in a public speaking group. In contrast, Rekert and Begnal (1990), who compared the effects of various types of training on vocal delivery, found oral interpretation training significantly reduced vocal disfluencies. In short, evidence regarding the effects of oral interpretation training on public speaking skills is inconclusive.

Dating anxiety. A considerable body of research indicates that ST can be used effectively to treat dating anxiety (Bander, Steinke, Allen, & Moser, 1975; Cappe & Alden, 1986; Christensen & Arkowitz, 1974; Christensen, Arkowitz, & Anderson, 1975; Curran, 1977; Curran & Gilbert, 1975; MacDonald, Lindquist, Kramer, McGrath, & Rhyne, 1975; Martinson & Zerface, 1970; McGovern, Arkowitz, & Gilmore, 1975; Montgomery & Haemmerlie, 1986; Twentyman & McFall, 1975). For a review of the use of ST to reduce dating anxiety see Kelly (1984).

Unassertiveness. Researchers have found social skills training to be an effective way of reducing unassertive behavior (Hersen, Eisler, Miller, Johnson, & Pinkston, 1973; Kazdin, 1974; McFall & Lillesand, 1971; McFall & Marston, 1970; Wolpe & Fodor, 1977). For a review of the use of ST to reduce unassertive behavior see Cipani (1988); Delmater and McNamara (1986); Erin, Dignan, and Brown (1991); and Kelly (1984).

The literature shows that ST is an effective model for treating a wide variety of problems such as public speaking anxiety, interpersonal communication problems, dating anxiety and unassertiveness. Research supports the conclusion that the PSU Reticence Program, a skills deficit treatment approach, is effective. In general, studies of rhetoritherapy and other skills-training programs have relied on self-report of feelings and behavior and have not assessed behavioral changes directly. Future research needs to evaluate the degree of behavioral change trainees exhibit immediately after treatment and the longevity of that change.

REDUCING CONDITIONED ANXIETY

The second treatment model focuses on reducing conditioned anxiety. Anxiety-reducing techniques assume that individuals already possess the skills necessary to cope in communication situations (Glaser, 1981); however, anxiety inhibits their effective use of these skills. Conditioned anxiety treatments also assume that individuals with high levels of anxiety learned to associate a particular communication situation with psychological discomfort (anxiety). Because of the discomfort, the anxious individual tends to avoid communication situations. When the anxious individual avoids communicating, his or her level of anxiety decreases; subsequently, communication avoidance behavior is reinforced by a reduction in anxiety. These events form the following causal chain:

High $\longrightarrow$ Discomfort $\longrightarrow$ Avoidance
anxiety   behavior

The most widely used treatment technique for reducing speech anxiety is systematic desensitization (Hoffman & Sprague, 1982).

Systematic Desensitization

Systematic desensitization (SD) is a treatment designed to reduce anxiety associated with a particular stimulus (Wolpe, 1958). Although SD was not originally designed for the treatment of communication anxiety, it has been successfully used to reduce communication anxiety without much modification to Wolpe's original design.

The goal of SD is to inhibit the anxious response (Wolpe, 1958) to a specific communication situation. By inhibiting the response, individuals should be less anxious and, therefore, less likely to avoid the specific communication situation. In order to inhibit a negative response to a communication situation, anxious communicators follow an SD training process that typically includes the following three components:

- Learning how to relax through the use of progressive muscle relaxation (Jacobson, 1938)
- Constructing a hierarchy of relevant stimuli, organized from nonanxious communication situations (talking to a best friend on the phone) to extremely anxious communication situations (losing your notes before giving a televised speech; see Paul, 1966; Richmond & McCroskey, 1992)
- Learning to associate or "pair" the anxious communication situations with psychological comfort (relaxation)

In a typical SD program (Richmond & McCroskey, 1992), the facilitator overviews the SD process. The facilitator also might emphasize that participants do not have to take part in any communication activity (Richmond & McCroskey, 1992). After an overview, participants learn how to relax by tightening and relaxing major muscle groups throughout the body, such as the hands, shoulders, back, neck, and so on. If a person at any time feels tension, he or she is told to lift the index finger of the right hand.

Once participants have learned how to relax, they are asked to visualize a nonthreatening communication situation (such as talking to a good friend). If at any point a participant feels tension, the facilitator asks all participants to stop visualizing the communication situation, and the group goes back to muscle relaxation exercises. For the remaining portion of the SD program, participants work through the hierarchy of communication situations until they can visualize the most threatening communication situation without experiencing anxiety. For a step-by-step description of this process see Richmond and McCroskey (1992). For information regarding the implementation of an SD program see McCroskey (1972) and Barrick (1971).

Research investigating the effectiveness of SD shows that it is a successful way of reducing anxiety (Bander et al., 1975; Curran & Gilbert, 1975; McCroskey, 1972; McCroskey, Ralph, & Barrick, 1970; Myers, 1974; Paul, 1968; Paul & Shannon, 1966; Watson, 1988). Researchers have also investigated variations in the format of an SD program. Results indicate that SD can be used effectively with a tape recorder rather than a facilitator

(Lohr & McManus, 1975). Furthermore, watching others being treated for SD on videotape is nearly as effective as going through the actual treatment process (Weissberg, 1977).

Researchers also have studied how a participant's expectations of treatment influence its effectiveness (see Friedrich & Goss, 1984). Evidence suggests that a positive expectation might affect self-reports of anxiety (Hemme & Boor, 1976). Kirsch and Henry (1979) found that the participant's evaluation of the credibility of an SD program was significantly related to physiological manifestations of anxiety. Those who found an SD program credible, demonstrated fewer physiological manifestations of anxiety.

Flooding

Another way of treating an anxious response is to "flood" the participant with the anxiety provoking stimulus (e.g., public speaking) until the participant has extinguished or neutralized the anxious response. Out of all the treatment methods discussed in this chapter, *flooding*, also known as implosion therapy, is probably the least used treatment for reducing speech anxiety. Despite its infrequent use, research indicates that flooding is an effective way of treating anxiety disorders (Marshall, Gauthier, & Gordon, 1979).

Although SD and flooding are successful in the reduction of anxiety, Fremouw and Scott (1979) identified two problems with these treatment strategies. First, SD and flooding do not allow the therapist to explain why the treatment is effective in reducing anxiety. Second, once the treatment is over, the therapist can "suggest little more than relaxation practice" (p. 130). However, it is possible that SD and flooding can indirectly help the participant to develop coping statements (Friedrich & Goss, 1984) by changing the way he or she thinks about communicating.

NEGATIVE COGNITIVE APPRAISAL

As previously discussed, the key assumption of SD and flooding is that an individual has learned to associate a particular communication situation with anxiety. Negative cognitive appraisal techniques, on the other hand, assume that anxiety is caused by irrational thoughts about a particular communication situation. Whereas conditioned anxiety treatments (SD and flooding) adopt a stimulus-response (S-R) model, NCA treatments use a stimulus-process-response model, the emphasis resting on the thought processes of the individual. Changing the way people think about communication is thus the focus of negative cognitive appraisal treatment programs. A causal chain for NCA models might look like the following:

$$\text{Negative thoughts} \longrightarrow \text{High anxiety} \longrightarrow \text{Discomfort} \longrightarrow \text{Avoidance behavior}$$

Four methods for treating NCA are rational emotive therapy (RET), cognitive restructuring (CR), visualization, and positively biased interaction.

Rational Emotive Therapy

Rational emotive therapy, founded by Ellis (1962), focuses on the rational and problem-solving aspects of the anxiety disorder. The goal of RET is to replace irrational thoughts about communication with rational thoughts. Ellis identified 11 irrational beliefs that underscore emotional problems. The therapist's role in RET is to identify the irrational beliefs that cause an anxious response and challenge those beliefs until the client replaces irrational beliefs with rational ones.

RET as a treatment for speech anxiety can be summarized by the A-B-C model (Ellis & Greiger, 1977). An individual experiences an activating event (A of the A-B-C model) and subsequently forms beliefs (B) about the activating event that are either rational or irrational, yielding some consequence (C) such as anxiety. The therapist prompts the individual to challenge or dispute (D) the irrational beliefs and replace them with rational beliefs, bringing about both positive effects (E) and a new philosophy of communication.

For example, an individual might be confronted with speaking to a group of strangers (activating event). The individual believes that everyone must love him or her all the time or else he or she is a bad person (belief), and, therefore, the individual experiences anxiety as the result of this irrational thinking (consequence). The therapist challenges the irrational belief that "everyone must love me in order to be a good person," making statements such as, "It is not possible for everyone to love you because people have different opinions and points of view," or "It is impossible to please everyone" (dispute). The client subsequently replaces the irrational belief with a rational belief such as, "Rather than focusing my attention on the evaluations of another, I will concentrate on what I am saying" (effect).

Research suggests that RET is an effective way of treating speech anxiety. Initial studies by Karst and Trexler (1970) and Trexler and Karst (1972) found that RET was more effective at reducing public speaking anxiety than both attention-placebo and waiting list conditions. Meichenbaum, Gilmore, and Fedoravicius (1971) found that group insight treatment (a derivative of RET) was as effective as desensitization in reducing speech anxiety.

Watson and Dodd (1984) compared three types of treatments: RET, SD, and ST. The results suggested that all three techniques produce a significant decrease in self-reported shyness. However, none of the techniques was clearly superior to the rest. Ayers and Hopf (1987) also found that RET was as effective as SD for treating communication apprehension. In short, research consistently shows that RET is an effective way of reducing anxiety.

Cognitive Restructuring

Another way of treating irrational thoughts is CR. Similar to RET, CR (Meichenbaum, 1976) focuses on the thinking processes of the individual. However, CR differs from RET by helping the individual to develop coping statements rather than by replacing irrational thoughts with rational ones. Because CR focuses on the development of coping statements, the therapist is not required to challenge the irrational thoughts of participants (Fremouw & Scott, 1979).

Fremouw and Scott envision cognitive restructuring as a four-step process:

Step 1. The first duty of the trainer is to explain the process of CR. The trainer states that negative self-statements cause people to fear communication situations. One way to combat this problem is to replace the negative self-statements with coping statements. The trainer explains that participants will identify negative self-statements, learn how to use coping statements, and practice coping statements.

Step 2. In Step 2 the trainer teaches the participant how to identify negative self-statements. In discussion the trainer identifies several negative self-statements and asks participants to add other negative self-statements they have heard. Once a series of statements has been generated, the trainer discusses the consequences of negative self-statements.

Step 3. In Step 3 participants learn coping statements that can be used before, during, and after a communication situation. Before communicating, the participant might replace negative self-statements with coping statements such as, "Speak slowly and I'll be fine," or "We're all equals here." During a conversation, participants might use coping statements like, "This is a little easier than last time," or "I was a little anxious, but now I've calmed down." After the conversation the participant uses coping statements like, "It was not a big deal," or "Each time it will get easier."

Step 4. The final step is to practice the coping statements through the use of role-playing exercises and small group discussion. Participants are asked to discuss topics that are controversial. They are encouraged to practice coping statements between training sessions and to keep a diary that details their experiences.

There is some dispute over which component of CR is most responsible for its effectiveness. Some researchers suggest that learning coping statements is the key to CR (Glogower, Fremouw, & McCroskey, 1978), whereas others suggest that insights into the role of maladaptive self-statements is most responsible for its effectiveness (Thorpe, Amatu, Blakey, & Burns, 1976).

Although there is dispute over which component of CR is most responsible for its effectiveness, research clearly indicates that CR is an effective way of treating communication problems (Fremouw, 1984). Specifically, evidence suggests that CR is as effective as ST in decreasing self-reported and behavioral anxiety (Elder, Edelstein, & Fremouw, 1981; Fremouw & Zitter, 1978). CR is also more effective than SD in reducing both irrational beliefs and anxiety levels (Kanter & Goldfried, 1979).

Visualization

Standard visualization. Another way of reducing negative thoughts is through visualization. Visualization (Assagioli, 1973, 1976) is closely related to SD. As discussed previously, the third step in SD is visualizing several anxiety-provoking situations and associating these situations with a state of relaxation. In a visualization program participants are asked to "imagine performing some action successfully" (Ayres & Hopf, 1985, p. 319). Visualization, unlike SD, focuses on positive thinking. Ayers and Hopf noted that the use of visualization as a strategy for reducing communication apprehension is quite similar to the visualization techniques used by athletes to improve their performance.

In a typical visualization program (Ayers & Hopf, 1989), subjects are first taught how to relax, and then guided through a visualization narrative, typically a visualization of the day on which they will give a speech. The visualization starts with getting up in the morning and proceeds through giving of the speech. At each visualization step, participants are asked to visualize positive images. For example, the trainer presents the positive image of waking up in the morning with high energy and confidence. The trainer also asks participants to visualize giving an excellent speech.

Research indicates that visualization is an effective way of reducing public speaking anxiety. Ayers and Hopf (1985) found that visualization, in addition to a public speaking class, was more effective at reducing self-reported anxiety than a public speaking class alone. Research also indicates that the positive effects of visualization are long lasting (Ayers & Hopf, 1990). In comparing visualization, SD, and RET, Ayers and Hopf (1987) found that all three treatment modes were effective in reducing communication apprehension, but the differences in effectiveness between the three treatments were not statistically significant. Ayers and Hopf asserted that there is no significant difference between treatments (SD, RET, and visualization), and that visualization is easier to implement than other techniques. Therefore, Ayers and Hopf concluded that a visualization program might be superior to other treatments in situations where time and resources are limited.

Performance visualization. Ayers and Hopf (1992) developed an alternative method for visualization designed to improve performance as well as reduce anxiety levels. They reported that performance visualization is similar to standard visualization, except that it includes additional steps: (a) visualizing a conversation with a close friend, (b) watching a video clip of an outstanding speaker (focusing on the speaker's delivery), (c) making a "mental movie" of the outstanding speaker, and (d) visualizing themselves giving a speech as well as the outstanding speaker.

To assess the effectiveness of performance visualization, Ayers and Hopf (1992) compared three experimental groups: performance visualization, standard visualization, and control group. Results indicated that both forms of visualization, standard and performance, reduced both anxiety and negative thinking. However, performance visualization was more effective than either standard visualization or the control group in reducing physical manifestations of anxiety (disfluency, rigidity, and inhibition). Although more research is needed to assess the consistency and general applicability of these results, performance visualization appears to be a relatively simple treatment procedure that yields cognitive, affective, and behavioral change.

Positively Biased Interaction Techniques

Haemmerlie and Montgomery (1986) developed a treatment methodology based on the theory of self-perception (Bem, 1972). The theory of self-perception asserts that a person's attitudes and emotions are derived from thoughts regarding his or her behavior. That is, beliefs and feelings are shaped by perceptions of behavior. According to this theory, people must change the way they act to change the way they feel.

This approach is in direct contrast to other approaches such as SD and flooding, because self-perception theory asserts that changes in behavior result in changes in attitude rather than changes in attitude resulting in changes in behavior. As Hammerlie and Montgomery asserted:

> Instead of assuming a reduction in fear results in an increase in approach behavior and a decrease in avoidance behavior, as a more traditional model might do, self-perception theory instead suggests the opposite. An increase in approach behavior and/or a decrease in avoidance behavior might cause a decrease in perceived anxiety. (p. 329)

To treat shyness, Haemmerlie and Montgomery (1986) suggested positively biased social interactions. For example, in one study the shy subjects participated in a series of six, 10- to 12-minute positive interactions with a member of the opposite gender. In order to ensure a positive interaction, members of the opposite gender (confederates) were selected based on their "ability to carry on a pleasant conversation" (p. 332). Confederates were told to "initiate conversation topics and to be as friendly and natural as possible" (p. 332); however, confederates were not told the nature of the investigation.

Results indicate that the positively biased interaction technique is an effective way of reducing anxiety (Haemmerlie, 1983; Haemmerlie & Montgomery, 1982, 1984). The treatment effects were long lasting, and subjects reported that they enjoyed participating in the research.

However, using a positively biased interaction technique to test the applicability of self-perception theory is problematic. According to the theory of self-perception, changing a person's behavior (increasing approach behavior) will result in a reduction of anxiety. Therefore, if a person interacts with a person who is unfriendly, his or her level of anxiety should still decrease because of the increase in approach behavior. Because Hammerlie and Montgomery (1986) used confederates that were friendly and initiated conversation topics, it is quite possible that the subjects' perception of the consequences of communication lowered their levels of anxiety rather than their perceptions of behavior.

For example, John has found that almost every time he communicates, something goes wrong. Over time, John has developed an anxious response to communication because of negative consequences. John then goes through a positively biased interaction program in which he communicates with a person who is friendly and shows interest in talking with him (maintains the conversation by initiating new topics). John begins to learn that communicating does not necessarily lead to negative consequences and, therefore, his level of anxiety concerning communication decreases. This explanation is just as feasible as the explanation offered by self-perception theory.

In order to test the central premise of this theory, four experimental groups should be compared: positive interaction, positive and negative interaction, negative interaction, and control. If the theory of self-perception holds true, then highly anxious subjects in the first three treatment groups (increased approach behavior) should experience decreases in anxiety levels.

In short, four methods for reducing negative cognitive appraisal were reviewed. Each of these strategies shows significant ability to reduce self-reported anxiety.

Combination Techniques

As studies indicated that a variety of techniques reduce apprehension, scholars started to investigate the effects of multiple treatments. For example, Worthington, Tipton, Cromley, Richards, and Janke (1981) found that the combination of coping skills and ST was more effective in reducing anxiety than SD or ST alone. Newhouse and Spooner (1982) tested a treatment program that used both SD and rhetoritherapy. Multiple measures indicated that this combination treatment was superior to regular classroom instruction.

Watson and Dodd (1984) compared three types of treatment: ST and RET, ST and SD, and ST. They found that all three groups reported significant decreases; however, one type of treatment was not significantly better than another.

Allen et al. (1989) used meta-analysis to assess the relative effectiveness of treatments of public speaking anxiety. Meta-analysis is a technique that allows for statistical comparisons across research studies. Allen et al. (1989) compared the effectiveness of seven combinations of treatments: ST, SD, CM, ST+SD, ST+CM, SD+CM, and ST+SD+CM. Perhaps the most important result of the review was that the use of two or more treatment models (e.g., ST and CM) is more effective than one treatment model in reducing public speaking anxiety. Furthermore, there is tentative evidence suggesting that the use of all three treatment models (ST, SD, and CM) is the most effective treatment strategy for reducing public speaking anxiety (Allen et al., 1989).

SUMMARY AND SUGGESTIONS FOR FUTURE RESEARCH

The many treatment strategies for treating communication problems (e.g., rhetoritherapy, SD, flooding, visualization, RET, etc.) can be summarized by three treatment models (skills deficit, conditioned anxiety, and negative cognitive appraisal). Treatment models can be differentiated by the assumptions made concerning the causes of communication difficulties. The skills deficit model assumes that a lack of social skills causes communication problems such as anxiety. Another treatment model assumes that individuals have learned to associate communication with anxiety and that anxiety inhibits the use of effective communication skills (conditioned anxiety). A third treatment model assumes that negative or irrational thoughts cause anxiety, which also inhibits the use of effective communication skills (negative cognitive appraisal).

Although the treatment models adopt different assumptions and strategies, a substantial body of research indicates that all three treatment models significantly reduce self-reported reticence, communication apprehension, and the like. Research also indicates that combinations of treatment strategies are superior to single strategies in treating communication problems. Although the research indicates that a variety of treatment strategies helps to solve communication problems, more research is needed in critical areas.

Subject by Treatment Interactions

Researchers have made many suggestions concerning directions for future research (Curran, 1977; Friedrich & Goss, 1984; Glaser, 1981; Kelly, 1984; Page, 1980). Glaser suggested that some people will respond to certain types of treatment better than others because of differences in communication difficulties (subject X treatment interaction). For example, a person with negative thoughts might not respond as well to ST as a person lacking in skills. To test the effects of the subject by treatment interaction, researchers need to complete two steps: fully assess the communication difficulties of participants in a treatment program, and expose people with certain communication problems to a variety of treatment strategies.

One way of completing the first step is to develop instrumentation that assesses the general types of individual communication problems. Are the problems cognitive (negative thoughts), affective (anxiety), behavioral (lack of skills), or some combination of the three? Assuming that all participants in a treatment program have similar communication problems is erroneous, yet few programs formally assess participants for multiple communication problems. Most programs admit participants based on a single measure of communication problems (skills deficit, anxiety, negative thoughts). One way of solving this evaluation problem is to develop instrumentation that assesses multiple communication problems. Researchers could then assess the communication problems of the participants in a treatment program and determine the effectiveness of the treatment for certain types of individuals.

Isolating Treatment Components

Most treatment programs consist of more than one treatment component. For example, rhetoritherapy includes an ST component and a CM component (Phillips, 1986), and cognitive therapy may include an SD component (Glaser, 1981). Therefore, research indicating that a treatment strategy is effective is not very specific. For example, finding that rhetoritherapy is an effective treatment strategy does not indicate which component or set of components are most responsible for its effectiveness. Formal investigations need to isolate and assess the relative contributions of treatment components. Isolating treatment components also will allow for more accurate comparisons across research studies.

Multifaceted Assessment of Treatment

Although some researchers have assessed cognitive, affective, and behavioral improvements, most studies have concentrated on the reduction of self-reported anxiety (Glaser, 1981). Research needs to assess the effects of treatment on thoughts, feelings, and behaviors. Furthermore, the effects of treatment need to be assessed both outside the laboratory and over an extended period of time (Glaser, 1981; Kelly, 1984).

Experimental Bias

Because of interactions with subjects during a treatment program, it is likely that experimenters unintentionally influence the results of their research (Rosenthal, 1977). Research is needed to assess the influence of the researcher-subject interaction. Here is a discussion of some ways that researchers might influence the results of their research.

Researchers can unintentionally give cues that demand certain behaviors or responses of participants in a treatment program (Rosenthal & Rosnow, 1969). Research must be conducted into the effect of "demand cues" on self-reports. It is also possible that people who avoid communication are more likely to respond to demand cues because of their fear of negative evaluation or negative consequences. Reporting to an authority figure (the researcher) that a treatment program is ineffective is a tension-filled communication situation that many reticent or apprehensive individuals might avoid.

In addition to demand cues, the very fact that participants chose to participate in a treatment program might bias their evaluation of the program. Cialdini (1984) stated that "Once we have made a choice or taken a stand, we will encounter personal and interpersonal pressures to behave consistently with that commitment. Those pressures will cause us to respond in ways that justify our earlier decision" (p. 66). In this case, the choice or stand Cialdini referred to would be to participate in a treatment program. Once the decision to participate in a program has been made, participants act in ways that reinforce their decision, and form positive expectations of the program. Positive expectations would very likely bias their assessment of the program (Rosenthal, 1969, 1977). If a participant did not form positive expectations of the program, then his or her attitudes (this program is ineffective) would contradict the person's actions (choosing to participate), placing the person in the uncomfortable state of cognitive dissonance. To remove the uncomfortable state of cognitive dissonance, the participant has two options: change his or her attitudes toward the treatment program (this program is effective), or drop out of the treatment program. No matter the option taken, those participants who complete the treatment program would have positive attitudes toward it.

Another factor that might influence the evaluation of the program is the use of *positive feedback by an authority*. If an experimenter in a position of authority continually tells participants that they are improving, they are likely to believe him or her. This process is known as the pygmalion effect (Rosenthal & Jacobson, 1968). Furthermore, the fact that an authority figure is telling them that they are improving might amplify the pygmalion effect. Studies show that a person in the position of authority has considerable influence over the behavior of an individual (Cialdini, 1984).

It is important to note that filling out a self-report instrument is an evaluated behavior, and responses do not necessarily reflect the attitude of the respondent. That is, reports of the effectiveness of a treatment program by a participant might be significantly influenced by both the amount and type of feedback given from the experimenter.

Many issues surrounding the effectiveness of programs designed to alleviate communication problems need to be investigated. Researchers need to assess thoroughly the communication problems of participants in their treatment programs, isolate effective treatment components, and assess the role of experimenter bias. In doing so, programs can be revised and refined so that those who suffer from communication problems will have more effective and efficient treatment alternatives.

APPENDIX A
SAMPLE SYLLABUS

SPCOM 100: SPECIAL SECTION SYLLABUS

TEXTS: Kelly, L. & Watson, A.K. (1986). *Speaking with confidence and skill.* Lanham, MD: University Press of America.
Kougl, K. (1988). *Primer for public speaking.* New York: Harper & Row.

INTRODUCTION

This section of Speech Comm 100 is designed for intensive work in communication situations in which you feel your performance needs to be improved. This course is not a means by which you can avoid speaking situations that you find difficult and uncomfortable. On the contrary, it is a course designed to teach you the skills that you need to perform effectively in most speaking situations. Course assignments require that you practice the skills you are taught both within and outside of the classroom. The syl-

labus is quite flexible because the course is tailored to your individual needs. Once I get to know you and your communication
strengths and weaknesses, we can work together on an individual basis to determine what specific assignments you should
complete during the course.

The following communication concepts will be covered:

1. *The Context*: How do time and place shape behavior in a
    communication situation?
2. *The Goal*: What specifically do you want to accomplish
    through talk?
3. *The Sayables*: What can you talk about in a given situa-
    tion?
4. *The Order*: How do you structure (organize) messages?
5. *The Practice*: How do you rehearse before entering a
    speaking situation?
6. *The Evaluation*: Did you achieve your goal? How can you
    improve in your next attempt?

REQUIREMENTS

1. Conference with the instructor.
    Each of you will meet with me in my office for a 15- to
    20-minute conference. The purpose of the conference is
    to discuss your communication strengths and weak-
    nesses, your goals for the course, and to get you started
    on your first assignment. Sign-up for the conferences
    will be held today. I would like to try to complete all con-
    ferences before the end of the week.

2. Self-as-Communicator Paper 1.
    When you come in for the conference, you are to bring a
    paper in which you discuss your communication
    strengths and weaknesses, your goals for the course,
    and so forth. Tell me in what ways you are not satisfied
    with your communication and how you would like to
    improve. We will use this paper as the basis for our con-
    ference discussion. The paper is designed to get you to
    think specifically about these matters before you meet
    with me. The paper will not be graded but it is required.

3. Self-as-Communicator Paper 2.
    At the end of the course you will turn in a paper in
    which you discuss the ways that you have improved as

a communicator, areas in which you feel you still need improvement, etc. This paper is not graded but must be handed in. It will not be read until final grades have been submitted to the Registrar.

4. Exams.
There will be a midterm and final exam on course content and reading. The date of the midterm is on the attached schedule of classes and the final exam will be at the regularly scheduled exam time.

5. Quiz.
There will be one quiz on goal analysis very early in the semester. The date for the quiz is on the attached schedule.

6. Goals.
A. You are required to complete three out-of-class goals from the following categories unless waived by the instructor:
1. Social conversation: initiating and maintaining conversations in a variety of settings; talking to persons in authority, etc.
2. Group discussion: class participation, small group problem solving, committee work, etc.
3. Interviewing: job interviews, appraisal interviews, internship interviews, etc.
4. Public speaking: speeches, technical reports, etc.

B. You are required to complete two in-class goals, one of which must be an individual public speech. Other possibilities include:
1. Oral interpretation: performing a piece of literature (reading it aloud to the class).
2. Group oral presentation.

NOTE: At the conference you and I will negotiate how many goals you should do from the different categories based on your needs.

7. Goal Analysis and Report Papers.
For each goal that you complete, both in and out of class, you need to hand in two papers. The specific format of these papers will be given to you in class.

a. Goal analysis paper: turned in and approved before you complete your goal.
b. Goal report paper: turned in after you complete your goal.

8. Group Activity.
    Each of you will be involved in a group project. You will be assigned to a group and will be given a task. Your group will prepare one paper to be handed in. Details will be presented in class.

9. Attendance and Due Dates.
    Attendance is required. This is a performance course, and there will be a lot of activity in class that requires your participation. If you miss more than three classes, your final grade will be lowered. If a goal analysis is not turned in and approved and returned to you before you complete the goal, it will not count as a completed assignment. Late papers will not be accepted.

GRADING

You are guaranteed a "C" in class if you do the following:

1. Three satisfactory out-of-class goals.
2. Two satisfactory in-class goals, at least one of which is a speech.
3. Miss no more than three classes.
4. Turn in both self-as-communicator papers.
5. Get satisfactory grades on the tests and quiz.
6. Do a satisfactory job on the group assignment.

To get a higher grade in the course, you need to complete more goals, get above average grades on the tests, and do a thorough job on the goal analysis and report papers.

APPENDIX B
PREDISPOSITIONS
TOWARD VERBAL
COMMUNICATION SCALE*

All of us have certain images or impressions of ourselves. Some of these inner mental pictures relate to matters of our body image, personality, physical appearance, role style, mannerisms, and the like. This task involves social images, namely the way you see yourself reacting to face-to-face encounters with others. More specifically, we are interested in the image or impression you have of your speech communication; that is, the picture you have of your own verbal behavior.

In the following items, we are asking you to describe your conception of the way you tend to express yourself orally to others. Do not think of what you might happen to say or do to a given individual in a particular type of social situation but rather concentrate on the larger picture you have of your verbal behavior in social situations generally.

Please do not spend too much time on the following items. Try to answer as honestly as possible. All answers will be strictly confidential.

There is no right or wrong answer. Some questions will be difficult to answer because you honestly do not know. On those questions, however, please try to determine which way you are leaning and answer in the appropriate direction.

The following scale is used: YES! = very strong agreement with the statement; YES = strong agreement with the statement; yes = mild agreement with the statement; ? = don't know or neutral feelings about the statement; no = mild disagreement with the statement; NO = strong disagreement with the statement; NO! = very strong disagreement with the statement.

For example, if you agree strongly with the following statement, you would circle "YES."

Wisconsin winters are too cold. YES! YES yes ? no NO NO!

SCORING KEY:

*1. I am inclined to let other people   YES! YES yes ? no NO NO!
     start conversations.

2.   I have a tendency to dominate   YES! YES yes ? no NO NO!
     informal conversations with other
     people.

3.   When I am with other people I   YES! YES! yes ? no NO NO!
     generally talk often.

4.   In most social situations I tend to   YES! YES yes ? no NO NO!
     direct the course of conversation.

*5. When I am with others it generally   YES! YES yes ? no NO NO!
     takes me quite a while to warm up
     enough to say very much.

* 6. I generally rely on others to keep   YES! YES yes ? no NO NO!
     conversations going.

7.   In most social situations I general- YES! YES yes ? no NO NO!
     ly speak quite frequently.

* 8. I tend to hesitate when I speak.   YES! YES yes ? no NO NO!

* 9. I generally prefer to listen rather   YES! YES yes ? no NO NO!
     than to speak.

10. In most social situations I tend to   YES! YES yes ? no NO NO!
     come on strong.

*11. I find myself pausing often when I   YES! YES yes ? no NO NO!
     speak.

12. I am inclined to jump into infor-   YES! YES yes ? no NO NO!
     mal conversations.

*13. I tend to feel inhibited when I talk YES! YES yes ? no NO NO!
     to others.

14. I generally find that I express myself quite freely.   YES! YES yes ? no NO NO!

15. I try to take charge of things when I am with people.   YES! YES yes ? no NO NO!

*16. I often don't express my views in normal conversations with others.   YES! YES! yes ? no NO NO!

17. I would describe myself as dominant in social situations.   YES! YES yes ? no NO NO!

18. When I am with others I am inclined to talk forcefully.   YES! YES yes ? no NO NO!

*19. I have a tendency to let other people determine the course of conversation.   YES! YES yes ? no NO NO!

20. In one-to-one conversations I tend to talk more than half the time.   YES! YES yes ? no NO NO!

21. In most social situations I tend to speak for long periods of time.   YES! YES yes ? no NO NO!

*22. I am inclined to let other people talk for long periods of time.   YES! YES yes ? no NO NO!

*23. I prefer to keep my comments brief.   YES! YES yes ? no NO NO!

*24. I probably speak for shorter periods of time than the average person.   YES! YES yes ? no NO NO!

*25. In most social situations I am inclined to let other people get in the last word.   YES! YES yes ? no NO NO!

Items are scored: YES! = 7, YES = 6, yes = 5, ? = 4, no = 3, NO = 2, NO! = 1. Starred items indicate reverse scoring.

*See Mortensen, D.C., Arnston, P.H., & Lustig, M. (1977). The measurement of verbal predispositions: Scale development and application. *Human Communication Research, 3,* 146-158.

APPENDIX C
PRCA-24 SCALE*

Directions: This instrument is composed of 24 statements concerning your feelings about communication with other people. Please indicate in the space provided the degree to which each statement applies to you by marking whether you (1) Strongly Agree, (2) Agree, (3) Are Undecided, (4) Disagree, or (5) Strongly Disagree with each statement. Please put the number of your response (from 1 to 5) in the space. There are no right or wrong answers. Many of the statements are similar to other statements. Do not be concerned about this. Work quickly; just record your first impression.

———— 1. I dislike participating in group discussions.
———— 2. Generally, I am comfortable while participating in a group discussion.
———— 3. I am tense and nervous while participating in group discussions.
———— 4. I like to get involved in group discussions.
5. Engaging in a group discussion with new people

259

_____   makes me tense and nervous.

6. I am calm and relaxed while participating in group
_____   discussions.

7. Generally, I am nervous when I have to participate
_____   in a meeting.

8. Usually, I am calm and relaxed while participating
_____   in meetings.

9. I am very calm and relaxed when I am called upon
_____   to express an opinion at a meeting.

10. I am afraid to express myself at meetings.

_____11. Communicating at meetings usually makes me
_____   uncomfortable.

12. I am very relaxed when answering questions at a
_____   meeting.

13. While participating in a conversation with a new
_____   acquaintance, I feel very nervous.

14. I have no fear of speaking up in conversations.

_____15. Ordinarily I am very tense and nervous in conver-
_____   sations.

16. Ordinarily I am very calm and relaxed in conversa-
_____   tions.

17. While conversing with a new acquaintance, I feel
_____   very relaxed.

18. I'm afraid to speak up in conversations.

_____19. I have no fear of giving a speech.

_____20. Certain parts of my body feel very tense and rigid
_____   while giving a speech.

21. I feel relaxed while giving a speech.

_____22. My thoughts become confused and jumbled when I
_____   am giving a speech.

23. I face the prospect of giving a speech with confi-
_____   dence.

24. While giving a speech I get so nervous, I forget facts
_____   I really know.

*See Richmond, V.P., & McCrosky, J.C. (1992). *Communication: Apprehension, avoidance, and effectiveness* (3rd ed.). Scottsdale, AZ: Gorsuch Scarisbrick.

APPENDIX D
SOCIAL RETICENCE
SCALE*

Directions: Please respond to the following questions by indicating the extent to which they are true or typical of you, using the following format:

> 5 — Very typical of me
> 4 — Somewhat typical of me
> 3 — Sometimes true, sometimes not true of me
> 2 — Somewhat atypical of me
> 1 — Very atypical of me

———— 1. I frequently have difficulties in meeting new people.
———— 2. I frequently feel depressed or sad.
———— 3. I have a hard time expressing my opinions to others.
———— 4. Even my friends don't seem to know me very well.
———— 5. Many people apparently think that I am unfriendly.
———— 6. It is difficult for me to think clearly in the presence of others.

_____ 7. I am very self-conscious.

_____ 8. It is difficult for me to make new friends.

_____ 9. I frequently feel isolated from other people.

_____ 10. I have difficulty being assertive, even when it is appropriate or I need to be.

_____ 11. Most people don't know what I am really like.

_____ 12. Many people may think I'm snobbish or bored because I'm not more outgoing.

_____ 13. It is difficult for me to know what to say in a group.

_____ 14. Frequently I am preoccupied with my own feelings and reactions.

_____ 15. I frequently avoid or don't enjoy potentially good experiences.

_____ 16. I often feel lonely.

_____ 17. I usually keep quiet in groups, even when I have something to say.

_____ 18. Even many of my friends don't know any of my true assets.

_____ 19. I'm afraid many people think I am weak.

_____ 20. I often have difficulty in communicating effectively.

_____ 21. I wish that I wasn't so sensitive to my own thoughts and feelings.

_____ 22. Basically I am a shy person.

*See Jones, W.H., & Russell, D. (1982). The social reticence scale: An objective instrument to measure shyness. *Journal of Personality Assessment, 46*, 628-631.

APPENDIX E
BEHAVIORAL
ASSESSMENT OF
SPEECH ANXIETY
(BASA)*

Observers rate speakers on each of the following variables, which are potential indicators of speech anxiety.

Voice

        Quivering or tense voice
        Too fast
        Too soft
        Monotonous, lack of emphasis

Verbal fluency

        Nonfluencies, stammers, halting
        Vocalized pauses
        Hunts for words, speech blocks

Mouth and throat
    Swallows
    Clears throat
    Breathes heavily

Facial Expression
    Lack of eye contact, extraneous eye movements
    Tense face muscles, grimaces, twitches
    "Deadpan" facial expression

Arms and hands
    Rigid or tense
    Fidgeting, extraneous movement
    Motionless, lack of appropriate gestures

Gross bodily movement
    Sways, paces, shuffles feet

Overall
    Overall anxiety estimate

*See Mulac, A., & Sherman, A.R. (1974). Behavioral assessment of speech anxiety. *Quarterly Journal of Speech, 60,* 134-143.

APPENDIX F
OPTION D (PSU
RETICENCE PROGRAM)
HANDOUT

<u>Speech Communication 100: Option D</u>

Option D is an emphasis of Speech Communication 100 established to assist students who have special communication needs. It is designed to work directly on specific problems in communication within academic and social settings. In Option D, students are expected to set individual goals to accomplish communication tasks which they have heretofore been reluctant to try and unable to do. Check the following kinds of communicative concerns:

1. You may have difficulty asking questions in class and participating in class discussions. You may be reluctant to strike up acquaintances with classmates.

2. You may shy away from speaking to professors after class and avoid office conferences.

3. You may feel apprehensive at employment interviews and uncertain about how to communicate on the job with your boss and fellow employees.

4. You may be uneasy about committee work and feel that you don't contribute your fair share in group problem-solving discussions.

5. You may have difficulty meeting strangers and opening up new friendships. In social situations, you may find yourself a non-participant on the fringe of the group.

6. You may be unusually troubled, feel physically ill, shake, or sweat when you have to present formal reports in public situations.

7. You may experience difficulty with shyness.

If you feel any or all of these communication concerns are yours and if you wish to work specifically on solving them, you are eligible for an interview for Option D. IF YOU ARE IN DOUBT ABOUT WHETHER OR NOT YOU HAVE SPECIAL COMMUNICA-TION NEEDS, COME FOR THE INTERVIEW. There is no obligation to enter Option D; it is entirely voluntary. However, you cannot enroll in Option D without an interview.

Interviews are confidential and will be conducted in Room 225 Sparks any time between 9:00 a.m. and 4:00 p.m. on Thursday (date) and Friday (date), and between 9:00 a.m. and noon on Monday (date). The interviewer will discuss your communicative needs with you, and the two of you will decide whether or not Option D can be useful to you. If you elect to enter Option D, your transfer will be automatic; you will not need to go through a drop-add procedure.

APPENDIX G
FORCED-CHOICE
EXERCISE

Below are several statements about human communication. The task for your group is to read each item, discuss it, and try to reach consensus as to whether you: **SA** (strongly agree), **A** (agree), **D** (disagree), or **SD** (strongly disagree).

_____ 1. Communication is the process by which we form our self-concepts.

_____ 2. Good communicators always speak spontaneously.

_____ 3. Communication skills cannot be taught; you either have them or you don't.

_____ 4. Being a good listener is much more important than being a good speaker.

_____ 5. The most effective communicators are people who can adapt to their "audience" and the situation.

_____ 6. Being a good communicator has little to do with achieving your goals in this world.

_____ 7. It is only through the process of communication that we are able to build close relationships with others.

_____ 8. Nervousness about speaking is a normal part of the process.

APPENDIX H
GOAL ANALYSIS
PREPARATION SHEET

STEP 1:

     State your end goal in a single sentence. (Be sure to include who your audience will be and how long the goal will last.)

STEP 2:

     List your criteria for success of this goal. Describe the performances that you would have to see happen in order to agree that the goal had been accomplished. "I will know that I have accomplished my goal when I have done the following:"

STEP 3:

     Give details of the goal:
     a. When will you attempt the goal?
     b. Where will you attempt the goal?
     c. What is it that you want to accomplish by talking to this person?

d. Why did you select this person to talk to?

e. Is there anything special you must do because of the communication context?

f. Is there anything special you should avoid because of the communication context?

STEP 4:

Give details for preparation and practice:

a. List the activities necessary to prepare and practice.

b. Describe how you will start your goal.

c. Describe how you will progress with your goal. What behaviors will you engage in as you carry out your goal?

d. How will you end your goal?

STEP 5:

Try to account for possible outcomes of your goal.

a. What's one possible positive response you could get? What will you do if you get it?

b. What's one negative response you could get? What will you do if you get it?

c. What's the most likely response you will get? What will you do if you get it?

d. If something goes wrong, when would it be your fault? the other person's fault? the fault of circumstances?

APPENDIX I
GOAL REPORT
FORMAT SHEET

STEP 1:

    State your end goal.

STEP 2:

    Describe what happened when you tried to carry out the goal.

    a. How did you begin?

    b. How did you proceed from there?

    c. How did the audience react?

    d. How did you adjust to audience response?

    e. How did you end your goal?

STEP 3:

    Evaluate your success.

    a. How do you think it went? Were you successful? Why or why not?

    b. If you were unsuccessful, was it your fault, the fault

of the other, or the fault of circumstances? (Explain)

c. Did you achieve all of the performances that you had listed as criteria for success? Which ones did you achieve?

d. Would you do anything differently if you were to do the goal again? Are there any specific performances you would like to improve? How do you intend to improve them?

STEP 4:

Are there any additional comments you would like to make?

APPENDIX J
SAMPLE GOAL
ANALYSIS FOR SOCIAL
CONVERSATION

I. END GOAL:

> I will have a 5-minute conversation with a stranger at a Halloween party.

II. CRITERIA FOR SUCCESS:

> A. The conversation will last at least 5 minutes.
> B. I will contribute about 50% of the conversation.
> C. I will maintain about 50% eye contact while talking and 75% while listening.
> D. I will tell the other person my name and ask for his or hers.
> E. I will break pauses by bringing up a topic. I will do this for about half of the pauses that occur.

III. DETAILS OF THE GOAL:

A. My audience will be any stranger at the Halloween party.

B. I will attempt my goal on Friday, November 1.

C. My goal will take place at H.J.'s Halloween party, which will be held at his house.

D. My goal will last for at least 5 minutes.

E. I will be talking about the party, the costumes people are wearing, the costume my conversational partner is wearing, the music and activities at the party, then "safe" topics such as where the person is from, where I am from, etc.

F. My purpose for speaking is to develop my conversation skills, meet a new person, and have more fun at the party.

IV. DETAILS OF PREPARATION, PRACTICE, AND IMPLEMENTATION:

A. Preparation:

1. I will read the newspaper that morning so I am aware of what is going on in the area, the country, and internationally. This will help give me some possible topics of conversation.

2. I will think about some other possible topics such as where I got the idea for my costume, Halloween itself and trick-or-treating, upcoming events in Hartford, and so forth.

3. I will prepare a costume to wear to the party.

B. Practice:

For this goal, I will not need to practice as long as I spend time thinking about some possible topics and what I have to say about them.

C. Implementation:

1. I will start my goal by looking for someone who is standing alone but looking around.

2. I will approach the person and make a comment about his or her costume.

3. I will continue the conversation by bringing up topics I have thought of such as costumes, Halloween, the party, and so on.

4. I will indicate that I am interested in the conversation by nodding and smiling when I agree or understand.
5. I will make comments and ask questions about each topic we talk about.
6. I will end the conversation by using either a temporary or permanent closing.
—If I use a permanent closing, I will say, "It's been nice talking to you. I'm going to go get a refill. See you later."
—If I use a temporary closing, I will suggest getting together again for lunch or to play a game of tennis (or whatever activity I discovered we have in common during our conversation).

V. POSSIBLE OUTCOMES:

A. The best thing that could happen is that we talk for more than 5 minutes and end with a temporary closing. If this happens I'll let the other person know that I enjoyed meeting them and am looking forward to seeing them again.
B. The worst thing that could happen is that the person I approach might brush me off by saying he or she doesn't feel like talking or is waiting for someone so would I please leave them alone. If this happens, I will say, "Have a nice time at the party. I hope your friend shows up" or something to that effect.
C. The most likely outcome is that our conversation lasts for about 5 minutes and we end with a permanent closing.
D. If I do not accomplish my goal, it will be:
1. My fault if I do not think about possible topics or do not take the initiative to approach someone.
2. The other person's fault if he or she does not want to talk.
3. The fault of circumstances if I know everyone at the party or our conversation is interrupted by someone else.

APPENDIX K
SAMPLE AUDIENCE
AND SITUATION
ANALYSIS EXERCISE

<u>Directions</u>: Read the goal listed below and then answer each question. What would you do if you had to carry out this goal? Put yourself in the situation as you answer each question.

<u>Your Goal</u>: I will have a face-to-face conversation with the person I have been dating for 6 months in order to break off the relationship.

<u>Questions</u>:

1. Among the possible places for carrying out the goal, what place seems most suitable? Why?
2. Given the place that you listed above, explain how the place might influence what happens when you attempt

to carry our your goal. Are there any physical features or distractions that might have an impact?

3. Among the possible times for carrying out the goal, what time seems most suitable? Why?

4. How might the time of day affect what happens when you carry out this goal?

5. Are there any norms operating in the place you have chosen that might have an impact on how you carry out your goal?

6. Talk about some possible ways that the type of relationship you have had with this person may affect how you go about carrying out your goal.

7. What are some possible ways that the person might react to this discussion? How will you handle each one?

APPENDIX L
THE STANDARD
AGENDA*

PHASE 1: UNDERSTANDING THE CHARGE

I. Goals
    A. To figure out what our task is
    B. To determine how much authority we have as a group
    C. To identify what it is that we have to turn out and when
    D. To identify who is to get what we turn out
    E. To determine what that person(s) will do with it
II. Outcomes
    A. Questions addressed to a higher authority
    B. A written specification of the final task
    C. A record of our understanding of the task

*This material was adopted from a very excellent group discussion book by Julia T. Wood, Gerald M. Phillips, and Douglas J. Pedersen, *Group Discussion: A Practical Guide to Participation and Leadership* (2nd ed.), New York: Harper & Row, 1986. Used with permission.

III. Members' Tasks
   A. To raise questions about the nature of the group task
   B. To raise questions about personal responsibility to the group
   C. To raise questions to be addressed to higher authorities
   D. To raise questions about schedule or agenda
IV. Leaders' Obligations
   A. To raise necessary questions pertinent to understanding the task
   B. To transmit and interpret information from higher authorities
   C. To act as a liaison to higher authorities
   D. To insure that agreements and understandings of the group are written into the record

PHASE 2: UNDERSTANDING AND PHRASING THE QUESTION

I. Goals
   A. To agree on what the problem is
   B. To phrase a question specifying the problem that allows the maximum range of possible answers
   C. To agree on the type of question (fact, value, or policy)
   D. To agree on a focus (symptoms or causes)
II. Outcomes
   A. A precisely worded question to guide the group to the most appropriate solution
   B. A record of any symptoms and/or causes generated in the discussion
III. Members' Responsibilities
   A. To raise questions about the nature of the problem
   B. To register preliminary attitudes about the problem, its nature and its severity
   C. To offer information about the history and causes of the problem
   D. To point out what information is needed to begin to study the problem and to assist in obtaining it
   E. To make proposals about the wording of the question
IV. Leaders' Obligations
   A. To ascertain that all members understand the problem
   B. To guide members to tasks that they can perform that will equip them to participate in future phases of the discussion

C. To make sure that the group understands the cause-symptom issue and how it has been resolved

D. To make sure that the group understands the level of its discussion: fact, value, or policy

E. To make sure that group understandings are reflected in the wording of the question

F. To make sure the question is written into the record

G. To raise issues about operationalizing terms in the question

PHASE 3: FACT-FINDING

I. Goals

A. To gather factual information about the nature of the problem

B. To critically evaluate the factual information obtained

C. To revise the problem-question, if necessary, following factual analysis

II. Outcomes

A. A written fact sheet or listing of available information for all members

B. Optional: A recommendation on whether the discussion is to continue

C. Optional: rewording of the problem-question if necessary

III. Members' Tasks

A. To do research and gather information on the problem using libraries, polls, experiments, reading, interviewing; work is coordinated with others as directed or planned

B. To analyze information presented; to apply tests of evidence

C. To prepare, when necessary, individual positions or statements on the problem and share them

D. To order information into a coherent body of data that fully describes the problem

IV. Leaders' Obligations

A. To direct and expedite the gathering of information

B. To direct the group in the preparation of the fact sheet

C. To provide opportunity for examination and evaluation of information presented to the group

D. To raise questions relevant to aborting the discussion or rephrasing the question if either appears warranted

E. To generate a recommendation about whether the group needs to continue its discussion

PHASE 4: SETTING CRITERIA AND LIMITATIONS

I. Goals
    A. To place various limitations on the group for legal,
    moral, institutional, logistical, or suasory reasons
    B. To compare the ideal solution with possible ones
    C. To develop standards against which proposed solu-
    tions can be tested
    D. To predict undesirable concomitants
II. Outcomes
    A. A list of restrictions on group activities
    B. A list of standards for testing solutions
III. Members' Tasks
    A. To suggest and discuss suggestions that limit the
    group for moral, legal, logistical, institutional, and sua-
    sory reasons
    B. To suggest and develop standards for judging solutions
    C. To discover and suggest possible hazards inherent in
    solutions to the problem
    D. To suggest reworking previous steps if necessary
IV. Leaders' Obligations
    A. To make sure the group understands its limitations
    and does not exceed them
    B. To seek input from external authorities regarding
    limitations
    C. To examine the possibility that the group needs to
    return to previous steps in order to improve its work
    D. To generate and enter into the record a set of criteria
    against which the group can test proposed solutions

PHASE 5: DISCOVERING AND SELECTING SOLUTIONS

I. Goals
    A. To lay on the table for examination as many solutions
    as possible
    B. To use special techniques to generate even more
    alternative solutions
    C. To test each solution against the criteria and rate it
    D. To select a final solution to the problem
    E. To recommend methods of checking on the effective-
    ness of the final solution
II. Outcomes
    A. A set of proposals detailing solutions and rationale
    for solutions

B. A draft of headings for the final report
III. Members' Tasks
A. To review factual data and propose specific solutions
B. To fit together parts of solutions to prepare different solutions
C. To examine historical data for precedential solutions
D. To produce position papers where necessary
E. To test each solution against criteria and limitations and to reject solutions that do not measure up or refine them to fit the requirements
IV. Leaders' Obligations
A. To prevent the group from making a premature agreement
B. To direct the group through various ways to deriving solutions
C. To moderate disagreement and argument about various proposals
D. To point out similarities and agreements among proposed solutions
E. To help the group test its solutions against the criteria and limitations
F. To insure that agreements embodied in the final solution are entered into the record

PHASE 6: PREPARING AND DELIVERING THE FINAL REPORT

I. Goals
A. To do whichever of the following are necessary given the nature of the group:
1. Demonstrate to the public what the group accomplished
2. Demonstrate to the higher authority that the group has done its job
3. Decide whether the group goes out of business, takes on a new problem, prepares an administrative plan, or implements its own report
B. Optional: An oral presentation of the solution
II. Outcomes
A. A report containing whichever of the following elements the group deems necessary:
1. A preamble containing a review of the problem solving
2. The background of the question
3. A detailed presentation of the final solution containing, if necessary, an implementation plan, organization chart, and budget

4. An argued defense, including a presentation of need, demonstration that the plan can remedy the need as well as fit within limitations, and further, that the plan brings no undesirable concomitants

B. Optional: An oral presentation of the solution

III. Members' Tasks

A. To participate as before. The group problem has changed to either or both of the following:

1. What should be the contents of the final report?

2. What should be the contents of the program to implement our solution?

IV. Leaders' Obligations

To guide in the preparation of the final report, an administrative plan, or whatever else is warranted to conclude the group discussion

APPENDIX M
SAMPLE GROUP
EXERCISE

PROBLEM:

> Your group must choose one of the following people to receive an $8,000 scholarship so she or he may attend the university as an undergraduate. This scholarship is renewable for a total of 4 years as long as academic progress is satisfactory to the university.

NOTE:

> It will help to establish a set of criteria, which, when applied to all five people, will point to one individual as the best solution.

Duane, 17, finished high school in 3 years because, he says, he "couldn't have stood another year of the b.s." His mother, a registered nurse, is a widow with two younger children. In spite of finishing a year early, Duane made a 3.0 in high school. University tests predict he is likely to earn a 2.6 in a science curriculum,

3.1 in nonscience. His mother is determined that he become a physician; Duane says his mind isn't made up. Because of the cost of babysitting for her youngest child, his mother can provide almost nothing for his college education. Duane has had some emotional troubles; a psychiatrist recommends college because she feels that Duane "needs an intellectual challenge."

Carla, 18, has very high recommendations from a small-town high school where she earned a 3.8 average. In her senior year she accepted an engagement ring from a local truck driver who wants her to get married and forget about college. University tests predict she is likely to earn a 3.3 in science and a 2.6 in nonscience. She wants to become a mechanical engineer. Her parents are uneducated, industrious, and very poor. They think Carla has a fine mind but predict that she will drop out of college before she finishes and get married.

Roy, 48, earned the Silver Star and lost his right hand in Vietnam. He earned a high school diploma in the army. The university tests predict a 2.0 in science and a 2.3 in nonscience. He is eligible for veteran's assistance, but his family needs his help to support a large brood of younger children. Roy wants to major in business, "to make enough money in my life so I won't have to worry constantly like my parents had to do."

Melissa, 26, is a divorcee with a 7-year-old son. She made a 2.8 in high school, because "I goofed around." Tests predict she will earn a 2.9 in science and a 3.6 in a nonscience major. She wants to become a teacher, "probably in high school but in college if I'm lucky." She says she is bitter toward men and will never remarry. She receives no financial help toward caring for her son. Her present employer, a dress shop owner, gives her a good character reference.

Sam, 19, was offered several football scholarships to Southern colleges, but they were withdrawn in the spring when he had his legs injured in an automobile accident. He can get around well but cannot compete in athletics. He made low high school grades but entrance test scores for the university are good; he is predicted to average 2.5 in science and 3.0 in nonscience majors. His father, a laborer, refuses to contribute to college for him. Now that he can no longer play, Sam is determined to become a football coach, although he had been advised that it may be difficult without a college playing record.

APPENDIX N
FIFTY QUESTIONS
ASKED BY EMPLOYERS
DURING INTERVIEWS
WITH COLLEGE SENIORS

1. What are your long-range and short-range goals and objectives, when and why did you establish these goals, and how are you preparing to achieve them?
2. What specific goals, other than those related to your occupation, have you established for yourself for the next 10 years?
3. What do you see yourself doing 5 years from now?
4. What do you really want to do in life?
5. What are your long-range career objectives?
6. How do you plan to achieve your career goals?
7. What are the most important rewards you expect in your business career?
8. What do you expect to be earning in 5 years?
9. Why did you choose the career for which you are preparing?

10. Which is more important to you, the money or the type of job?
11. What do you consider to be your greatest strengths and weaknesses?
12. How would you describe yourself?
13. How do you think a friend or professor who knows you well would describe you?
14. What motivates you to put forth your greatest effort?
15. How has your college experience prepared you for a business career?
16. Why should I hire you?
17. What qualifications do you have that make you think that you will be successful in business?
18. How do you determine or evaluate success?
19. What do you think it takes to be successful in a company like ours?
20. In what ways do you think you can make a contribution to our company?
21. What qualities should a successful manager possess?
22. Describe the relationship that should exist between a supervisor and those reporting to him or her.
23. What two or three accomplishments have given you the most satisfaction? Why?
24. Describe your most rewarding college experience.
25. If you were hiring a graduate for this position, what qualities would you look for?
26. Why did you select your college or university?
27. What led you to choose your field of major study?
28. What college subjects did you like best? Why?
29. What college subjects did you like least? Why?
30. If you could do so, how would you plan your academic study differently? Why?
31. What changes would you make in your college or university? Why?
32. Do you have any plans for continued study? An advanced degree?
33. Do you think that your grades are a good indication of your academic achievements?
34. What have you learned from participation in extracurricular activities?
35. In what kind of work environment are you most comfortable?
36. How do you work under pressure?

37. In what part-time or summer jobs have you been most interested? Why?

38. How would you describe the ideal job for you following graduation?

39. Why did you decide to seek a position with this company?

40. What do you know about our company?

41. What two or three things are most important to you in your job?

42. Are you seeking employment in a company of a certain size? Why?

43. What criteria are you using to evaluate the company for which you hope to work?

44. Do you have a geographical preference? Why?

45. Will you relocate? Does relocation bother you?

46. Are you willing to travel?

47. Are you willing to spend at least 6 months as a trainee?

48. Why do you think you might like to live in the community in which our company is located?

49. What major problems have you encountered and how did you deal with them?

50. What have you learned from your mistakes?

APPENDIX O
THE GREVITZ EXERCISE

Following are the 62 statements of the Grevitz Exercise in the order in which they are presented:

The Composition, History, Uses, and Operation of the Grevitz

1. Another use for the Grevitz is to put out forest fires.
2. The salt should be dropped from a height of 6 inches.
3. The Grevitz has a long and distinguished history.
4. The Blugars use the Grevitz to induce euphoria at spring orgies.
5. If the Grevitz shell wiggles in the water, the water is too hot.
6. The third step is to blow hard at the fire.
7. In 1955 the Wallonians contracted for Grevitz sales with the Common Market.
8. Still another use for Grevitzes is bifurcation of the ego.
9. Female Grevitzes are light purple.
10. The water used for soaking Grevitz shells should be lukewarm.

11. The first Grevitz cost 34,069 grozziks (14¢ U.S.).
12. The Swiss use Grevitzes to induce translucability at chocolate euphoria rites.
13. Great care should be taken in removing the Grevitz shell.
14. Andreas Klorp marketed the first Grevitz at Krbitzke.
15. Grevitzes stimulate bifurcation at libidinous denouements.
16. The first step in operating a Grevitz is to remove the shell.
17. Grevitzes are composed of shell, body, and maffle.
18. There are four main uses for the Grevitz.
19. The Grevitz may be used in winter to eliminate earwigs.
20. When inserting the Grevitz, do not twist.
21. When the shell has been soaked, install Grevitz in the left ear.
22. The first step in firefighting is throw the Grevitz over your right ear.
23. Klorp perfected the Grevitz with the help of Denigram Geech.
24. It is easy to identify the composition and color of Grevitzes.
25. Grevitzes do an excellent job of bifurcation in plenifors libido.
26. When inserting the Grevitz, use a gentle pressure.
27. The body of the Grevitz lodges inside the shell.
28. Twisting may injure the ear.
29. Finster developed the Grevitz in his lab at Gezornemplatz.
30. The second step in using Grevitzes in firefighting is to stamp the ground.
31. The second step in operating the Grevitz is to soak the shell.
32. Shells are three times larger than body and maffle combined.
33. Geeks and other pagans use the Grevitz to induce euphoria at bar mitzvahs.
34. Use voodoo with your Grevitz to seduce earwig males.
35. Klorp reduced Grevitz cost to 4,000,577 grozziks. (11¢)
36. The first Grevitz was developed by Sigwald Finster in 1801.
37. Twisting may break off the maffle.
38. A final use for the Grevitz is to eliminate earwigs.
39. To operate a Grevitz takes considerable skill.

40. Finster used a distillation process to produce the first Grevitz.

41. Water used to soak Grevitz shells should be lukewarm (85 degrees).

42. Male Grevitzes are bright purple.

43. Grevitz shells should not be discarded because they are delicious with Kaltmede.

44. Today the Grevitz accounts for 60% of the Wallonian economy.

45. Grevitzes can bifurcate the libido in cases of DTs.

46. Push on Grevitz with left elbow.

47. The Grevitz was perfected in 1906 by Andrejas Klorp.

48. The first use of the Grevitz is to induce euphoria.

49. Salt should be dropped at two grains per corner.

50. After the earwig has been seduced via voodoo, stamp on it with foot.

51. The maffle sticks out of the shell, one-fifth the length of the shell.

52. In 1951 Grevitzes were included in the free trade agreement with South Pludge.

53. Grevitz shells should not be discarded for they provide protection for fleebs.

54. From 1951 to the present, Grevitzes have sustained the Wallonian economy.

55. Other Grevitzes are mauve.

56. A pinch of salt should be dropped into Grevitz soaking water.

57. In 1962, the Wallonians enacted the Grevitz Protection Bill.

58. The salt should be dropped at 8 grains per second.

59. Use right index finger to guide insertion.

60. The temperature of water used to soak shells should be tested with the elbow.

61. Grevitzes' colors range from bright to dull associated with gender.

62. After the shells have been removed they should not be discarded.

This is the blank structural form for the exercise.

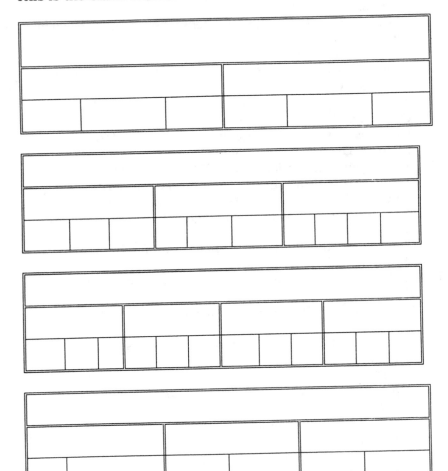

The statements can be inserted appropriately in the blank outline as follows:

I

24					
17 (A)			61 (B)		
32 (1)	27 (1)	51 (1)	42 (1)	9 (2)	55 (3)

II

3									
36 (A)			47 (B)			54 (C)			
29 (1)	11 (2)	40 (3)	35 (1)	14 (2)	23 (3)	52 (1)	7 (2)	57 (3)	44 (4)

III

18											
48 (A)			1 (B)			8 (C)			38 (D)		
33 (1)	12 (2)	4 (3)	22 (1)	30 (2)	6 (3)	45 (1)	15 (2)	25 (3)	19 (1)	34 (2)	50 (3)

IV

39												
16 (A)			31 (B)			21 (C)						
13 (1)	(2) 62		(1) 10	(2) 56		(1) 20	(2) 26					
	a 43	b 53	a 5	a 60	a 41	a 58	a 2	a 49	a 28	b 37	a 46	b 59

Note how the boxes in the structures can be coordinated into a formal outline.

OUTLINE OF THE GREVITZ COMPOSITION

I. 24
  A. 17
    1. 32
    2. 27
    3. 51
  B. 61
    1. 42
    2. 9
    3. 55

II. 3
  A. 36
    1. 29
    2. 11
    3. 40
  B. 47
    1. 35
    2. 14
    3. 23
  C. 54
    1. 52
    2. 7
    3. 57
    4. 44

III. 18
  A. 48
    1. 33
    2. 12
    3. 4
  B. 1
    1. 22
    2. 30
    3. 6
  C. 8
    1. 45
    2. 15
    3. 25
  D. 38
    1. 19
    2. 34
    3. 50

IV. 39
  A. 16
    1. 13
    2. 62
      a. 43
      b. 53
  B. 31
    1. 10
      a. 5
      b. 60
      c. 41
    2. 56
      a. 58
      b. 2
      c. 49
  C. 21
    1. 20
      a. 28
      b. 37
    2. 26
      a. 46
      b. 59

The sentences on the outline can be put together into the complete composition as follows.

The Composition, History, Uses, and Operation of the Grevitz

24. It is easy to identify the composition and color of Grevitzes
  17. Grevitzes are composed of shell, body, and maffle.
    32. Shells are three times larger than body and maffle combined.
    27. The body of the Grevitz lodges inside the shell.
    51. The maffle sticks out of the shell, one-fifth the length of the shell.
  61. Grevitz colors range from bright to dull, associated with gender.
    42. Male Grevitzes are bright purple.
    9. Female Grevitzes are light purple.

55. Other Grevitzes are mauve.

3. The Grevitz has a long and distinguished history.

36. The first Grevitz was introduced by Sigwald Finster in 1801.

29. Finster developed the Grevitz in his lab at Gezornemplatz.

11. The first Grevitz cost 34,069 grozziks (14¢ U.S.).

40. Finster used distillation process to produce the first Grevitz.

47. The Grevitz was perfected in 1906 by Andrejas Klorp.

35. Klorp reduced Grevitz cost to 4,000,577 grozziks (11¢).

14. Klorp marketed the first Grevitz at Krbitzke.

23. Klorp perfected the Grevitz with the help of Denigram Geech.

54. From 1961 to the present, Grevitzes have sustained the Wallonian economy.

52. In 1951 Grevitzes were included in the free trade agreement with South Pludge.

7. In 1955 The Wallonians contracted for Grevitz sales with the Common Market.

57. In 1962, the Wallonians enacted the Grevitz Protection Bill.

44. Today, the Grevitz accounts for 60 percent of the Wallonian economy.

18. There are four main uses for the Grevitz.

48. The first use of the Grevitz is to induce euphoria.

33. Geeks and other pagans use the Grevitz to induce euphoria at bar mitzvahs.

12. The Swiss use Grevitzes to induce translucability at chocolate euphoria rites.

4. The Blugars use Grevitzes to induce euphoria at spring orgies.

1. Another use for the Grevitz is to put out forest fires.

22. The first step in firefighting is throw the Grevitz over your right ear.

30. The second step in using Grevitzes in firefighting is to stamp the ground.

6. The third step is to blow hard at the fire.

8. Still another use for Grevitzes is bifurcation of the ego.

45. Grevitzes can bifurcate libido in cases of DTs.

15. Grevitzes stimulate bifurcation at libidinous denoue-ments.

25. Grevitzes do an excellent job of bifurcation in pleni-

fors libido.
38. A final use for the Grevitz is to eliminate earwigs.

19. The Grevitz may be used in the winter to eliminate earwigs.

34. Use voodoo with your Grevitz to seduce earwig males.

50. After earwig has been seduced via voodoo, stamp on it with foot.

39. To operate a Grevitz takes considerable skill.

16. The first step in operating a Grevitz is to remove the shell.

13. Great care should be used in removing the shell.

62. After the shells are removed, they should not be discarded.

43. Grevitz shells should not be discarded because they are delicious with Kaltmede.

53. Grevitz shells should not be discarded because they provide protection for fleebs.

31. The second step in operating the Grevitz is to soak the shell.

10. The water used for soaking Grevitzes should be lukewarm.

5. If the Grevitz shell wiggles in the water, it is too hot.

60. The temperature of the water used to soak shells should be tested with the elbow.

41. Water used to soak Grevitz shells should be heated with propane.

56. A pinch of salt should be dropped into Grevitz soaking water.

58. The salt should be dropped into the water at 8 grains/sec.

2. The salt should be dropped from a height of 6 inches.

49. Salt should be dropped at two grains per corner.

21. When the shell has been soaked, insert Grevitz in left ear.

20. When inserting the Grevitz, do not twist.

28. Twisting may injure the ear.

37. Twisting may break the maffle.

26. When inserting use a gentle pressure.

46. Push on Grevitz with left elbow.

59. Use right index finger to guide insertion.

APPENDIX P
IDENTIFICATION OF FUZZIES

Each of the following statements contains words or phrases that we would label "fuzzies" or abstractions. Rewrite each statement so that it represents a behavior.

1. I will be a stimulating conversationalist.

2. I will feel comfortable when I introduce myself to a stranger.

3. I will bring up interesting topics of conversation.

4. I will not be nervous when I talk to people.

5. I will be a good listener when I talk to acquaintances.

APPENDIX Q
SELF-ASSESSMENT
FORM

Please answer each question as honestly as you can so I can get to know you as an individual and what specific concerns you have about communication.

1. Why did you enroll in this workshop?

2. What specific difficulties do you have with communication?

3. What types of communication situations do you find difficult?

4. What are your strengths as a communicator?

5. What would you like to get out of this workshop?

REFERENCES

Adler, R.B. (1977). *Confidence in communication: A guide to assertive and social skills*. New York: Holt, Rinehart & Winston.

Adler, R.B. (1980). Integrating reticence management into the basic communication curriculum. *Communication Education, 29,* 215-221.

Aitken, J.E., & Neer, M. (1992). A faculty program of assessment for a college level competency-based communication core curriculum. *Communication Education, 41*(3), 270-286.

Alden, L., & Cappe, R. (1986). Interpersonal process training for shy clients. In W.H. Jones, J.M. Cheek, & S.R. Briggs (Eds.), *Shyness: Perspectives on research and treatment* (pp. 343-355). New York: Plenum Press.

Allen, M., Hunter, J.E., & Donohue, W.A. (1989). Meta-analysis of self-report data on the effectiveness of public speaking anxiety treatment techniques. *Communication Education, 38,* 54-76.

Assagioli, R. (1973). *The act of will.* New York: Viking Press.

Assagioli, R. (1976). *Psychosynthesis: A manual of principles and techniques.* New York: Penguin Books.

Ayers, J. (1988). Coping with speech anxiety: The power of positive thinking. *Communication Education, 37,* 289-296.

Ayres, J., & Hopf, T.S. (1985). Visualization: A means of reducing speech anxiety. *Communication Education, 34,* 318-323.

Ayres, J., & Hopf, T.S. (1987). Visualization, systematic desensitization, and rational emotive therapy: A comparative evaluation. *Communication Education, 36,* 236-240.

Ayres, J., & Hopf, T.S. (1989). Visualization: Is it more than extra-attention? *Communication Education, 38,* 1-5.

Ayres, J., & Hopf, T.S. (1990). The long-term effect of visualization in the classroom: A brief research report. *Communication Education, 39,* 75-78.

Ayres, J., & Hopf, T.S. (1992). Visualization: Reducing speech anxiety and enhancing performance. *Communication Reports, 5,* 1-10.

Babbie, E. (1992). *The practice of social research* (6th ed.). Belmont, CA: Wadsworth.

Bander, K.W., Steinke, G.V., Allen, G.J., & Moser, D.L. (1975). Evaluation of three dating specific approaches for heterosexual dating anxiety. *Journal of Consulting and Clinical Psychology, 43,* 259-266.

Barrick, J.E. (1971). A cautionary note on the use of systematic desensitization. *Speech Teacher, 20,* 280-281.

Bashore, D. (1971). *Relationships among speech anxiety, trait anxiety, IQ, and high school achievement.* Unpublished master's thesis, Illinois State University, Normal, IL.

Beatty, M.J., & Dobos, J.A. (1992). Adult sons' satisfaction with their relationships with fathers and person-group (father) communication apprehension. *Communication Quarterly, 40,* 162-176.

Beatty, M.J., Dobos, J.A., Balfantz, G.L., & Kuwabara, A.Y. (1991). Communication apprehension, state anxiety, and behavioral disruption: A causal analysis. *Communication Quarterly, 39,* 48-57.

Beck, A.T. (1976). *Cognitive therapy and the emotional disorders.* New York: International Universities Press.

Beez, W.V. (1968). Influence of biased psychological reports on teacher behavior and pupil performance. *Proceedings of the 76th Annual Convention of the American Psychological Association, 3,* 605-606.

Begnal, C.F. (1983). *A comparison of reticent and nonreticent women's communication about friendships and relationships.* Unpublished doctoral dissertation, The Pennsylvania State University, University Park, PA.

Bem, D.J. (1972). Self-perception theory. In L. Berkowitz (Ed.), *Advances in experimental social psychology* (Vol. 6, pp. 183-200). New York: Academic Press.

Berger, C.R., & Bradac, J.J. (1982). *Language and social knowledge: Uncertainty in interpersonal relations.* London: Edward Arnold.

Booth, R. (1990). A short-term peer model for treating shyness in college students: A note on an exploratory study. *Psychological Reports, 66,* 417-418.

Booth-Butterfield, M. (1986). Stifle or stimulate? The effects of communication task structure on apprehensive and non-apprehensive students. *Communication Education, 35,* 337-348.

Booth-Butterfield, M. (1989). The interpretation of classroom performance feedback: An attributional approach. *Communication Education, 38,* 119-131.

Booth-Butterfield, S. (1988). Inhibition and student recall of instructional messages. *Communication Education, 37,* 312-324.

Bowers, J.W., & Members of 36C:099. (1986). Classroom communication apprehension: A survey. *Communication Education, 35,* 373-378.

Brenes, A., & Cooklin, A.I. (1983). Videotape feedback effects in interpersonal perception accuracy in families undergoing therapy. *Journal of Psychiatric Treatment and Evaluation, 5,* 345-352.

Brown, S.D. (1980). Video-tape feedback: Effects on assertive performance and subjects' perceived competence and satisfaction. *Psychological Reports, 47,* 455-461.

Buerkel-Rothfuss, N.L., & Yerby, J. (1982, November). *PSI vs. a more traditional model for teaching the basic course.* Paper presented at the annual meeting of the Speech Communication Association, Louisville, KY.

Burgoon, J.K. (1976a). The unwillingness-to-communicate scale: Development and validation. *Communication Monographs, 43,* 60-69.

Burgoon, J.K. (1976b). Coping with communication anxiety and reticence in the classroom. *Florida Speech Communication Journal, 4,* 13-21.

Burgoon, J.K., & Hale, J.L. (1983). A research note on the dimensions of communication reticence. *Communication Quarterly, 31,* 238-248.

Burgoon, J.K., & Koper, R.L. (1984). Nonverbal and relational communication associated with reticence. *Human Communication Research, 10,* 601-626.

Burgoon, J.K., Pfau, M., Birk, T., & Manusov, V. (1987). Nonverbal communication performance and perceptions associated with reticence: Replications and classroom implications. *Communication Education, 36,* 119-130.

Buss, A.H. (1984). A conception of shyness. In J.A. Daly & J.C. McCroskey (Eds.), *Avoiding communication: Shyness, reticence, and communication apprehension* (pp. 39-50). Beverly Hills, CA: Sage.

Butt, D.E. (1965). *A survey to determine the basis for criticism practices in the beginning speech course.* Unpublished master's thesis, The Pennsylvania State University, University Park, PA.

Calhoun, J.E. (1973, September). *Elemental analyses of the Keller method of instruction.* Paper presented at the annual meeting of the American Psychological Association, Montreal.

Cappe, R.F., & Alden, L.E. (1986). A comparison of treatment strategies for clients functionally impaired by extreme shyness and social avoidance. *Journal of Consulting and Clinical Psychology, 54,* 796-801.

Carroll, J. (1964). Words, meanings, and concepts. *Harvard Educational Review, 34,* 178-202.

Cheek, J.M., & Buss, A.H. (1981). Shyness and sociability. *Journal of Personality and Social Psychology, 41,* 330-339.

Christensen, A., & Arkowitz, H. (1974). Preliminary report on practice dating and feedback as treatment for college dating problems. *Journal of Counseling Psychology, 21,* 92-95.

Christensen, A., Arkowitz, H., & Anderson, J. (1975). Practice dating as treatment for college dating inhibitions. *Behavior Research and Therapy, 13,* 321-331.

Cialdini, R.B. (1984). *Influence: How and why people agree to things.* New York: William Morrow.

Cipani, E. (1988). Research and practice in three areas of social competence: Social assertion, interviewing skills, and conversational ability. *Child and Youth Services, 10,* 123-149.

Clevenger, T. (1984). An analysis of research on the social anxieties. In J.A. Daly & J.C. McCroskey (Eds.), *Avoiding communication: Shyness, reticence, and communication apprehension* (pp. 219-236). Beverly Hills, CA: Sage.

Comadena, M.E., & Prusank, D.T. (1988). Communication apprehension and academic achievement among elementary and middle school students. *Communication Education, 37,* 270-277.

Combs, A.W., & Snygg, D. (1959). *Individual behavior: A perceptual approach to behavior.* New York: Harper & Brothers.

Condon, J.C., Jr. (1973). When people talk with people. In C.D. Mortensen (Ed.), *Basic readings in communication theory* (pp. 45-63). New York: Harper & Row.

Conville, R. (1974). Linguistic nonimmediacy and communicators' anxiety. *Psychological Reports, 35,* 1107-1114.

Curran, J.P. (1977). Social skills training and systematic desensitization in reducing dating anxiety. *Behavior Research and Therapy, 13,* 140-157.

Curran, J.P., & Gilbert, F.S. (1975). A test of the relative effectiveness of a systematic desensitization program with date anxious subjects. *Behavior Therapy, 6*, 510-521.

Daly, J.A., & Buss, A.H. (1984). The transitory causes of audience anxiety. In J.A. Daly & J.C. McCroskey (Eds.), *Avoiding
communication: Shyness, reticence, and communication
apprehension* (pp. 67-80). Beverly Hills, CA: Sage.

Daly, J.A., & Lawrence, S. (1985, May). *Understanding stage
fright: Self-focused cognitions and speech anxiety.* Paper presented at the annual meeting of the International
Communication Association, Honolulu.

Daly, J.A., Vangelisti, A., Neel, H., & Cavanaugh, D. (1987,
November). *Pre-performance concerns associated with public
speaking anxiety.* Paper presented at the annual meeting of
the Speech Communication Association, Boston.

Davis, G. (1977). *Communication apprehension, intelligence, and
achievement among secondary school students.* Unpublished
master's thesis, West Virginia University, Morgantown, WV.

Delmater, R.J., & McNamara, J.R. (1986). The social impact of
assertiveness: Research findings and clinical implications.
Behavior Modification, 10, 139-158.

Domenig, K.M. (1978). *An examination of self-reports of reticent
and non-reticent students before and after instruction.*
Unpublished master's thesis, The Pennsylvania State
University, University Park, PA.

Duran, R.L., & Kelly, L. (1989). The cycle of shyness: A study of self-
perceptions of communication performance. *Communication
Reports, 2*, 30-38.

Dusek, J.B. (1975). Do teachers bias children's learning? *Review
of Education Research, 45*, 661-684.

Ekman, P., & Friesen, W. (1975). *Unmasking the face: A guide to
recognizing emotions from facial expressions.* Englewood
Cliffs, NJ: Prentice-Hall.

Elder, J., Edelstein, B., & Fremouw, W. (1981). Response acquisition and cognitive restructuring in the enhancement of
social competence. *Cognitive Therapy and Research, 5*, 203-
210.

Ellis, A. (1962). *Reason and emotion in psychotherapy.* New York:
Citadel.

Ellis, A., & Greiger, R. (1977). *Handbook for rational-emotive therapy.* New York: Springer.

Erin, J.N., Dignan, K., & Brown, P.A. (1991). Are social skills
teachable? A review of the literature. *Journal of Visual
Impairment and Blindness, 85*, 58-61.

Freimuth, V.S. (1976). The effects of communication apprehension
on communication effectiveness. *Human Communication
Research, 2*, 289-298.

Fremouw, W.J. (1984). Cognitive-behavioral therapies for modification of communication apprehension. In J.A. Daly & J.C. McCroskey (Eds.), *Avoiding communication: Shyness, reticence, and communication apprehension* (pp. 209-218). Beverly Hills, CA: Sage.

Fremouw, W.J., & Harmatz, M.G. (1975). A helper model for behavioral treatment of speech anxiety. *Journal of Consulting and Clinical Psychology, 43*, 652-660.

Fremouw, W.J., & Scott, M.D. (1979). Cognitive restructuring: An alternative method for the treatment of communication apprehension. *Communication Education, 28*, 129-133.

Fremouw, W.J., & Zitter, R.E. (1978). A comparison of skills training and cognitive restructuring-relaxation for the treatment of speech anxiety. *Behavior Therapy, 9*, 248-259.

Frey, L.R., Botan, C.H., Friedman, P.G., & Kreps, G.L. (1991). *Investigating communication: An introduction to research methods*. Englewood Cliffs, NJ: Prentice-Hall.

Friedrich, G., & Goss, B. (1984). Systematic desensitization. In J.A. Daly & J.C. McCroskey (Eds.), *Avoiding communication: Shyness, reticence, and communication apprehension* (pp. 173-187). Beverly Hills, CA: Sage.

Garrison, J.P., & Garrison, K.R. (1979). Measurement of oral communication apprehension among children: A factor in the development of basic speech skills. *Communication Education, 28*, 119-128.

Glaser, S.R. (1981). Oral communication apprehension and avoidance: The current status of treatment research. *Communication Education, 30*, 321-341.

Glaser, S.R., Biglan, A., & Dow, M.G. (1983). Conversational skills instruction for communication apprehension and avoidance: Evaluation of a treatment program. *Communication Research, 10*, 582-613.

Glogower, F.D., Fremouw, W.J., & McCroskey, J.C. (1978). A component analysis of cognitive restructuring. *Cognitive Therapy and Research, 2*, 209-223.

Goulden, N.R. (1992). Theory and vocabulary for communication assessments. *Communication Education, 41*(3), 258-269.

Gray, P.L., Buerkel-Rothfuss, N., & Yerby, J. (1986). A comparison between PSI-based and lecture-recitation formats of instruction in the introductory speech communication course. *Communication Education, 35*, 111-125.

Haemmerlie, F.M. (1983). Heterosocial anxiety in college females: A biased interactions treatment. *Behavior Modification, 7*, 611-623.

Haemmerlie, F.M., & Montgomery, R.L. (1982). Self-perception theory and unobtrusively biased interaction: A treatment for heterosocial anxiety. *Journal of Counseling Psychology, 29*, 362-370.

Haemmerlie, F.M., & Montgomery, R.L. (1984). Purposefully biased interaction: Reducing heterosocial anxiety through self-perception theory. *Journal of Personality and Social Psychology, 47*, 900-908.

Haemmerlie, F.M., & Montgomery, R.L. (1986). Self-perception theory and the treatment of shyness. In W.H. Jones, J.M. Cheek, & S.R. Briggs (Eds.), *Shyness: Perspectives on research and treatment* (pp. 329-342). New York: Plenum Press.

Hanser, S., & Furman, C.E. (1980). The effect of videotape-based feedback on the development of applied clinical skills. *Journal of Music Therapy, 17*, 103-112.

Hay, E.A. (1992). A national survey of assessment trends in communication departments. *Communication Education, 41*(3), 247-257.

Hemme, R.W., & Boor, M. (1976). Role of expectancy set in the systematic desensitization of speech anxiety: An extension of prior research. *Journal of Clinical Psychology, 32*, 400-404.

Hersen, M., Eisler, R.M., Miller, P.M., Johnson, M.B., & Pinkston, S.G. (1973). Effects of practice, instructions, and modeling on components of assertive behavior. *Behavior Research and Therapy, 11*, 443-451.

Hittleman, D.R. (1988, March). *Silent participants: Understanding students' nonoral responses.* Paper presented at the annual meeting of the International Reading Association, Toronto.

Hoffman, J., & Sprague, J. (1982). A survey of reticence and communication apprehension treatment programs at U. S. colleges and universities. *Communication Education, 31*, 185-193.

Homans, G.C. (1974). *Social behavior: Its elementary forms.* New York: Harcourt, Brace, Jovanovich.

Hurt, H.T., Preiss, R., & Davis, B. (1976, May). *The effects of communication apprehension of middle-school children on sociometric choice, affective, and cognitive learning.* Paper presented at the annual meeting of the International Communication Association, Portland, OR.

Jacobson, E. (1938). *Progressive relaxation.* Chicago: University of Chicago Press.

Johnson, E. (1981). Invidious mirror? Ethical problems in the use of videorecording. In J.L. Fryrear & B. Fleshman (Eds.), *Videotherapy in mental health* (pp. 305-316). Springfield, IL: Charles C. Thomas.

Jones, W.H., & Russell, D. (1982). The social reticence scale: An objective instrument to measure shyness. *Journal of Personality Assessment, 46*, 628-631.

Jordan, W.J., & Powers, W.G. (1978). Verbal behavior as a function of apprehension and social context. *Human Communication Research, 4*, 294-300.

Kanter, N.J., & Goldfried, M.R. (1979). Relative effectiveness of rational restructuring and self-control desensitization in the reduction of interpersonal anxiety. *Behavior Therapy, 10,* 472-490.

Karst, T.O., & Trexler, L.D. (1970). Initial study using fixed-role and
rational-emotive therapy in treating public speaking anxiety.
Journal of Consulting and Clinical Psychology, 34, 360-366.

Kazdin, A.E. (1974). Effects of covert modeling and model rein-
forcement on assertive behavior. *Journal of Abnormal
Psychology, 83,* 240-252.

Keller, F.S., & Sherman, J.G. (1974). PSI: *The Keller plan handbook.* Menlo Park, CA: W. A. Benjamin.

Keller, F.S., & Sherman, J.G. (1982). *The PSI handbook: Essays
on personalized instruction.* Menlo Park, CA: W. A. Benjamin.

Kelly, L. (1982). A rose by any other name is still a rose: A comparative analysis of reticence, communication apprehension,
unwillingness to communicate, and shyness. *Human
Communication Research, 8,* 99-113.

Kelly, L. (1984). Social skills training as a mode of treatment for
social communication problems. In J.A. Daly & J.C.
McCroskey (Eds.), *Avoiding communication: Shyness, reticence, and communication apprehension* (pp. 189-208).
Beverly Hills, CA: Sage.

Kelly, L. (1992). *The long-term effects of rhetoritherapy.*
Unpublished manuscript, University of Hartford, Hartford,
CT.

Kelly, L., Duran, R.L., & Stewart, J. (1990). Rhetoritherapy revis-
ited: A test of its effectiveness as a treatment for communication problems. *Communication Education, 39,* 207-226.

Kelly, L., & Keaten, J. (1992). A test of the effectiveness of the
Reticence Program at The Pennsylvania State University.
Communication Education, 41, 361-374.

Kelly, L., Keaten, J., & Begnal, C. (1992, November). *Toward a typology of reticent communicators.* Paper presented at the annual
meeting of the Speech Communication Association, Chicago.

Kelly, L., Keaten, J., & Begnal, C. (1994, November). *Refinement
of a typology of reticent communicators.* Paper presented at
the annual meeting of the Speech Communication
Association, New Orleans.

Kelly, L., & Watson, A.K. (1986). *Speaking with confidence and
skill.* New York: Harper & Row.

Kinzer, H.J. (1985, February). *Video feedback in the classroom:
Possible consequences for the communication apprehensive.*
Paper presented at the annual meeting of the Western
Speech Communication Association, Fresno, CA.

Kirsch, I., & Henry, D. (1979). Self-sensitization and mediation in
the reduction of public speaking anxiety. *Journal of
Consulting and Clinical Psychology, 47,* 536-541.

Kougl, K.M. (1980). Dealing with quiet students in the basic college speech course. *Communication Education, 29,* 234-238.

Lazarus, A.A. (1973). On assertive behavior: A brief note. *Behavior Therapy, 4,* 697-699.

Leary, M.R. (1983). *Understanding social anxiety: Social, personality, and clinical perspectives.* Beverly Hills, CA: Sage.

Lerea, L.A. (1956). A preliminary study of the verbal behavior of stage fright. *Speech Monographs, 23,* 220-233.

Lohr, J.W., & McManus, M.L. (1975). The development of an audio-taped treatment for systematic desensitization of speech anxiety. *Central States Speech Journal, 26,* 215-220.

Lustig, M.W. (1980). Computer analysis of talk-silence patterns in triads. *Communication Quarterly, 28,* 3-12.

Lustig, M.W., & Grove, T.G. (1975). Interaction analysis of small problem-solving groups containing reticent and non-reticent members. *Western Journal of Speech Communication, 39,* 155-164.

Lutz, J.M. (1967). *Students' reaction to criticism in the high school speech class.* Unpublished master's thesis, The Pennsylvania State University, University Park, PA.

MacDonald, M.L., Lindquist, C.U., Kramer, J.A., McGrath, R.A., & Rhyne, L.D. (1975). Social skills training: Behavior rehearsal in groups and dating skills. *Journal of Counseling Psychology, 22,* 224-230.

Mager, R.F. (1972). *Goal analysis.* Belmont, CA: Fearon Publishers.

Malinowski, B. (1923). The problem of meaning in primitive languages. In C.K. Ogden & I.A. Richards (Eds.), *The meaning of meaning* (pp. 296-336). New York: Harcourt Brace Jovanovich (Harvest Books).

Marshall, W.L., Gauthier, J., & Gordon, A. (1979). The current status of flooding therapy. *Progress in Behavior Modification, 7,* 205-275.

Martinson, W.D., & Zerface, J.P. (1970). Comparison of individual counseling and a social program with nondaters. *Journal of Counseling Psychology, 17,* 36-40.

McCroskey, J.C. (1970). Measures of communication-bound anxiety. *Speech Monographs, 37,* 269-277.

McCroskey, J.C. (1972). The implementation of a large-scale program of systematic desensitization for communication apprehension. *Speech Teacher, 21,* 255-264.

McCroskey, J.C. (1976). The effects of communication apprehension on nonverbal behavior. *Communication Quarterly, 24,* 39-44.

McCroskey, J.C. (1977a). Classroom consequences of communication apprehension. *Communication Education, 26,* 27-33.

McCroskey, J.C. (1977b). Oral communication apprehension: Summary of recent theory and research. *Human Communication Research, 4,* 78-96.

McCroskey, J.C. (1980). Quiet children in the classroom: On helping not hurting. *Communication Education, 29,* 237-244.

McCroskey, J.C. (1981). *Oral communication apprehension: Reconceptualization and a new look at measurement.* Paper presented at the annual meeting of the Central States Speech Association, Chicago.

McCroskey, J.C. (1982). Oral communication apprehension: A reconceptualization. In M. Burgoon (Ed.), *Communication yearbook 6* (pp. 136-170). Beverly Hills, CA: Sage.

McCroskey, J.C. (1984a). The communication apprehension perspective. In J.A. Daly & J.C. McCroskey (Eds.), *Avoiding communication: Shyness, reticence, and communication apprehension* (pp. 13-38). Beverly Hills, CA: Sage.

McCroskey, J.C. (1984b). Self-report measurement. In J.A. Daly & J.C. McCroskey (Eds.), *Avoiding communication: Shyness, reticence, and communication apprehension* (pp. 81-94). Beverly Hills, CA: Sage.

McCroskey, J.C., & Andersen, J. (1976). The relationship between communication apprehension and academic achievement among college students. *Human Communication Research, 3,* 73-81.

McCroskey, J.C., Andersen, J.F., Richmond, V.P., & Wheeless, L.R. (1981). Communication apprehension of elementary and secondary students and teachers. *Communication Education, 30,* 122-132.

McCroskey, J.C., Booth-Butterfield, S., & Payne, S.K. (1989). The impact of communication apprehension on college student retention and success. *Communication Quarterly, 37,* 100-107.

McCroskey, J.C., & Daly, J.A. (1976). Teacher's expectations of the communication apprehensive child in the elementary school. *Human Communication Research, 3,* 67-72.

McCroskey, J.C., Daly, J.A., & Sorensen, G. (1976). Personality correlates of communication apprehension. *Human Communication Research, 2,* 376-380.

McCroskey, J.C., & Payne, S.K. (1986). The impact of communication apprehension on student retention and success: A preliminary report. *ACA Bulletin, 56,* 65-69.

McCroskey, J.C., Ralph, D.C., & Barrick, J.E. (1970). The effect of systematic desensitization on speech anxiety. *Speech Teacher, 19,* 32-36.

McCroskey, J.C., & Richmond, V.P. (1982). Communication apprehension and shyness: Conceptual and operational distinctions. *Central States Speech Journal, 33,* 458-468.

McCroskey, J.C., & Richmond, V.P. (1987). Willingness to communicate. In J.C. McCroskey & J.A. Daly (Eds.), *Personality and interpersonal communication* (pp. 129-156). Newbury Park, CA: Sage.

McCroskey, J.C., & Richmond, V.P. (1991). Willingness to communicate: A cognitive view. In M. Booth-Butterfield (Ed.), *Communication, cognition, and anxiety* (pp. 19-37). Newbury Park, CA: Sage.

McCroskey, J.C., & Sheahan, M.E. (1976, May). *Seating position and participation: An alternative theoretical explanation.* Paper presented at the annual meeting of the International Communication Association, Portland, OR.

McCroskey, J.C., & Vetta, R.D. (1978). Classroom seating arrangements: Instructional communication theory versus student preferences. *Communication Education, 27,* 99-111.

McFall, R.M., & Lillesand, D.B. (1971). Behavior rehearsal with modeling and coaching in assertion training. *Journal of Abnormal Psychology, 77,* 313-323.

McFall, R.M., & Marston, A.R. (1970). An experimental investigation of behavior rehearsal in assertive training. *Journal of Abnormal Psychology, 76,* 295-303.

McGovern, K.B., Arkowitz, H., & Gilmore, S.K. (1975). Evaluation of social skills training programs for college dating inhibitions. *Journal of Counseling Psychology, 22,* 505-512.

McKinney, B.C. (1980). *Comparison of students in self-selected speech options on four measures of reticence and cognate problems.* Unpublished master's thesis, The Pennsylvania State University, University Park, PA.

McKinney, B.C. (1982). The effects of reticence on group interaction. *Communication Quarterly, 30,* 124-128.

Mehrley, R.S. (1984, November). *The relationship between communication apprehension and voluntary attrition among first semester college students.* Paper presented at the annual meeting of the Speech Communication Association, Chicago, IL.

Meichenbaum, D. (1976). Toward a cognitive theory of self-control. In G.Schwartz & D. Shapiro (Eds.), *Consciousness and self-regulation: Advances in research* (pp. 223-260). New York: Plenum Press.

Meichenbaum, D., Gilmore, J.B., & Fedoravicious, A. (1971). Group insight versus desensitization in treating speech anxiety. *Journal of Consulting and Clinical Psychology, 36,* 415-419.

Merriam, M.L., & Friedman, P. (1969). *Title III, United States Education Act of 1965. Project Report, Alameda County PACE Study.* Hayward, CA: Alameda County Board of Education.

Metzger, N.J. (1974). *The effects of a rhetorical method of instruction on a selected population of reticent students.*

Unpublished doctoral dissertation, The Pennsylvania State University, University Park, PA.

Miller, G.R. (1984). Some (moderately) apprehensive thoughts on avoiding communication. In J.A. Daly & J.C. McCroskey (Eds.), *Avoiding communication: Shyness, reticence, and communication apprehension* (pp. 237-246). Beverly Hills, CA: Sage.

Mino, M. (1982). *The effects of oral interpretation training on public speaking effectiveness of reticent and non-reticent students.* Unpublished manuscript, The Pennsylvania State University, University Park, PA.

Monroe, C., & Borzi, M.G. (1988). Communication apprehension and avoidance of postsecondary education. *School Counselor, 36,* 118-124.

Montgomery, R.L., & Haemmerlie, F.M. (1986). Self-perception theory and the reduction of heterosocial anxiety. *Journal of Social and Clinical Psychology, 4,* 502-512.

Morris, C.G. (1982). *Assessment of shyness.* Unpublished manuscript, University of Michigan, East Lansing, MI.

Mortensen, C.D., & Arnston, P.H. (1974). The effects of predispositions toward verbal behavior in interaction patterns in dyads. *Quarterly Journal of Speech, 61,* 421-430.

Mortensen, D.C., Arnston, P.H., & Lustig, M. (1977). The measurement of verbal predispositions: Scale development and application. *Human Communication Research, 3,* 146-158.

Muir, F.L. (1964). *Case studies of selected examples of reticence and fluency.* Unpublished master's thesis, Washington State University, Seattle, WA.

Mulac, A., & Sherman, A.R. (1974). Behavioral assessment of speech anxiety. *Quarterly Journal of Speech, 60,* 134-143.

Murray, D.C. (1971). Talk, silence, and anxiety. *Psychological Bulletin, 75,* 244-260.

Myers, R.M. (1974). Validation of systematic desensitization of speech anxiety through galvanic skin response. *Speech Monographs, 41,* 233-235.

Neer, M.R. (1987). The development of an instrument to measure classroom apprehension. *Communication Education, 36,* 153-166.

Neer, M.R., & Hudson, D.D. (1981, November). *A method for teaching apprehensive students to lead classroom discussion.* Paper presented at the annual meeting of the Speech Communication Association, Anaheim, CA.

Neer, M.R., Hudson, D.D., & Warren, C. (1982, November). *Instructional methods for managing speech anxiety in the classroom.* Paper presented at the annual meeting of the Speech Communication Association, Louisville, KY.

Neer, M.R., & Kircher, W.F. (1989, April). *The effects of delivery skills instruction on speech anxiety.* Paper presented at the annual meeting of the Central States Communication Association, Kansas City, MO.

Nelson, T.F., & Bennett, M.L. (1973). Unit size and progress rates in self-paced instruction. *Journal of College Science Teaching, 3,* 130-133.

Newhouse, T.L., & Spooner, E.W. (1982). *A skills development and apprehension reduction program for communication apprehensive/reticent students: An alternative to basic course instruction.* Paper presented at the annual meeting of the Western Speech Communication Association, Denver, CO.

Oerkvitz, S.K. (1975). *Reports of continuing effects of instruction in a specially designed speech course for reticent students.* Unpublished master's thesis, The Pennsylvania State University, University Park, PA.

O'Neill, G.W., Johnston, J.M., Walters, W.M., & Rasheed, J.A. (1975). The effects of quantity of assigned material on college student academic performance and study behavior. In J. M. Johnston (Ed.), *Behavioral research and technology in higher education* (pp. 283-299). Springfield, IL: Charles C. Thomas.

Ortiz, J. (1988, March). *Creating conditions for student questions.* Paper presented at the National Seminar on Successful College Teaching, Orlando, FL.

Padgett, V.R. (1983). Videotape replay in marital therapy. *Psychotherapy: Theory, Research & Practice, 20,* 232-242.

Page, W.T. (1980). Rhetoritherapy versus behavior therapy: Issues and evidence. *Communication Education, 29,* 95-104.

Paivio, A. & Lambert, W.E. (1959). Measures and correlates of audience anxiety ("stage fright"). *Journal of Personality, 27,* 1-17.

Paul, G.L. (1966). *Insight vs. desensitization in psychotherapy: An experiment in anxiety reduction.* Stanford, CA: Stanford University Press.

Paul, G.L. (1968). Two-year follow-up of systematic desensitization in therapy groups. *Journal of Abnormal Psychology, 73,* 119-130.

Paul, G.L., & Shannon, D. (1966). Treatment of anxiety through systematic desensitization in therapy groups. *Journal of Abnormal Psychology, 71,* 124-135.

Pedersen, D.J. (1965). *Some effects of the knowledge of grades on certain aspects of student learning as measured by performance in the basic college course in speech.* Unpublished master's thesis, The Pennsylvania State University, University Park, PA.

Phillips, G.M. (1965). The problem of reticence. *The Pennsylvania Speech Annual, 22,* 22-38.

Phillips, G.M. (1968). Reticence: Pathology of the normal speaker. *Speech Monographs, 35,* 39-49.

Phillips, G.M. (1977). Rhetoritherapy versus the medical model: Dealing with reticence. *Communication Education, 26,* 34-43.

Phillips, G.M. (1984a). Reticence: A perspective on social withdrawal. In J.A. Daly & J.C. McCroskey (Eds.), *Avoiding communication: Shyness, reticence, and communication apprehension* (pp. 51-66). Beverly Hills, CA: Sage.

Phillips, G.M. (1984b). A competent view of "competence." *Communication Education, 33,* 25-36.

Phillips, G.M. (1986). Rhetoritherapy: The principles of rhetoric in training shy people in speech effectiveness. In W.H. Jones, J.M. Cheek, & S.R. Briggs (Eds.), *Shyness: Perspectives on research and treatment* (pp. 357-374). New York: Plenum Press.

Phillips, G.M. (1991). *Communication incompetencies: A theory of training oral performance behavior.* Carbondale: Southern Illinois University Press.

Phillips, G.M., Butt, D.E., & Metzger, N.J. (1974). *Communication in education: A rhetoric of schooling and learning.* New York: Holt, Rinehart & Winston.

Phillips, G.M., Kougl, K.M., & Kelly, L. (1985). *Speaking in public and private.* Indianapolis, IN: Bobbs-Merrill.

Phillips, G.M., & Metzger, N.J. (1973). The reticent syndrome: Some theoretical considerations about etiology and treatment. *Speech Monographs, 40,* 220-230.

Phillips, G.M., & Sokoloff, K.A. (1979). An end to anxiety: Treating speech problems with rhetoritherapy. *Journal of Communication Disorders, 12,* 385-397.

Phillips, G.M., & Zolten, J.J. (1976). *Structuring speech: A how-to-do-it book about public speaking.* Indianapolis, IN: Bobbs-Merrill.

Pilkonis, P.A. (1977a). Shyness, public and private, and its relationship to other measures of behavior. *Journal of Personality, 45,* 585-595.

Pilkonis, P.A. (1977b). The behavioral consequences of shyness. *Journal of Personality, 45,* 596-611.

Powers, W., & Smythe, M.J. (1980). Communication apprehension and achievement in a performance-oriented basic communication course. *Human Communication Research, 6,* 146-152.

Rekert, D.M., & Begnal, C.F. (1990). *Speech modification training for reticent speakers: A comparison of three methods.* Paper presented at the annual meeting of the Eastern Communication Association, Philadelphia.

Richmond, V.P., & McCroskey, J.C. (1992). *Communication: Apprehension, avoidance, and effectiveness* (3rd ed.). Scottsdale, AZ: Gorsuch Scarisbrick.

Rosenfeld, L.B. (1983). Communication climate and coping mechanisms in the college classroom. *Communication Education, 32*, 167-174.

Rosenthal, R. (1969). Interpersonal expectations. In R. Rosenthal & R.L. Rosnow (Eds.), *Artifact in behavioral research* (pp. 187-277). New York: Irvington Publishers, Jalsted Press Division of Wiley.

Rosenthal, R. (1977). Biasing effects of experimenters. *Et cetera, 34*, 251-264.

Rosenthal, R., & Jacobson, L. (1968). *Pygmalion in the classroom: Teacher expectations and pupils' intellectual development.* New York: Holt, Rinehart & Winston.

Rosenthal, R., & Rosnow, R.L. (1969). *Artifact in behavioral research.* New York: Irvington Publishers, Jalsted Press Division of Wiley.

Rubin, R.B. (1982). Assessing speaking and listening competence at the college level: The communication competency assessment instrument. *Communication Education, 31*, 19-32.

Schaller, K.A., & Comadena, M.E. (1988, April). *Teacher expectations of the communication apprehensive student.* Paper presented at the annual meeting of the Central States Speech Association, Schaumburg, IL.

Scott, M., & Wheeless, L.R. (1977). The relationship of three types of communication apprehension to classroom achievement. *The Southern Speech Communication Journal, 42*, 246-255.

Semb, G. (1974). Personalized instruction: The effects of mastery criteria and assignment length on college student test performance. *Journal of Applied Behavior Analysis, 7*, 61-70.

Sherman, J.G., & Ruskin, R.S. (1978). *Personalized system of instruction.* Englewood Cliffs, NJ: Education Technology Publications.

Simon, S.B., Howe, L.W., & Kirschenbaum, H. (1972). *Values clarification: A handbook of practical strategies for teachers and students.* New York: Hart.

Sondel, B. (1958). *The humanity of words.* New York: World Publishing Co.

Sours, D.B. (1979). *Comparison of judgments by placement interviewers and instructors about the severity of reticence in students enrolled in a special section of a basic speech course.* Unpublished master's thesis, The Pennsylvania State University, University Park, PA.

Stacks, D.W., & Stone, J.D. (1984). An examination of the effects of basic speech courses, self-concept, and self-disclosure on communication apprehension. *Communication Education, 33*, 317-331.

Sullivan, H.S. (1953). *The interpersonal theory of psychiatry.* New York: W. W. Norton.

Thelen, M.H., & Lasoski, M.C. (1980). The separate and combined effects of focusing information and videotape self-confrontation feedback. *Journal of Behavior Therapy & Experimental Psychiatry, 11*, 173-178.

Thorpe, G., Amatu, H., Blakey, R., & Burns, L. (1976). Contribution of overt instructional rehearsal and "specific insight" to the effectiveness of self-instructional training: A preliminary study. *Behavior Therapy, 7*, 501-511.

Toulmin, S.E. (1958). *The uses of argument.* Cambridge: Cambridge University Press.

Trexler, L.D., & Karst, T.O. (1972). Rational-emotive therapy, placebo, and no-treatment effects on public speaking anxiety. *Journal of Abnormal Psychology, 79*, 60-67.

Trower, P., & Kiely, B. (1983). Video feedback: Help or hindrance? A review and analysis. In P.W. Dowrick & S.J. Biggs (Eds.), *Using video* (pp. 181-197). Chichester: Wiley.

Twentyman, C.T., & McFall, R.M. (1975). Behavioral training of social skills in shy males. *Journal of Clinical Psychology, 43*, 324-395.

Van Riper, C., & Emerick, L. (1984). *Speech correction: An introduction to speech pathology and audiology.* Englewood Cliffs, NJ: Prentice-Hall.

Warren, C.A.B. (1982). *The court of last resort: Mental illness and the law.* Chicago: University of Chicago Press.

Watson, A.K. (1988). *Effects of systematic desensitization in the alleviation of communication apprehension.* Paper presented at the annual meeting of the Eastern Communication Association, Baltimore, MD.

Watson, A.K., & Dodd, D.H. (1984). Alleviating communication apprehension through rational-emotive therapy: A comparative evaluation. *Communication Education, 33*, 257-266.

Weissberg, M. (1977). A comparison of direct and vicarious treatments of speech anxiety: Desensitization, desensitization with coping imagery, and cognitive modification. *Behavior Therapy, 8*, 606-620.

Weissberg, M., & Lamb, D. (1977). Comparative effects of cognitive modification, systematic desensitization, and speech preparation in the reduction of speech and general anxiety. *Communication Monographs, 44*, 27-36.

Winans, J. (1938). *Speech-making.* Englewood Cliffs, NJ: Prentice-Hall.

Wolpe, J. (1958). *Psychotherapy by reciprocal inhibition.* Stanford, CA: Stanford University Press.

Wolpe, J., & Fodor, I.G. (1977). Modifying assertive behavior in women: A comparison of three approaches. *Behavior Therapy, 8*, 567-574.

Wood, J.T., Phillips, G.M., & Pedersen, D.J. (1986). *Group discus-*

sion: A practical guide to participation and leadership (2nd ed.). New York: Harper & Row.

Worthington, E.L., Tipton, R.M., Cromley, J.S., Richards, T., & Janke, R. (1981). *Treatment of speech anxiety: A sequential dismantling of speech skills training, coping skills training, and paradox.* Paper presented at the annual meeting of the Southeastern Psychological Association, Atlanta, GA.

Zimbardo, P.G. (1977). *Shyness: What it is, what to do about it.* Reading, MA: Addison-Wesley.

Zimbardo, P G. (1982). Shyness and the stresses of the human connection. In L. Goldberger & S. Breznitz (Eds.), *Handbook of stress: Theoretical and clinical aspects* (pp. 466-481). New York: The Free Press.

Zimbardo, P.G. (1986). The Stanford shyness project. In W.H. Jones, J.M. Cheek, & S.R. Briggs (Eds.), *Shyness: Perspectives on research and treatment* (pp. 17-25). New York: Plenum Press.

Zolten, J.J. (1982). *The use of premeditated humor in interpersonal relationships.* Unpublished doctoral dissertation, The Pennsylvania State University, University Park, PA.

Zolten, J., & Mino, M. (1981). *Oral reading as a prelude to public speaking for reticent students.* Paper presented at the annual meeting of the International Communication Association, Minneapolis, MN.

Zolten, J.J., & Phillips, G.M. (1985). *Speaking to an audience: A practical method of preparing and performing.* Indianapolis, IN: Bobbs-Merrill.

Author Index

Subject Index

and maintaining conversation, 58

M

medical model of communication incompetence, 147-150
memory, *see* canons of rhetoric
message characteristics associated with reticence, 191-192
duration of message, 191
immediacy, 191
nonverbal behavior, 192
mock interviews, *see* job interviewing
modification of behavior, *see* behavior modification
monologue, *see* oral interpretation, types of

N

narrative, *see* oral interpretation, types of
narcissism, *see* resistance to training
negative cognitive appraisal, *see* treatment research
nonsense dialogue, *see* oral interpretation
nonverbal communication, *see* delivery skills

O

observing inept communication behavior
choosing the observer, 23
choosing the setting, 23-24
formal observation, 23-24
global versus specific observation, 24-25
limitations, 25-26
open-ended questions, 82
oral interpretation
conceptual clarity, 113-115
emotional clarity, 115
functions of training in, 105

nonsense dialogue, 105-107
preparation for, 111-117
rehearsal for, 117-119
types of, 110-111
See also delivery skills; treatment research
organization, 12
See also canons of rhetoric; structuring ideas
organizing ideas, *see* canons of rhetoric; structuring ideas

P

paraverbal communication, *see* delivery skills
performance assignments, *see* communication climate in the classroom
performance criticism, 167-183
and rhetorical canons, 176-180
classical conception of, 173-176
critical questions for teachers, 180-181
gist, 181
labeling, 170-171
physiology, 182
requirements for, 169-176
social clichés, 182
performance visualization, *see* treatment research; visualization
Personal Report of Communication Apprehension-24, *see* assessing inept communication behavior
personality, 2, 10, 142
defined, 2, 10
phatic communion, *see* social conversation, value of small talk
physiology, *see* performance

criticism
pitch, *see* delivery skills
poetry, *see* oral interpretation,
   types of
posture, *see* delivery skills
Pennsylvania State University
   Reticence Program
   assessment procedures, 34-
      36
   background, 5-9
   current status, 9-13
   grading, 38
   inception, 5
   pedagogical premises of,
      150-157
   resistance to training, 159-
      165
   screening interviews, 26-31
   self-as-communicator paper,
      34-35
   student characteristics, 5,
      136-138
   student conference, 38-39
   student difficulties, 6-7
   trainer role, 39-40
   training contract, 38-39
   See also communication
      workshop; treatment
      research
Predispositions Toward Verbal
   Communication scale, *see*
   assessing inept communication behavior
public speaking, 73-77
   as enlarged conversation,
      73-77
   building confidence for, 76
   delivery, 199-123
   impromptu speeches, 75
   practice for, 75-76
   preparation for, 74-75
   problems with, 141-142
   rehearsal process for, 76-77,
      123

R

rate, speaking, *see* delivery
   skills
rational emotive therapy, *see*
   treatment research
rationalization, *see* resistance
   to training
reducing public speaking anxiety, *see* treatment research
resistance to training 159-165
   compulsive activity, 164
   denial, 160
   hostility to criticism, 165
   narcissism, 165
   rationalization, 161-162
   refusal to participate, 163-
      164
   self-fulfilling prophecy, 164
   suspicion of skill, 161
   transference, 162-163
resume writing, *see* job interviewing
reticence, 1, 128-129, 130,
   131, 188
   compared to communication
      apprehension, 130
   definition of, 129
   See also communication
      incompetence;
      Pennsylvania State
      Reticence Program; reti-
      cent communicators
reticent communicators
   behavioral characteristics of,
      191-193
   effect of anticipated interac-
      tion on, 193
   preference for seating
      arrangement, 193
   types of, 136-138
   See also communication
      incompetence;
      Pennsylvania State